▼

Nightmares

and

Secrets

The Real Story of the 1984 Child Sexual
Abuse Scandal in Jordan, Minnesota

▼

Tom Dubbe, Ph.D.

Memorial Press
Shakopee, Minnesota

Nightmares and Secrets
The Real Story of the 1984 Child Sexual
Abuse Scandal in Jordan, Minnesota

Memorial Press
Post Office Box 131
Shakopee, Minnesota 55379

ISBN 0-9770685-0-1

Library of Congress Control Number 2005931854

First Edition
1 2 3 4 5 6 7 8 9 10

Cover Design and Layout by Patrick Kendall
Text Design and Composition by Words & Deeds Inc.
Printed by BANTA Book Group

Photographs courtesy of Scott County Sheriff's Department (1983); Minnesota Department of Corrections (2005) Washington Post/United Press International-Corbis Professional Licensing; Greg Rademacher, photographer; Jordan Fire Department and artist Al Stelton; Mary Margaret Lambright as well as author's personal collection.

To order additional copies of this book, see order form at the back of the book or go to www.tomdubbe.com.

Dedication

This book that I've spent more than 20 years collecting articles, talking to people, reading other books, researching and becoming a "reporter" is dedicated to the entire population of Jordan–past, present and future.

– Tom Dubbe

Table of Contents

Prologue

Something very, very bad happened in Jordan, Minnesota in 1983 and 1984. Children were sexually abused.

When one child is abused, it's a tragedy, but this case crossed the line and became a monster of monsters. It took on a breath of its own, a horrific tale with tentacles that pointed to so many people. Distrust, fear and shame took over and filled the town's air.

We lived together in a small, ancient valley and walked the same streets in the midst of turmoil so rampant that it overwhelmed us.

During every minute of this time, fear prevailed. It was inhaled and exhaled in our every waking moment.

Some people were falsely accused of criminal child sexual abuse. Yet, not all injustice can be fixed. Ruined reputations, both on a personal level and as a community, suffered from the repercussions and stigma of the child-abuse allegations.

After two adults accused of child sex abuse were found innocent by a jury in 1984, the prosecuting county attorney, Kathleen Morris, attacked the jury in an outburst of frustration. "This means we live in a society that doesn't believe children," she said.

Since that time, studies have shown that when skilled interrogators persist, some "suggestions" can become firm and seem real to a small child. Can the power of suggestion imprint a false memory within a child's mind? If so, could it be turned on an innocent parent to ruin their reputation, friendships, and career–their life?

To this day, the cowardice and apathy of some people still infuriates me. They are those who could have stepped up and done something about the Jordan child sexual abuse scandal. Their silence shamefully speaks volumes. A few people did courageously speak the truth at this challenging time. To them, I extend my appreciation and admiration.

Today the fear that gripped the village of Jordan in 1984 has lessened. But lurking in the back of many Jordanites' minds is the uneasy concern that justice has been denied. We fear that another gross miscarriage of justice could revisit the community. Why? Maybe the guilty have not all been punished. Maybe an overzealous county attorney could again arrest innocent citizens.

When you visit the beautiful town of Jordan, the surface may appear calm. But underneath the façade of politeness and civility, there's turmoil, resentment, frustration, hostility, and suppressed rage that eats away at our body and spirit.

Some Jordan residents, especially those considered by law as mandatory reporters of child abuse, have tried to discourage me from writing this book. I've been advised "not to rattle old bones," or to "let sleeping dogs lie." But their attitude of denial and support for a cover-up became my determination to find and tell the truth.

Today, more than 20 years later, I talked to one of the children who was removed from his parents' home and placed in foster care in 1984. He was removed because they were presumed guilty of criminal child sexual abuse. Now a 30-year-old man, he is truly one of many who still suffer the aftermath.

Though the charges against his parents were dismissed in October 1984, it was still many months before they were reunited. Today, he continues to be haunted by what he considers "his abduction" and is adamant that no sexual abuse ever happened. Yet he still suffers from its trials and tribulations–and his suffering comes out: several treatments for drug and alcohol abuse, failed relationships and attempted suicides. It is not hard to understand! In his search to numb his pain, heal his scars and discover his self-worth, he may create his own self-hate in response to the false allegations he and others made, especially about his mother and father.

A story of this magnitude directly involves hundreds of people, too many to all be named. I hope those who were falsely accused and abused by the authorities will step forward and tell their stories. Keeping secrets will not make the nightmares go away.

I've recapped some previously recorded objective data, including chronological timelines, government and judicial activities, reports and names. I quote or transcribe information from my personal interviews. I respected the privacy and anonymity of those who asked. Their anonymity in no way diminishes the credibility of their words.

Those I didn't identify explained that if their names, present address, and other specific information were made public, they fear the jeopardy of losing their jobs. This is not unwarranted as guilt by association, identification with the accused or even an innocent connection to the community of Jordan, caused some innocent people to lose their jobs in 1984.

Hurtful words and shunning may be some of the deepest human hurt. Today comments of perversion, abnormality and evil are still directed at past and present Jordan residents.

Pastor Fritz Sauer and Father Tomas Carolan, local clergy-men who ministered in Jordan during the scandal, encouraged me to write the book. My hope is that *Nightmares and Secrets* will lead to the next steps in my hometown's further healing. I try to bring some comfort to those who unjustly suffered so much heartache and heartbreak, while at the same time I'm quite comfortable to inflict some discomfort on persons responsible for the gross miscarriage of justice.

This book is meant to set the record straight about the Jordan, Minnesota child sexual abuse scandal of 1984. I want to open the eyes and enlighten those who serve in public roles. It's no accident that the judicial system is represented by the blindfolded goddess Themes holding aloft her scales. Surely serious blind spots in our entire court system tip the scales in opposition to true justice.

Communities all over the world have their moments where justice does not prevail. The guilty remain unpunished and the innocent are presumed guilty.

This happened in Jordan with such a magnitude that twenty years later, the town still bears the scars. We have collective, timeless nightmares we can't wake up from, and we wonder about secrets we never heard.

But the secrets aren't just from the alleged sex offenders who were charged with gross criminal sexual conduct with children. No, the secrets also lie with the authorities who shelter and block the truth.

Acknowledgments

During the past two decades, more than a thousand people have helped me write this book. Without their feedback, helpful suggestions, ideas, recollections and encouragements, I could not have finished. Thank you all.

I would like to extend my deepest thanks and appreciation to a number of people who made special contributions and would not let me quit.

Special thanks to my editor, Connie Anderson. She resurrected a wounded project and critically and surgically edited a plethora of data. She cut out the fluff and baloney and condensed twenty years of research and writing into a very reader-friendly text.

Judge Richard J. Menke assisted in interpreting and understanding the law and legal jargon. He was a real stickler for getting it right.

Brendan Suel, a veteran Scott County employee, shared his insider knowledge of some of the courthouse politics and shenanigans.

I thank the philosopher Jack Buss, a.k.a. the Jordan barber, who early on encouraged me to tell this story while I got my $3 haircut.

Special thanks to former Mayor Gail Andersen for sharing documents, as well as giving me her unvarnished opinions about the Jordan sex scandal. She was and is a courageous lady.

The late Anna Sandey provided me with much printed information from newspapers and magazines. She was a treasure trove of information. She saved every scrap of news about the Jordan sex abuse scandal. Anna, please read this book to your fellow angels.

I thank Anita M. Anderson, Law Librarian at the State Attorney General Library for her assistance in uncovering and providing documents and reports of the Jordan sex cases.

I must thank my writer friends at the Minneapolis Writer's Workshop who critiqued my writing and more often than not, told me to go back and re-write and make a better manuscript.

My friends at the Midwest Independent Publisher's Association (MIPA) encouraged me to keep writing and assured me the book would be published.

Many members of the Jordan High School graduating class of 1984 shared how the Jordan child sexual abuse scandal affected their senior year and remains a troubling memory.

Senator Norm Coleman explained how the Humphrey report was compiled. He stands on his record of the Scott County cases. He insist his remarks about Prosecutor Kathleen Morris made in 1985 were true and accurate.

Assistant Attorney General Bernard E. Johnson provided redacted copies of James Rud's confession, his recantation of his confession, and notes on the homicide investigation.

Writer Bruce Rubenstein shared his thoughts and recollections about his reporting on the sex abuse scandal.

A special thanks to John Paul Dubbe, Patricia Kendall and Patrick Kendall for providing their computer expertise in preparing this manuscript.

Many people shared reflections, opinions and comments, but refused to permit me to identify them by name and cite direct quotations in this book. They remain anonymous.

Some people simply refused to answer any questions or be interviewed. Professionals, psychologist, medical doctors, therapist, some lawyers and judges, child protection workers cited client confidentiality or legal considerations. They would not give any general comments about justice or injustice or innocence or guilt. Even when I assured them their comments would be off the record, and they would not be quoted, they refused to discuss the cases and offer any information and insights.

Some people made it difficult to get full and accurate information. After many requests, Sheryl Miller of the Scott County Sheriff's department, provided me with some incomplete and inaccurate information. Some records, reports and mug shots have been "lost."

One deputy sheriff refused to talk to me and warned me that I could be interfering with an ongoing homicide investigation. He reminded me that Minnesota has no statute of limitations on murder.

County Commissioner Bill Koniarski refused to comment on the case. Commissioner Tony Worm said his memory was faded, and he had discarded all his old records.

Some key players refused to be interviewed. One of the lead investigators, Deputy Sheriff Patrick Morgan, simply said he is not talking about his participation in specific interrogations or the results of the cases.

Patrolman Larry Norring, who did extensive interrogations and signed several of the official complaints, refused to be interviewed.

County Attorney Kathleen Morris refused to be interviewed. So did her chief assistant and now law partner,

Mariam Wolf.

Many people who worked on the Scott County sex cases told me they refused to be interviewed after the charges were dismissed and still will not comment because their attorneys advised them to say nothing. Any acknowledgement or admission of mistakes or wrongdoings could be used in law-suits against them. A courthouse employee said she was told, "Keep your mouth shut and don't apologize to anybody about anything."

Although there may be some understandable reasons for remaining silent about this scandal, I suspect some reasons for keeping secrets are not so honorable.

Why won't some police talk about their methods and partic-ipation in the investigation? Did they make mistakes or do some-thing illegal? Do they have something to hide and cover up?

Why are Kathleen Morris and Miriam Wolf silent? Is someone forcing them to be silent? Are they simply too embar-rassed by the results. Are they reticent because they are ashamed?

No one is obligated to talk to a writer, but they must realize their refusal to comment may be interpreted in itself as a state-ment and may raise additional questions. Recent history tells us that stonewalling and covering up are destructive: Richard Nixon and Watergate scandal or President Clinton's Monica Lewinsky shocker. It is better to be upfront, open and honest.

The lurking question remains. What is there to be so silent and secretive about? Nightmares are caused by secrets. Ignoring the truth does not make it go away. People mistake a "short memory" for a clear conscience.

Disclaimer

Much material included in this book was previously reported in the media, newspapers, magazines, TV, and published reports. In one sense this book is about reporting on what was reported.

Now we all know that what we hear on radio, see on TV, or read in newspapers and magazines is not always accurate and true. Just ask Dan Rather about his reporting on forged and untrue documents designed to disparage President Bush. Or ask the *New York Times* to explain the false reporting by one of their star reporters, Jason Blair.

Great effort was extended to verify the authenticity and accuracy of what was reported, especially in the print media. A lot of minor inaccuracies got printed. Population figures of Jordan and Valley Green Park were incorrectly reported. Sand Creek was incorrectly referred to as the Jordan River or the meandering Minnesota River. Dates of events were sometimes inaccurate.

Reporters were questioned when they used unidentified and confidential sources. Bernie Grace of KARE-TV referenced the Minnesota Shield law for journalists and would not name his confidential sources. Some publications acknowledged their errors and published corrections. For example, The September 9, 1984 *Shakopee Valley News* printed a correction about Judge Fitzgerald's son. The preceding week the newspaper printed a story that said Fitzgerald's son was given a lighter sentence for drunken driving because County Attorney Kathleen Morris prosecuted the case. The correction properly said that no alcohol was mentioned in the incident and that defense attorney Marc Kurzman was incorrect. Records at the courthouse show that Fitzgerald's son was charged with obstructing the legal process, and pleaded guilty to a reduced charge of disorderly conduct.

Some reporters acknowledged changed attitudes and perspectives about what they previously wrote, but they did not write follow-up explanations and their original articles have been unchallenged.

It is the author's intention to write a true and accurate account of what happened in the Jordan sex abuse scandal of 1984. Reference and comments on the historical reportage is well documented and substantiated. Reported material can be verified by the bibliography of Special Reports, Magazine and Periodicals, and Newspapers included in the Appendix.

The author believes all persons involved in the investigation and arrest of alleged child abusers sincerely wanted to do everything possible to protect children. Author met no one during his twenty-year investigation of these cases who said child sexual abuse should in any way be ignored or tolerated. Some say this abominable crime is unforgivable. Minnesota Attorney General Hubert Humphrey III said, "Most child sexual abuse cases pursued by Minnesota prosecutors were properly handled and the delicate balance between the interest of the children and the rights of the accused had been properly struck. However, something clearly went awry in the Scott

County cases."

The Scott County Investigation, a.k.a. the Humphrey Report published February 12, 1985, is perhaps the most exhaustive, authoritative and definitive account of the Jordan child sexual abuse scandal. This report can be ordered from State Attorney General's office and can be found on several web sites: www.tomdubbe.com or www.a-team.org/scott_ county.html.

Official documents, public trial records, court transcripts, jail records, municipal, state and federal agency rules, opinions, records and proceedings are available under The Freedom of Information Act 5 U.S.C. Í 552 As Amended By Public Law No. 104-231, 110 Stat. 3048.

Nightmares and Secrets is not meant to malign anyone's good intentions to protect children. Child sexual abuse is a heinous crime, and such criminals must be arrested and convicted. This is an examination and elaboration of what happened in the Jordan child sexual abuse scandal. Hopefully uncovering some of the secrets and exposing the nightmare will prevent another such scandal and pursuant debacle.

What Else Happened in 1984?

Just to give you a barometer of the times, I've collected some national news.

1. Apple Macintosh introduced.

2. Indian Prime Minister, Indira Gandhi, is assassinated.

3. Soviets boycott Los Angles Olympics.

4. Bishop Desmond Tutu is awarded the Nobel Peace Prize.

5. The AIDS virus is discovered.

6. Geraldine Ferraro becomes the first woman Vice-President running mate.

7. Reagan is reelected in a landslide election. Walter Mondale is never heard from again politically.

8. Old nude photos of Vanessa Williams, the current Miss America surface. She is forced from her throne.

9. Mary Lou Retton wins two gold, two silver and two bronze medals at the Olympics.

10. The term cyberspace is coined by William Gibson in his novel, "Neuromancer."

11. Bernhard Goetz, the "subway vigilante," shoots four young men on a New York subway after they threatened him.

12. James Huberty shoots 40 people at a McDonald's restaurant in San Ysidro, California. He kills 21 people before he was shot to death by police.

13. Marvin Gaye, the Motown legend, is shot and killed by his father in a domestic dispute.

14. Minnesota Governor Rudy Perpich appoints Phillip T. Kanning to a judgeship in Scott County, Minnesota.

15. Cardinal Bernard F. Law sends pedophile priest John J. Geoghan to a Weston parish after abruptly removing him from a Dorchester (Mass.) parish where he had molested children.

16. Prince Rogers Nelson puts Minneapolis on the pop-music map with his album Purple Rain, which tops the American charts for 24 weeks.

17. The book, 1984, written by Eric Arthur Blain under the pen name George Orwell, is required reading at many high schools and colleges.

18. Richard Burton, actor and Liz Taylor's ex-husband, dies.

19. Child abuse sex scandals are under way. Media focus is on a nursery school at a synagogue in Miami, the infamous McMartin case in California, and the expanding investigation in Jordan, Minnesota.

20. The book, Hubert Humphrey: A Biography by Carl Solberg is printed by Borealis Books.

21. Doug Flutie of Boston College wins the Heisman Trophy.

22. The Jordan Independent newspaper celebrates its centennial.

23. Most popular fiction book is The Talisman by Stephen King.

24. Most popular nonfiction book is Iacocca: An Autobiography by Lee Iacocca.

25. David Mamet was awarded a Pulitzer Prize for Glengarry Glen Ross.

26. Michael Jackson's hair caught on fire during the shooting of a Pepsi commercial.

27. Los Angles Raiders defeat the Washington Redskins in Super Bowl XVIII by a score of 38-9.

28. Most popular Television shows: 1) Dynasty on ABC, 2) Dallas on CBS and 3) The Cosby Show on NBC.

29. The top-rated news story of 1984 was the allegations regarding two sex rings, pornography, tortures, and murder of children in Jordan, Minnesota.

What would this horrible time have been like if every day something new did not hit the papers in Jordan, surrounding communities, the nearby metro area, nationwide and around the world. Did the story feed the media, or did the media feed the story?

1

Media Coverage

"How did things ever get so far? I don't know.
It was so unfortunate, so unnecessary."
– Vito Corleone, "The Godfather"

The media, newspapers, magazines, radio and TV, reported extensively on the child sexual abuse scandal in Jordan.

Newspaper stories of the Jordan sex abuse scandal were carried by the major wire services. Associated Press articles were printed in almost every major newspaper in America. Many foreign newspapers picked up the sensationalized stories. American tourists were astounded to see many articles in newspapers in France, Germany, Italy, England, Ireland, Japan, Amsterdam, South Africa, and other places in the literate civilized world describing, and sometimes adding, to the Jordan child sexual abuse stories.

Many national magazines such as Time Magazine, US Magazine, People Magazine, Newsweek wrote extensively about the Jordan sex cases.

Local magazines and periodicals such as Mpls. St. Paul,

Twin City Reader, and the Minneapolis Star Tribune Sunday
Magazine did investigative reporting, and published intriguing
stories.

Specialty publications such as Fidelity Magazine and The
New Federalist published exhaustive articles about specific
aspects of the Jordan sex cases. Fidelity Magazine reported
much about the work of therapist involved in the investigation.
The New Federalist did a scathing piece on State Attorney
General Skip Humphrey's involvement and failure to prosecute persons guilty of child sexual abuse.

Local weeklies such as the Jordan Independent, the
Shakopee Valley News, the Prior Lake American, the Belle
Plaine Herald and others kept the story a headline feature.

The two major metropolitan newspapers, the St. Paul
Pioneer Press and the Minneapolis Star Tribune kept their
readers informed with some objective and some opinionated
writing and photographs. The Jordan story enticed some big-
league reporters.

John Camp, better known today as the famous author John
Sanford, wrote a less-than-complimentary article about Jordan
for the St. Paul Pioneer Press. Rival newspaper, the
Minneapolis Star Tribune provided more reporters and more
coverage.

In 1984, Minneapolis Star Tribune reporters Paul McEnroe,
David Peterson and Mike Zerby rented a house in Jordan and lived
in the community and reported first-hand accounts on developments of the Jordan sex abuse cases.

Paul Sunder, editor of the Jordan Independent in 1984,
speaks well of the many reporters who visited Jordan. Many of
the reporters used the office facilities of the hometown newspaper to phone in stories and connect with their editors. Paul
said they would come digging, looking for some dirt on some-

one or on the community. Soon after these visiting reporters talked with the local townspeople, or visited the scenic majesty, and visited community events, they stopped looking for dirt and marveled at the beauty, cleanliness, and hospitality of the Jordan community.

Sunder commented how a reporter from the Chicago Tribune told him she had come to Jordan thinking it was some sort or an incestuous, hillbilly, dirt-road Hicksville. After talking with residents, driving on paved streets, walking on concrete sidewalks, and touring the modern schools, she would write that Jordan was a nice town inhabited by smart, civilized, kind, and decent people.

One reporter, Bernie Grace of KARE-TV, is not welcome today in Jordan or in the Scott County Courthouse. Judge Fitzgerald said he warned Bernie Grace to "watch his step and not overstep his rights as a reporter" or he would bar him from the Scott County Courthouse.

When someone was arrested and charged with child sexual abuse in Jordan, Bernie Grace would show up with camera, shooting much of the actual arrest scene, which would then show up on the 10 o'clock evening news. Sensationalized and derogatory commentary accompanied the Grace's video filming; Jordan was depicted as a sleazy place. Laurie Boyce of KARE-TV said no scripts from the broadcast are part of the archives at KARE-TV.

How Bernie Grace knew in advance who was going to be arrested, and when it was going to happen, is still a mystery today. Kathleen Morris accused Sheriff Doug Tietz of leaking information to defense attorneys, especially about accused Deputy Buchan. This led to suspicions that the Sheriff or one of his deputies tipped off reporter Bernie Grace.

Sheriff Tietz and other deputies suspect Kathleen Morris or one of her staff tipped off Grace about an impending arrest.

Maybe he had someone other than the sheriff or the county attorney or their staffs giving him inside information.

Bernie Grace said he would never reveal his confidential sources or even at the suggestion that he do a "Bob Woodward thing" and tell us who his source is after his "deep throat" is dead. Grace remained adamant that he would never reveal his source. He said his job was to report the news and let the public make up its mind based on the fact presented. Grace refused to speculate or identify innocent or guilty suspects. He did say, "It was a sad, complicated string of events that occurred in Scott County."

An old journalism cliché says bad news sells best. The Jordan child sexual abuse scandal got reported and sensationalized as a bad news big story. Without all the media hype, the Jordan sex scandal may have turned out differently.

> *"We must remember always that accusation is not proof.*
> *And that conviction depends upon evidence and the due*
> *process of law. We will not walk in fear, one of another.*
> *We will not be driven by fear into an age of unreason,*
> *If we dig deep in our history and doctrine, and remember*
> *that we are not descended from fearful men...."*
> – Edward R. Murrow, CBS broadcaster on March 29, 1954

This Place Called Jordan

"Hate evil and love good, and establish justice."
– Amos 5:15

In 1853, William Holmes staked a claim of 160 acres. Along with his brother Thomas, he laid out the town site in 1854. William Holmes is credited as the founder of Jordan. Jordan celebrated its sesquicentennial in 2004. William, his wife and oldest son, Orin, lived in a log home on what today is the corner of Water Street and Broadway Street. Holmes operated a mill, thus Jordan was originally known as "Holmes Mill." In 1854, the second family arrived. William Varner and his wife built a log home on what is now the corner of Varner Street and First Street. The Varners had 10 children. By 1855, William Varner was operating his own mill and the area began to prosper. Holmes and Varner each wanted the town to be named after the other, but decided together to call it Jordan.

Some say Jordan was named after the rich Jordan valley and Jordan River of the biblical Palestine. Other historians have speculated that Jordan was named after the Jordan River running through town that generated power to run the mills. There is some error in this thinking because the stream is called Sand Creek, and the only river nearby is the Minnesota River. Sand Creek feeds into the Minnesota River several miles from town.

Before the famous (or infamous) Jordan child sexual abuse scandal of 1984, Jordan was best known for beer and baseball. They seemed to go hand in hand or perhaps hand-in-glove. The Jordan Brewery Inc. started sometime during the mid-1800s by prominent local businessman, Frank Nicolin. In fact, Jordan around 1867 supported two breweries. Men named Shutz and Hilgers obtained control of the two breweries in 1902. The City Brewery built a beautiful park and pavilion near the brewery. Dances with live music were held every week. Commuter trains stopped by the park and dropped off visitors who enjoyed food and a glass or more of Jordan beer at the brewery.

In 1920, brewing stopped with Prohibition. The brewery park remained open and in 1926, Shutz and Hilgers sold the property to the Scott County Food Seed Association. The park became the original location of the Scott County Fairgrounds and was called "Fairgrounds Park."

Following Prohibition, at its peak in the late 1930s, Jordan Brewery Inc. was producing 40,000 barrels annually. In 1946 the Jordan Brewery was purchased by Mankato Brewing Company. New equipment was added and the output of Jordan beer increased from 40,000 barrels to 150,000 barrels. In 1955 making Jordan beer was discontinued by the Mankato Brewing Company.

In 1973, Jordan resident, Gail Andersen bought the property in a partnership for $6,000. A partnership breakup led Andersen to sell her interest in 1980. In early 1990, city officials announced plans to demolish the building. At the last minute, Gail Andersen re-purchased the property and is the sole owner. The sale included the brewery building and 12 acres of wooded hillside. She hopes to restore the building to its original pre-Prohibition grandeur to be used for an apartment or office space.

(In early 1984, Gail Andersen was mayor of Jordan. She voiced some strong opinions during the 1984 child sexual abuse scandal. Later in 1984 she was convicted on two gross misdemeanor charges and removed from office.)

Beer, the brewery, and baseball have been connected with each other since Jordan's beginning. The Jordan amateur team is named the Jordan Brewers, though the brewery has not brewed a beer in well over 50 years. The most famous player ever to wear a Jordan Brewer uniform during the late 1940s and early 1950s was Jim Pollard. Pollard, a star basketball player for the champion Minneapolis Lakers, smacked long home runs out of the park. He missed only two practices in seven years with the club. In 1954, Pollard showed up at the park for a Sunday game. The Lakers had won the NBA title the night before in Rochester, New York. Pollard was paid $45 a game, and if he figured he didn't earn it, he would donate it to the Boy Scouts.

In 1960, a devastating flood turned the baseball park, known as Fairgrounds Park into a large lake. After the water receded, the community pitched in and cleaned up the park. In 1962, the community further responded and expanded the old beer stand. Jordan would not let this "diamond in the rough" go to waste.

In 1969, Jordan hosted the State Amateur baseball tournament. With donations and contributions, local citizens turned Fairgrounds Park into a baseball gem. A huge crowd of 15,274

The welcoming sign by Jordan's Mini-Met ballpark.

– Author's collection

attended the tournament. Following the 1969 State tournament, the ballpark drew praise from the entire baseball world.
Comparisons were made to professional parks.

Bill Boni wrote an article that appeared in the St. Paul
Pioneer Press, which read, "It [Fairgrounds Park] could have
been the Met [Metropolitan Stadium, home of the Minnesota
Twins] in miniature–except that in a ball park such as this,
you're closer to the action, more part of the scene." The community responded to this article and soon baseball was being
played at the newly named Mini-Met.

Jordan successfully hosted the Babe Ruth State
Tournament in 1971. The Babe Ruth League developed many
future stars. Jordan also hosted the 50th anniversary of the
Minnesota State Amateur Baseball Tournament. In 1981
Jordan co-hosted the State Amateur Baseball Tournament with

the neighboring community of Belle Plaine. This was the first time a dual-site tournament had been tried. Officials said the tournament was a grand success and vowed to continue the dual-site format. In 2004, Jordan and Belle Plaine again hosted the State Amateur Baseball Tournament. Jordan won the championship. Maybe the most popular of the baseball heroes to play at the Mini-Met is Ron Beckman. When Beckman reached his milestone of 1,000 hits, the team shot off a grand display of fireworks.

Beer and baseball make up a lot of Jordan's history. Urban life may creep into the area and Jordan may grow into a larger city, but the Mini-Met will always remain a small-town baseball park. The many good memories or Jordan baseball overshadow the sad reminders of the Jordan child sexual abuse scandal of 1984.

Before the scandal of 1984, those chamber of commerce-style words and descriptions were used frequently: beautiful, scenic, pastoral, majestic, picturesque rolling hills, crystal clear streams, fish-filled ponds, tranquil, awesome, pleasant, gracious, hospitable, marvelous, wonderful, colorful, cordial, rustic, serene, peaceful, lovable and livable.

To preserve much of the history and historical sites in memory and to teach younger residents about the community, the Jordan Fire Department commissioned famous Minnesota artist Al Stelton to do a painting that reflected Jordan's 150-year history. A limited number of prints and artist proofs were printed and sold by the Jordan Fire Department. This fire department, which should be ranked as one of the greatest volunteer departments, has given me permission to include a photo of the print titled, "Our Town."

A wonderful mural commissioned
for Jordan's sesquicentennial.
– Courtesy of Jordan Fire Department and artist Al Stelton

3
▼

So Why Did This Happen?
And Why in Jordan?

"Not for every idle word must a man render an account, but for every silence."
– St. Ambrose

Michael Haeuser, head librarian at Gustavus Adolphus College, St. Peter, Minnesota, did major research in order to write a book about the Jordan child sexual abuse scandal (that he never finished).

In the October 16, 1994, *Minneapolis Star Tribune*, he said the Jordan case was another Salem witch hunt and mentioned ten important reasons for the debacle. In my interview with Haeuser in 2003, he still felt the reasons cited in 1994 were accurate.

Michael Haeuser's 10 Reasons

1. **The Times**. The rise of feminism brought with it the voices of anguished victims of child sexual abuse. It turned out to be shockingly common for people to rape

kids–even their own. Many people felt guilty that suffering had been allowed to go on. The accused had to be monsters, and its backlash was unavoidable.

2.   **Inexperience**. Everyone knew much less than is now known about prosecuting sexual abuse cases. There was a naiveté about the ability and willingness of children to lie about such things, and any hint of skepticism was to be against believing the child.

3.   **The makeup up Jordan**. Far from the idyllic, gently wooded Lake Wobegon that reporters loved to invoke, Jordan was town on the edge, an old-line farming community being overtaken by outer suburbs. People worried about urban problems moving in. The town seemed full of strangers, and ominous ones. There was a big trailer park across the highway, with a large transient population whom people didn't trust.

4.   **Local politics**. There were bitter divisions in town. Mayor Gail Andersen was allied with dissidents in the police department. A lot of people on her side of the dispute wound up as accused child molesters. (Haeuser avoids the word conspiracy, but said he feels that "various people's own agendas were being furthered down the line" as the case developed.) Some charges were filed, even though the children said to be involved, denied abuse or hadn't been interviewed.

5.   **Small-town police**. A rookie cop did the initial investigation. He saw a cache of videotapes and other material in the James Rud's trailer, but he didn't have a search warrant. The cache was never found. Haeuser suspects than only a handful of defendants were guilty, but that's more than the one who was actually convicted.

6.   **The nub of the truth**. Just as there was some witchcraft going on in Salem, some children were being abused in

Jordan. Children who repeated some of their very disturbing experiences and comments gave validity to the whole Jordan case.

7. **The Cermak case**. Attorney Morris had credibility, too, through having succeeded not long before in prosecuting several members of the Cermak family, including the grandparents, for repeated abuse of children. If grandmas in Scott County were doing such things, what else was going on down there?

8. **The cooperation of professionals**. Haeuser said interviews later on by the Minnesota State Crime Bureau psychologist and others who helped get the information made them sound "like zealots who knew the truth, regardless of any evidence."

9. **The children**. Haeuser said …despite references to scores of children supposedly involved, the case really came down to a core group of five kids who accused 36 people. In total, these five children were interviewed at least 128 times, and probably much more often. Three of the five had been sexually active themselves and were relieved that the police were not after them. (All children are 13 or younger.)

10. **Kathleen Morris**. Could it have happened without her? It has, all over the world. There have been several Jordans without Morris being present. Yet, Haeuser said he considers her the trigger that set off everything else. He has traced a multitude of ways in which her intense interest in sexual abuse created a climate of anxiety unique to Scott County–one that intensified the ultimate eruption.

More Reasons and Theories...
Experts Chime In

Some of the theories that were batted about in the Jordan scandal discussions included:
- Kinsey's Fault
- Politics of Jordan's Sex Scandal
- Self-serving Professionals
- Bad Water Theory

Kenneth R. Pangborn is a subject-matter expert for the defense in sex abuse trials, and provides services to people accused of child sexual abuse. He says the allegations of child sexual abuse in Jordan and elsewhere are the result of some bad legislation passed in 1974.

Panghorn is a certified member of the American Society of Trial Consultants, (ASTC) the American Professional Society on the Sexual Abuse of Children, (APSAC) the Association for the Treatment of Sex Abusers (ATSA) and the International Association on Mental Health and Law.

Minnesota Senator Walter Mondale sponsored the Child Abuse Prevention and Treatment Act (CAPTA). President Nixon signed Public Law 93-247, and this is commonly referred to as the Mondale Act. Pangborn, along with others who provide services to people accused of child sexual abuse, contend that the Jordan cases and other cases are partly the result of this law because it grants absolute immunity to those who make false allegations of child sexual abuse. Pangborn visited with some of the accused in Jordan, and concludes these were fine people who were falsely accused of a heinous crime.

Kinsey's Fault

Judith A. Reisman, Ph.D. in her book, *Kinsey: Crimes &*

Consequences states that Kinsey's claims about the harmlessness of adults having sex with children, and of even child rape, would lead to more child sexual abuse. Dr. Reisman documents that at least 317 infants and young boys were sexually abused at the Institute for Sex Research at the Indiana University under the supervision of Alfred C. Kinsey, sex expert and pioneer of the current sex education model.

Reisman points out how in May 1957, major German newspapers reported that Alfred Kinsey, our nation's "sex expert," was writing and guiding a German pedophile as he sexually abused innocent children. Dr. Von Balluseck, the former Nazi commandant, said Kinsey asked him to have sex with children and send details of his experiences. Dr. Von Balluseck recorded his crimes against 100 children in minute detail and sent the information regularly to sex researcher Kinsey.

Kinsey's position, when questioned about moral or legal considerations about child sexual abuse, was that one is not an offender, not a criminal, unless one is caught and convicted. In 1950, FBI director J. Edgar Hoover warned of a terrifying increase in sex crimes.

Kinsey contended that more harm was done to children by adult hysteria than by any criminal sexual activity against the child. Kinsey worked to change sex offender laws and codes. He stated that sexual activities such as mouth-genital contacts, anal coital acts, homosexuality, group activities, adult-child sex, and animal intercourse should not be legally defined as sexual perversion.

Dr. Reisman's account of Kinsey's pedophiles makes credible the theory that the Jordan child abuse sex scandal of 1984 evolved from the work of Alfred Kinsey.

The Politics of the Jordan Sex Scandal

Several people wrote about the Jordan sex scandal as a political issue. Scott County Attorney Morris may have been trying to improve her political stature and seek higher office. She was a politician and was elected the first female county attorney in the State of Minnesota and was reelected by a substantial majority. It was supposed she was seeking Skip Humphrey's State Attorney General job. Or she had designs on an even higher office.

A local historian believed Morris was duplicating former U.S. Attorney General Janet Reno's climb to higher office. Janet Reno successfully prosecuted child sexual abuse cases in Miami, and President Bill Clinton selected her to become the nation's first female U.S. Attorney General.

The political intrigue of the Jordan child sexual abuse scandal has some credence. It is a big story involving local politicians, the mayor of Jordan, the Jordan city council, the Jordan police chief and other police officers, such as Scott County Sheriff Doug Tietz and some deputies. It stretched to include elected school board officials, elected county commissioners, County Attorney Kathleen Morris, her staff, appointed and elected judges, and Minnesota State officials such as Attorney General Skip Humphrey, and Solicitor General Norm Coleman, now a United States Senator, Governor Rudy Perpich, and FBI investigators.

A then-prominent defense attorney, Patrick Leavitt (now deceased) said the Jordan case went forward because of the strong feminist support in Scott County. "If a man had been the Scott County Attorney, there would not have been national and international sensationalized news coverage."

A former employee of the Scott County Human Services contends that the Jordan sex abuse cases got blown way out of proportion because untrained Child Protection Service personnel zealously tried to impress their bosses.

Self-serving Professionals

A theory about making the Jordan story more than it was, suggests the professionals, especially the psychologist, had a commercial interest in keeping the story alive and multiplying. The County was a good employer and paid well. There may well be more than a kernel of truth in such a theory.

Bad Water Theory

The most out-to-lunch theory, sometimes humorously repeated, is that there must have been something in the water. Reporter John Camp, also known as suspense author, John Sandford, wrote in the *St. Paul Pioneer Press* February 19, 1984 that Don Shelby, WCCO-TV I-Team investigator, is a recognized expert in child-abuse investigations, and Shelby doesn't think there was anything in the water.

As of this date, to my knowledge, neither the Public Health, nor the Pollution Control Agency, nor any other governmental authority has found anything wrong with the drinking water in Jordan. So there is no credence that the drinking water in Jordan caused the scandal.

Jordan is not a place like Garrison Keillor's fictional Lake Wobegon: *"Where the women are strong, the men are good looking and all of the children are above average."*

Jordan is a real place. It was not, and is not, the home to a lot of deviates, perverts, child molesters and child sexual abusers. Jordan is inhabited by a lot of good solid citizens. It is, however, where a lot of its residents were accused of child sexual abuse.

After these charges were dismissed, these residents suffered the consequences of being charged with such a monstrous crime. Reputations were destroyed. Some experienced economic hardships and lost their jobs or any hopes of promotions or a better job. Some filed bankruptcy and lost their homes. Some suffered physical illness and some died at an early age. Marriages crumbled and divorce became another heart-wrenching story. Many experienced mental health problems and severe depression. Some lost all faith in God and religion. Some became substance abusers and required drug and alcohol treatment. All had to leave the community.

And here is why. Starting with one mother reporting the sexual abuse of her children by one man–this initial report mushroomed out of control until 24 adults were accused, arrested and charged with sexual abuse of their own–and other children. It is a story, that if you saw it on TV, you'd say, "This can't be true." But sadly, it is. It happened in 1984 to one town where nothing unusual happens on a day-to-day basis to hardworking people–and unfortunately it continues to happen in towns and cities around the country. Children making accusations, officials charging in and arresting people–WITHOUT thorough investigations. Children need to be protected, no doubt! But society must respect and enforce the rights that Americans have come to expect–to be considered innocent until proven guilty.

Later you'll read that one of the conclusions from the Humphrey Task Force on this issue is, that if at all possible, the perpetrator should be removed from the home, not the children. Lives were disrupted in a way no one could comprehend. Children were damaged–and pay the price even today. For those charged adults, none of their lives will ever be the same. The children's childhood was cut short by a zealous country prosecutor. The innocent were easily painted with the same broad brush of hysteria once the first charge was made, once

James Rud gave authorities the ammunition to arrest and charge his townsfolk.

Time Line of the Infamous Child Sexual Abuse Scandal

"I have learned silence from the talkative;
tolerance from the intolerant and kindness from the
unkind. I should not be ungrateful to those teachers."
– Kahlil Gibran, Sand and Foam

- September 1983: Christine Brown, a 25-year-old Jordan woman, informs Jordan Police that her children were sexually abused by James Rud, a resident of Valley Green Trailer Park in Jordan. He has a known history of child sexual abuse. The investigation begins.

- October 1, 1983: James Rud, 26, was arrested on 13 charges alleging sexual abuse of at least four children between the ages of 8 and 10.

- November 14-17, 1983: Rud's parents, Alvin and Rosemary Ann, are charged with sexual abuse of children. Christine Brown (the woman who made the first accusation) is charged with sexual abuse of children. Two other women Rud knows are charged with sexual abuse of children.

- November 1983: Scott County Attorney Kathleen Morris takes on the case.

- November 18, 1983: James Rud is charged with an additional 85 counts of criminal sexual abuse. Authorities characterize Rud as part of the largest juvenile sex ring ever discovered in Minnesota

- January 11, 1984: Helen Brown, 33, and her husband Tom, 39, are arrested and charged with child sexual abuse involving seven children. Helen Brown is Christine Brown's sister.

- January 20, 1984: Lois Bentz, 33, and her husband Robert, 39, are arrested and charged with child sexual abuse.

- January 25, 1984: James Brown, 36 of Jordan, brother of Tom Brown and ex-husband of Christine Brown, is charged with criminal child sexual abuse.

- February 6, 1984: Jordan police officer, Greg Myers, 30 is arrested and charged with four counts of first-degree and four counts of second-degree criminal sexual conduct.

- May 24, 1984: Jane Myers, 34, is charged with four counts of first-degree and four counts of second-degree criminal sexual conduct. Jane Myers is the wife of Jordan police officer Greg Myers who was arrested on similar charges on February 6,1984.

- June 4. 1984: Scott County Deputy Sheriff Donald Buchan, 37, and his wife Cindy, 27, are charged with child sexual abuse.

• June 4, 1984: Terry Morgenson, who worked in the Scott County Assessor's Office (last person arrested), was charged with two counts of criminal sexual conduct. His wife Paulette was not charged and their children were not removed from their home.

• July 1984: Two of the children from families arrested and charged indicated they had seen children tortured and murdered. This started a murder investigation that added to the upset in this community. (Read more about it in the Humphrey Report in chapter 38). There are references to this murder investigation throughout the book.

• August 15, 1984: James Rud pleads guilty to 10 counts of first-degree criminal sexual conduct involving children under age 13. For a reduced prison sentence, Rud agrees to testify against other adults. Rud says he attended an adult/child sex party with Lois and Robert Bentz. Rud volunteers that he has seen most of the others charged in the case at sex parties. The trial of Lois and Robert Bentz begins.

• August 1984: At the Bentz trial, one child admits his accusations were fabricated. James Rud who previously claimed to have been at sex parties with Robert Bentz, is unable to identify Bentz at trial.

• September 19, 1984: After a jury of eight men and four women deliberated for more than 20 hours over three days, they found Robert and Lois Bentz not guilty on 12 counts each of abusing one of their own children and four other Scott County children.

• October 15,1984: Opening arguments begin in the trial of Deputy Sheriff Donald and Cindy Buchan. Morris' office announces that the charges against the Buchans and the other 19 adult defendants are being dropped. Morris says she will try to use family court to keep the children of those charged from being returned home from foster care. After the Bentz trial Morris is on record as saying she thinks all are guilty of criminal child sexual abuse.

- October 15, 1984: Scott County Attorney Kathleen Morris claims she dropped the charges against all the accused because trying the cases would jeopardize a wider investigation involving child pornography and homicide.

- October 18, 1984: Morris announces she is turning over jurisdiction of the entire case to the state attorney general's office. Minnesota Attorney General Hubert Humphrey III will decide whether to re-file criminal charges against any of the defendants. The state attorney general will handle the prosecution of anyone accused of child pornography or murder.

- November 14, 1984: State and federal agents announce that they have found no credible evidence of homicides. They will continue to investigate sexual abuse allegations.

- November 14, 1984: State Attorney General's office disclosed that two boys admitted to authorities that they made up stories about the killings. Their stories were bizarre and inconsistent.

- January 1985: James Rud, the only person convicted, is sentenced to 40 years in prison. (He expects to be released in 2009.)

- February 12, 1985: State Attorney General Hubert Humphrey III released a report saying he cannot prosecute any remaining defendants, citing lack of evidence as well the children's damaged credibility. The report is critical of Scott County Attorney Kathleen Morris handling of the case.

Who Is James Rud– and What Is His History?

"Lying lips are abomination to the Lord; but they that deal truly are his delight."
– Proverbs 12:22

By November 18, 1983, he had been charged with a total of 108 counts of criminal sexual abuse. The Minneapolis Star Tribune December 2, 1983 reported that Rud was charged with two more counts, increasing the total to 110.

Born March 3, 1957, James Rud had a history of sexual misconduct long before the Jordan sexual abuse scandal. At age 8, he "checked out" a 7-year-old girl in his parents' garage. His parents discovered the incident and young James was sent to the Dakota County Mental Health Clinic at Mendota Heights to see if he needed psychiatric help.

Rud's criminal sexual history dates back to 1978 when he was 21-years old. He was in the U.S. Army stationed at Fort Eustice, Virginia. On May 14, and again May 18 and 19, he was charged with indecent liberties with children under age 13. (After his 1983 arrest, the Minneapolis Star Tribune reported that he had been convicted of these charges, but "received a suspended one-year sentence on the condition that he receive psychiatric treatment.")

Now here we are six years later. Rud has left the military and returned home to live near his parents and hometown. He is considered a hard-working trash collector. As a single man, he dated a lot of women, and true to form of a pedophile, the women always had young children.

On November 19, 1983, the same newspaper's Paul McEnroe writes, "In July 1980 Dakota County authorities charged Rud with second-degree criminal conduct stemming from charges that he fondled two girls under the age of 13. He pleaded guilty to the lesser charge and was sentence to 90 days in jail and five years probation on the condition that he attend behavioral therapy sessions for sex offenders."

He's been through some kind of sexual deviant treatment or therapy, once when he was 8 and again when he was 21, thanks to the military, and then again in 1980. When actually charged, he pleaded guilty to lesser charges and treatment. Who knows if he had offended again between that case and now, 1984? Most likely he did, but none was ever reported.

The woman who made the first report of abuse was a friend of Rud's girlfriend. The girlfriend had told Christine Brown that Rud "was a good babysitter."

James John Rud was arrested on October 1, 1983 and charged with 13 counts of alleged sexual and physical abuse of at least four children, ages 8 and 10. Many more charges followed.

– Mugshot Polaroid from Scott County
Sheriff's Department in 1983

6
▼

What Labels Someone a "Pedophile"?

*"If you bungle raising your children,
I don't think whatever else you do well matters much."*
– Jacqueline Kennedy

When I was researching this book, I thought it was important to give a little explanation about sexual abuse of a child by someone who fits the criteria of a pedophile.

Pedo is a Greek word that means "child, and phile means "love." People who abuse only young children (pre-teen) are pedophiles–as they lose interest when the child becomes a teenager.

The general consensus is that pedophiles can be "treated" but never cured. That means the urge to abuse little children is always there, although the treatment has tried to teach them to redirect that urge.

From the various things I've read, here are some significant characteristics of a pedophile:

- Usually well liked by all ages and appear to be respectable.

- Likely to have their homes filled with things children like to pay with like video games, outdoor play things, toys, etc.–even if they do not have children.

- They find a variety of ways and places to be with young children.

- Singles often date or marry women with children the age he prefers.

- Most often males may choose jobs that allow them access to children.

- Often are victims of some form of child abuse themselves.

- A female (infrequently) who is, is often with a male pedophile–and a victim of sexual abuse.

- Don't force or coerce the child, but usually have developed a friendship and trust, which then develops into sexual touching.

- Operates alone or is involved in a ring of pedophiles.

- When arrested (they never turn themselves in) they deny they did anything wrong!

The child victims are usually not forced–but remain silent–because they enjoy the gifts, the trust and the secrecy of the relationship. If the adult says anything, it might be that if the child reports him, he might go to jail (or that the child or the child's parent would go to jail), or he threatens to harm the child, their pet or other family members.

Many experts agree that sexual activity with an under-aged person (after puberty) is also illegal but the perpetrator is likely a homosexual.

Caveat: Just because a man offers to work with children does NOT mean he is a pedophile. However it is everyone's job to be observant of all people in our child's life.

Reporting Laws Today

*"Words are, of course, the most
powerful drug used by mankind."*
– Rudyard Kipling

Had stronger notification laws existed prior to the Jordan
sex abuse scandal, could have James Rud's sexual abuses been
prevented?

On December 30, 2003, the *Minneapolis Star Tribune*
published this definition of Level III sex offenders:

Level III sex offenders

Level III sex offenders are determined to be at the highest
risk of reoffending of all predatory offenders. They are
required to register when they move, and authorities distribute
information about such offenders throughout the communities
or neighborhoods in which they live.

Minnesota Stat. 244.052 (2004) Table 1.5: Public Notification
Requirements Regarding Level I, II and III offenders spells out
who must be notified about a sex offender.

Level III must be disclosed:

- Victims of the offense who have specifically requested disclosure

- Adult members of the offender's immediate family

- Witnesses to the victims of the offense

- Other law enforcement agencies

- Agencies and groups the offender is likely to encounter, including staff of educational institutions, day care establishments and organizations that serve persons likely to be victimized by the offender

- Individuals that law enforcement believes are likely to be victimized by the offender, based on the offender's previous pattern and victim preferences

- Other members of the community whom the offender is likely to encounter

James Rud is a Level III sex offender. Would you want him to move into your neighborhood? If you had young children or adolescents, would you want him in your community?

"Sex offenders are the worst of the worst," said Minnesota Governor Tim Pawlenty in 2004. My preference is to allow the voters of Minnesota a chance to re-establish the death penalty to deal with sex offenders who kill their victims. The legislature has prevented that, but we are taking steps to deal with sex offenders with strong measures that include longer prison terms and intensive supervision."

Highlights of Governor Pawlenty's proposal include:

- Life without release for heinous sex crimes

- Indeterminate life sentences for forcible rape and repeat sex offenders

- Enhanced sentencing guidelines that increase the presumptive prison terms for all categories of sex offenses

- Enhancing our ability to track and monitor sex offenders no longer in prison

Minnesota legislators have increased sentences for sex offenders in several ways since 1989 and are likely to support Governor Pawlenty's proposals:

1989: Sentence is now at least twice the usual sentence. Applied to people convicted of any criminal sexual felony–or of arson, assault, burglary or murder with a sexual motive–if they are judged a danger to public safety or in need of treatment or supervision beyond a normal prison term.

1992: Life in prison with the possibility of release after 30 years. For those convicted of forcible rape following two or more prior convictions for criminal sexual conduct in the first second or third degree.

1992: Mandatory 30-year sentence. For those convicted of aggravated assault following one previous conviction for criminal sexual conduct in the first, second or third degree.

1992: At least twice the usual sentence. For those convicted of aggravated sexual assault with no previous record of sex crimes.

2000: For first-time forcible rape, increased the standard sentence from 7 years and 2 months to 12 years.

2002: For first-time forcible sexual contact without penetration, increased standard sentence from 4 to 7 years.

IMPORTANT NOTE:

Two pedophiles who had lived in Scott County have release dates coming up. Both are inmates at the Moose Lake Correctional Facility.

John Jerry Cermak was found guilty, along with his parents, for abusing their children/grandchildren. The 1982 Cermak case made Kathleen Morris famous. Her case was helped along by the dozens and dozens of photos the adults took of the sex act with their children.

Cermak is expected to be released April 10, 2008.

James Rud is expected to be released October 1, 2009. For good or bad, I expect we have not heard the last of James Rud.

Of course...

Release dates are subject to change at any time based on jail credit, discipline violations or resentencing actions. Also, offenders are generally not released to supervision on Fridays, Saturdays, Sundays or state holidays.

John Jerry Cermak

James Rud

– Photos courtesy of Minnesota
Department of Corrections

Being Charged, and Then...
Naming Names!

*"Lying to ourselves is more deeply
ingrained than lying to others."*
– Feodor Dostoevsky

- Rud was arrested October 1, 1983 on 13 charges of abuse of at least four children ages 8 and 10.

- He was charged November 19, 1983 with 108 counts of criminal sexual abuse.

Now what happened next is right out of a horror film! James Rud "decided" to name other people. He started with his girlfriend, then the mother of the children he was charged with abusing... and from there–townsfolk he didn't even know. In the timeline listed earlier, you can see that many of these people are connected in one way or the other: neighbors, relatives, city and county employees.

Did he decide on his own to "name names" or was he coerced with promises? We'll never really know. That's another part of the secret!

Regardless, Rud's poison was out into the community, doing great damage. He claimed to have seen "those named" at sex parties where children were abused. This mess was being touted as the LARGEST JUVENILE SEX RING EVER DISCOVERED IN MINNESOTA.

After James Rud had been charged with 108 counts of sexual abuse, he was held on $100,000 bond in the Scott County Jail. During the 10 months from his being charged until the next August, he and his public defender attorney, William Christianson from Redwing, Minnesota talked with prosecuting attorney Kathleen Morris many, many times.

- Confession August 14, 1984: Charges reduced to 10 counts of first-degree criminal sexual abuse against a child under age 13

- Recanted confession to FBI and BCA officers November 20, 1984, saying he was coerced to confess.

Rud's confession and his recanting of that confession stirred up a hornet's nest that still has a buzz about it to this day.

After his arrest in October 1983, he was given a public defender for his lawyer. It's ironic that all the people whose names he gave had to pay for their own private attorneys–and then had no recourse against him or the county for false arrest!

9

Details on Who
and What Was Charged

*"'I can forgive, but I cannot forget' is only another way
of saying 'I cannot forgive.'"*
– Henry Ward Beecher

I believe Kathleen Morris is guilty of grossly overcharging the 24 adults accused of child sexual abuse. Morris filed a total of 402 felony charges.

If the accused had gone to trial and been convicted of all charges, the jail time sentence would have amounted to more than five thousand years. Of the 402 charges, only one of the accused, James Rud, pled guilty to reduced charges and was sentence to 40 years for 10 counts of criminal sexual abuse.

Many prosecutors initially overcharge suspects and use a proposed reduction in the number of offenses in plea bargain negotiations.

Morris' excesses did not convince 23 of the 24 accused to accept any offer for reduced charges and/or plea bargains for reduced or no jail time. They insisted they were falsely accused and were innocent of all felony charges of child sexual abuse. Of the 23 accused, two went to trial and were found innocent. Charges against 21 defendants were dismissed.

Were the charges against 21 other adults completely bogus? We'll never know!

Accused	D.O.B.	Number of Felony Charges
Robert Bentz	Not listed	12
Lois Bentz	Not listed	12
Christine Brown	4-22-58	10
Jim Brown	2-28-48	5
Tom Brown	7-27-44	14
Helen Brown	7-29-50	14
Donald Buchan	8-23-47 **	55*
Cindy Buchan	1-23-57 **	22*
Scott Germundson	5-7-57	8
Marlene Germundson	9-8-56	17
Judith Kath	9-2-44	18
Charles Lallak	Not listed *	6
Carol Lallak	Unknown	6
Irene Meisinger	10-12-51	11
Terry Morgenson	10-22-40	2
Greg Myers	7-12-53	16
Jane Myers	Not listed *	8
Duane Rank	4-8-26	6
Delia Rank	7-17-27	6

Accused	D.O.B.	Number of Felony Charges
Robert Rawson	11-29-30	18
Coralene Rawson	Not listed *	10
Alvin Rud	5-4-37	8
Rosemary Rud	9-25-33	8
James Rud	3-27-57	110

*   Not listed on official State of Minnesota complaint form

**   Why so many charges against Deputy Buchan and wife
     Cindy? Buchan arrested Jordan police officer Dean Johnson
     who was investigating the abuse allegations for Morris.
     What does that say about who was named, and why?

10

▼

Criminal Penalties

*"For nothing is secret that will not be revealed,
nor anything hidden that will not be known
and come to light."*
– Luke 8:17

Minnesota has five categories, or degrees, of "criminal sexual conduct." First-degree criminal sexual conduct is considered the most serious of these categories. Most criminal sexual conduct offenses are felonies, although certain fifth-degree offenses are gross misdemeanors. The categories of criminal sexual conduct are differentiated by factors such as the nature of the sexual contact, the age of the victim and the perpetrator, and the degree of force or coercion.

For example, according to the Minnesota House of Representatives Research Department:

"Criminal sexual contact in the first and second degree typically apply to conduct involving personal injury to the victim; the use or threatened use of force, violence, or a dangerous weapon; or victims who are extremely young. Criminal sexual conduct in the third, fourth and fifth degree typically address less aggravated conduct and apply to other situations in which the victim either did not consent to the sexual conduct, was relatively young, or was incapable of voluntarily consenting to the sexual conduct due to a particular vulnerability or due to the special relationship between the offender and the victim."

Categories of Criminal Sexual Conduct

Minn. Stat. (2004) 609.342-609.3451

Category	Description	Statutory Sentencing Provisions
First Degree	Involves (1) sexual penetration with another person, or (2) certain sexual contact with a person under 13 years old –as specified in Minn. Stat. (2004) 609-342	Mandatory minimum prison sentence of 144 months. Maximum sentence of 30 years in prison and/or a $40,000 fine.
Second Degree	Involves sexual contact with another person–as specified in Minn. Stat. (2004) 609.343	Mandatory minimum prison sentence of 90 months for certain offenses. Maximum sentence of 25 years in prison and/or a $35,000 fine.
Third Degree	Involves sexual penetration with another person– as specified in Minn. Stat. (2004) 609.344	Maximum sentence of 15 years in prison and/or a $30,000 fine.

Fourth Degree	Involves sexual contact with another person– as specified in Minn. Stat (2004) 609.345	Maximum sentence of 10 years in prison and/or a $20,000 fine.
Fifth Degree	Involves (1) non-consensual sexual conduct, or is (2) certain lewd conduct – as specified in Minn. Stat (2004) 609.3451	Maximum sentence for repeat violations 5 years in prison and/or a $10,000 fine. For non-repeat offenders, maximum sentence is one year in jail and/or a fine of $3,000.

11

Felony Complaints

"The wheels of justice...they're square wheels."
– Barbara Corcoran

These complaints, or charges, took place over nine months. The first arrest was James Rud in October 1983 and the last person charged was courthouse employee Terry Morgenson in June 1984.

Various people, deputy sheriffs, Jordan police officers, Shakopee police officers, special agents from the Bureau of Criminal Investigation, FBI agents, lawyers, child protection workers, medical doctors, and therapist were involved in the questioning of the accused and are referenced on the official complaint forms.

The official felony complaint form is signed by an individual and becomes part of the official court record. Felony complaints were signed by the following: (Sometimes more than one complaint is on record and signed by another individual.)

Complaint signed by:	Accused:
Deputy Sheriff Pat Morgan	Robert and Lois Bentz
	Coralene Rawson
	Terry Morgenson
	Tom and Helen Brown
Deputy Michael Busch	Duane and Delia Rank
	Robert Rawson
	Alvin and Rosemary Rud
	Irene Meisinger
	Jim and Christine Brown
	Marlene Germundson
	Judith Kath
	Greg and Jane Meyer
	Charles Lallak
Michael O'Gorman, BCA	Donald Buchan
Pat Shannon, BCA	Cindy Buchan
Patrolman Larry Norring	Scott Germundson
	James Rud
Deputy Norm Pint	Carol Lallak

Felony complaints were received and acknowledged by several judges and County Attorney Kathleen Morris. In fact her name is on many of the complaints.

Many other officers and other investigators are mentioned in the complaints, and some of the accused received multiply felony complaints.

Several deputies told me they had no involvement in the investigation but the felony complaints and other written reports show they were deeply involved. Why lie? What's the cover up? Some said their work was very minimal and recollections vague; hence they will offer no information or opinions. Patrolman Larry Norring and Deputy Pat Morgan, who signed felony complaints against the accused, refused to be interviewed or make any comment other than "No, I will not talk about it."

12

▼

Where People Lived When They Were Arrested

*"The world divides people into the people you tell
your secrets to and those you don't. And it further divides
into people you only tell a few secrets to
and those who know them all."*
– Laurence de Looze, Correspondence

A slanderous misconception was printed and promoted by much of the news media telling readers that most of those accused lived in the mobile home park. Only four of the 24 people arrested were residents of Valley Green Mobile Home Park in Jordan. Here is where those arrested lived at the time of their arrest:

Only Four of 24 Arrested Lived at Valley Green

Numbers below corresponds with number on map and the four who lived there have * by their name.

1. James Rud*
2. Irene Meisinger*
3. Marlene Germundson*
4. James Brown*
5. Greg & Jane Myers
6. Don & Cindy Buchan
7. Scott Germundson (Chaska)
8. Charles & Carol Lallak
9. Terry Morgenson
10. Duane & Dee Rank
11. Christine Brown
12. Tom & Helen Brown
13. Robert & Lois Bentz
14. Judith Kath (Prior Lake)
15. Bob & Coralene Rawson (Shakopee)
16. Alvin & Rosemary Rud (Shakopee)

Valley Green Mobile Home Park

The Minneapolis Star Tribune on November 21, 1984 reported that Valley Green Mobile Home Park had grown in the past 15 years to house about a thousand people in its 290 mobile homes. This was nearly 40 percent of Jordan's population.

The article went on to say, "Valley Green represents 'the other side of the tracks.' As it grew, the mobile park acquired an unfortunate reputation as a place occupied by the sorts of people who disappeared in the middle of the night without paying all their bills."

Valley Green had its crime problems. Deputy Police Chief

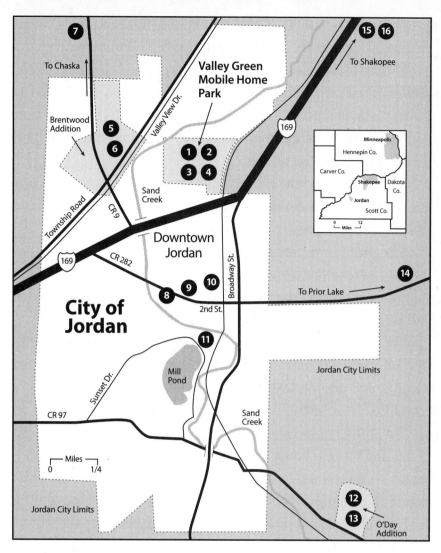

Map shows where people lived at time of their arrest

Dean Johnson admitted, "This is our highest call area."

An older fellow who does not want to be identified told me the trailer park is built upon a field where Mr. Alfred Sass spread "sludge," the human waste from the city-owned septic-sewer system. He said this field produced a beautiful bountiful corn crop and should have remained a cornfield. "Valley Green is located on a pile of shit. It's just shit on shit."

School Superintendent Ken Hanson said a great deal of low-income and subsidized housing had been added to the town. "Jordan seems to attract people whose lives are in transition, people who can't afford houses and apartments in more developed areas."

Some claimed the mobile home park was a haven for people with chemical dependency, people sort of "hiding out," and other kinds of unsavory characters.

In 1984, many Jordan residents, who had lived in the community before the development of Valley Green Mobile Park, felt the Park's inhabitants were not really Jordan people. Some still feel that way today.

In the fall of 1983, the first few people arrested in the Jordan child sexual abuse scandal came from Valley Green. Soon some people started calling that area of town "perverts paradise."

In 1984, reporters searched for dirty sensational stories about the mobile home park. One reporter told me of spending hours sitting on the elevated road bank of Highway 169 with a telescopic camera trying to get photos of some of the abusers and the abused. He never got what he was looking for.

The derogatory remarks about Valley Green led to some erroneous reporting and false conclusions. In spite of what was reported or even thought in town, some very upstanding, respectable people lived at Valley Green, including Ken Hicks, Jordan's School Board Chairman.

Not just everyone can move into Valley Green Park. On August 10, 2000, Charlene Koepp, editor of the Jordan Independent, wrote about a David Bateman in an article titled, "Where are we supposed to live?"

Valley Green routinely does criminal background checks on its potential renters. It was discovered that Mr. Bateman had some assault charges filed against him between 1991-1997 and had spent some time in jail.

Wendy Sonnier, manager at Valley Green, mentioned there are specific criteria that all applicants to Valley Green Park are subjected to before being admitted as residents of the Park. One of those criteria states that applicants must not have a felony conviction, history of drug use or dealing, physical violence to persons or property, or other conduct or behavior that would adversely affect the health, safety, or welfare of the park managers or the other residents.

Bateman acknowledged being abused as a child and eventually getting exposed to alcohol and drugs. Bateman and his wife, Linda, both martial arts instructors with black belts, had a mutually abusive relationship.

The question "Where are we supposed to live?" was reported in the Jordan Independent after the Batemans had been turned down at mobile home parks in Chaska, Watertown and Jordan, and even several apartment buildings.

Bateman claims the State's Attorney General told Linda to buy a mobile home in her name, and then he could move in with her and no one would know. Manager Wendy Sonnier said if management discovered that a person was living with someone else, and that person couldn't meet the specific criteria that all applicants must measure up to, the non-registered resident would have to leave the park.

Bateman said he had been through counseling for anger management and treatment for alcoholism, and spent three months in a halfway house. He contended that he was clean and sober and hadn't re-offended for 2-1/2 years. His past was behind him and Valley Green should permit him to move in.

Some Jordan residents agreed with the Batemans and a small group met and protested what they called "discrimination" at Valley Green Mobile Home Park.

On August 31, 2000 Judith A. Aune, a resident of Valley Green Park, wrote a letter to the editor of the Jordan Independent. She said she had lived in Jordan for about 15 years, and that everyone, including the Valley Green Park management, the police, and especially the kids, had knowledge about the flagrant drug dealing in the park.

She asserted no one had done a thing about the problem. She wrote that she had heard all the hype about the good life in a small town and how people help each other. She pleaded, "We should not turn our backs on Mr. Bateman who wants to do the right thing and has family members who want to help him." She concluded that giving Mr. Bateman a second chance would be the Christian thing to do.

This question of "Where are we supposed to live?" gets a lot of attention and discussion today as sex offenders are released from prison and treatment facilities and try to return to neighborhoods. Some offenders have repeated their criminal behavior, and have continued their patterns of abuse, rape and murder of innocent people.

Note: The present criteria (2005) for admission to Valley Green Park did not exist or were not enforced in 1983. If they had, James Rud would not have been permitted to live in Valley Green Park.

This is the question...

How did one man's arrest spread so convincingly to involve a total of 23 more people being accused, charged and then arrested? And then the worst of all–have their children forcibly removed from their homes before any investigation was conducted. So what happened?

Jordan, Minnesota, 1983-1984,
where 2,660 people lived the small-town life,
until James Rud was arrested–
and everything changed.

– Author's collection

13
▼

Witch Hunt:
Jordan 1984

*"Some people keep silent because they have
nothing to say, while others keep silent
because they know when to speak."*
– Sirach 20:6

Was there a witch hunt in Jordan in 1984?

Dr. Sharon Satterfield, a child psychiatrist, who directed a program in human sexuality in 1984 at the University of Minnesota, is quoted in the Minneapolis Star Tribune on August 13, 1984:

"Ten or fifteen years ago, people didn't believe children when they made these accusations. Now the pendulum has swung so far the other way that at times it has become a witch hunt. I just want to make sure we don't ignore the rights of people accused of abusing children, just as we used to ignore the complaints of the children who were abused."

Earlier in this article, Dr. Satterfield said: "Children do lie about sexual abuse. I know cases where children have brought charges to get attention or to be vindictive. Once you teach children about good touch and bad touch, you set them up to tell the story the way you want it told. Whenever you give a child a lot of attention, there is the danger they'll say what they think they're expected to say."

In US Magazine June 18, 1984, Patrolman Larry Norring, one of three investigators working full time on the Jordan cases said, "Some said we were on a witch hunt, arresting everybody and anybody."

Front page article in the Jordan Independent September 26, 1984 had this headline: "Sex Abuse Case Analysis: Was the Bentz trial a witch hunt?" The writer, Bruce Rubenstein was a freelancer who attended the Bentz trial and followed the Scott County child sexual abuse case for the Jordan Independent from the first arrest. Rubenstein states: "Of all the classic con games; the pigeon drop, the short-change, the bait and switch, the witch hunt, only the latter has real political potential. witch hunts have smoothed the road to power since the Inquisition and before. The recently concluded trial of Lois and Robert Bentz contained at least two elements of the witch hunt: charges so bizarre that they can't even be rationally discussed, let alone refuted; and a focus on sexuality.

"The jury fell for it and the result was something less than either side hoped for," Rubenstein said.

Rubenstein continued, "Scott County Attorney Morris lost the first trial against Bob and Lois Bentz, a critical event in the prosecution of the Jordan sex-ring cases. In summary, it was a dismal example of what is supposed to be the best legal system in the world. The defense argued the children were psychologically conditioned little dupes who entered against their will into a plot to imprison adults."

After the verdict, Morris said, "This doesn't mean the

Bentzes are innocent, it just means I failed to prove they were guilty."

Rubenstein goes on to say, "People who haven't been proven guilty are considered by our laws to be not guilty, as Morris is certainly aware. As for her assertion, she was unable to prove them guilty, a cynic could view the prosecution plan as an elaborate method to create a dramatic context for her final statement: 'I guess people just don't believe children.'

"That may be true, but no corroboration for the children's testimony was offered and little attempt was made to challenge the defense."

Bruce Rubenstein does not answer the question of whether or not the Scott County sex-ring abuse cases were a witch hunt, but he points out the defense successfully used a witch hunt theory in their arguments to get a not guilty verdict.

Newsweek February 18, 1988, page 72, showed a photo of Donald and Cindy Buchan with their children and this caption: "I'd like people to know we are not guilty." The article is titled, "The Youngest Witnesses. Is There A Witch Hunt Mentality in Sex Abuse Cases?" The text mentions that the most notable possible witch hunt sex abuse case was the Jordan child abuse scandal of 1984. The article reads, "In the most dramatic episode, lurid reports of child-abuse rings in Jordan, Minnesota resulted in criminal charges against 24 adults–most of which were dropped last fall after the first trial ended in an acquittal. The pendulum of enforcement, it seems, has swung too far."

Paul Abramson, a UCLA psychology professors who often works with prosecutors says, "Child protection services, the district attorney, and the police ignored child molestation charges for so long that now they are going the other way. They should take every accusation seriously, but they should avoid a rush to judgment."

Time Magazine February 25, 1985 page 22 headline read: "Disturbing End of a Nightmare: Under the supervision of Scott County Attorney, Kathleen Morris, the number of arrests for child sexual abuse grew. Fear spread through the once tranquil community. Children related incidents of sodomy, incest, and bestiality. One young girl reported being forced to eat a cat and a pet gerbil, fur and all." A ten-year-old boy said he was kidnapped and driven to a party where whip-wielding women in see-through clothes forced him into sexual acts with other children and adults, as they were photographed."

Jack Buss, the barber in Jordan in 1984, called Jordan "the new Salem." Women sometimes say their main confessor is their hairdresser. The majority of the male population of Jordan during the child sexual abuse scandal considered Jack to be the wise man with all the questions and answers. His shop was a gathering place for an exchange of ideas, insightful dialogue, humor, juicy gossip and detailed opinions about the newsworthy scandal.

Similarities with Salem's Witch Trials of 1692

The Salem, Massachusetts witch trials of 1692 have many similarities to the Jordan cases of 1984.

Samuel Parris, a pastor in Salem, had dealings in Barbados where he purchased two slaves. One of these slaves named Tituba was acquired to care for his nine-year-old daughter Elizabeth and his eleven-year-old niece Abigail.

Reverend Parris was a stern disciplinarian, and he allowed the girls virtually no game playing. The girls turned to Tituba and listened intently to her stories about voodoo practices in Barbados. They became fascinated and started playing voodoo with some of their friends. They started doing silly things such as fortune telling.

Elizabeth and Abigail started having fits in January 1692. The doctor suspected their behavior was caused by witchcraft. Other girls, friends of Elizabeth and Abigail, soon began having fits and making strange noises also.

The church congregation became frightened and begged the girls to tell them who or what was causing their distress. The girls shouted three names, Tituba, the slave, Sarah Good, a homeless woman; and Sarah Osborn, a woman who had married her servant.

After a beating by Reverend Parris, Tituba confessed to being a witch. Sarah Good and Sarah Osborn held on to their claims of innocence.

The three were moved to the Boston prison where Sarah Osborn died in chains. With Tituba's confession and admittance of other witches, the girls were pressured to tell the names of other witches. By the end of June, hysteria permeated the entire community and a hundred of Salem's residents would be incarcerated.

Local tavern owners, John and Elizabeth Proctor, were vocal about their opposition to the witch trials. Soon they were arrested along with others and would stand trial. A Mr. Giles Corey was pressed to death under a pile of rocks because he refused to stand trial.

The accusations and arrests continued to grow until they finally accused the wife of Governor Sir William Phips. At this time other ministers (prosecutors) took a stand and the trials were halted.

After the inquisition nineteen people were hanged, one pressed to death, and four others died in prison awaiting their trial. For those who had been accused, they continued to suffer until their deaths the stigma of possibly being a witch.

Ann Putman was the only girl to publicly address her part in the witch trials. In front of the Salem congregation, she said, "It was a great delusion of Satan" that caused her to act as she had.

In 1703, the colonial legislature of Massachusetts issued amnesties to all who had been accused and convicted, as well as to those accused who didn't survive prison life or had been put to death.

Five years after his testimony against a Salem woman helped put her to death, Reverend John Hale apologized. Salem declared a day of public contrition.

In 1709, the families of those who were executed received monetary reparations. In 1711, the colony passed a legislative bill restoring the rights and good names of those accused of witchcraft, and granted 600 pounds in restitution to their heirs.

In 1752, Salem Village was renamed Danvers.

In 1957, Massachusetts formally apologized for the events of 1692.

In 1992, on the 300th anniversary of the trials, a witchcraft memorial designed by James Cutler was dedicated in Salem.

Similarities of the Jordan Minnesota and Salem Massachusetts cases:

- Children telling wild stories believed by an overzealous prosecutor.
- Vigorous attempts by the prosecutors to obtain false confessions.
- Arrest of people who opposed the trials: John Proctor, Salem; Don and Cindy Buchan, Jordan.
- Community hysteria: people in both towns feared who would be arrested next.
- Suspicions and fear gripped the entire communities.

The Salem witch trial ended when new ministers (prosecutors) took over the cases. The Jordan witch hunt ended when

Attorney General Skip Humphrey and his associates took this case away from Scott County Attorney Morris.

The scary similarities of the Jordan and Salem trials are cause for much fear and trembling. People were falsely accused and arrested in Salem and in Jordan. The injustice in Salem happened. The injustice in Jordan happened. Could it happen again?

No Apology in Jordan

Unlike Salem, where some apologies were made to the accused, Kathleen Morris and her helpers have made no apologies to the accused in Jordan. In fact, she has spoken out loudly that she feels the accused in Jordan are guilty and the presumption of innocence in our justice system is a lot of nonsense.

While the displays of apology and repentance in Salem helped heal the community, there has been no apology or remorse from the accuser in the Jordan cases.

Minnesota Attorney General Skip Humphrey acknowledged that the Jordan community had been harmed by the scandal. However, he took no action to rectify the situation such as offering reparations or compensations to the innocent. The falsely accused in the Salem trials received monetary reparation. In Jordan, those found not guilty or had their charges dismissed have not received monetary compensation from Scott County or the State of Minnesota. Also, Humphrey took no decisive action to remove the overzealous prosecutor, Kathleen Morris.

Massachusetts formally apologized for the events of 1692 in Salem. No one in power or authority has formally apologized for the events of 1984 in Jordan. It is a grossly overlooked protocol that should be done.

14

Why People Don't Report Child Sexual Abuse– Even If They Are Mandated To

"A time comes when silence is betrayal."
– Martin Luther King

Why hadn't anyone seen and reported any suspected child abuse to authorities?

I pursued my inquiry, sometimes to the point of being a pest. Some interviewees considered me overbearing and obnoxious. I thought I was just being persistent and diligent in my quest for the truth. I challenged some with implications of cowardice if they had evidence of child abuse and failed to report such data to proper authorities.

I accused people of what is called the Genovese syndrome, a name that comes from what actually happened to a 28-year-old woman in New York on the morning of March 13, 1964. Catherine (Kitty) Genovese was returning home about

3:20 a.m. from her job as a bar manager.

She was about 35 yards from entering her apartment building when a man grabbed her. She yelled, "Oh my God, he stabbed me!" The attacker left, returned and stabbed her again. Lights came on and windows opened in many of the nearby apartments. The assailant again left and got in his car and drove away. At 3:35 a.m. he returned again and found her in a doorway at the foot of the stairs. He stabbed her a third time–this time fatally. Police received their first call at 3:50 a.m. and were at the scene within two minutes. The only person to call, a neighbor of Ms. Genovese, revealed that he had phoned only after much thought and an earlier phone call to a friend. He said, "I didn't want to get involved."

Detectives investigating Genovese's murder discovered that no fewer than 38 of her neighbors had witnessed at least one of her killer's three attacks but had neither come to her aid nor called the police. Kitty Genovese is a name that stands for Americans who are too indifferent, frightened or self-absorbed to "get involved" and help a fellow human being in trouble.

After accusing some people of having the Genovese syndrome, or just fear of getting involved, I gave them a copy of Pastor Martin Niemoler's writing:

"First they came for the Jew.
And I didn't speak up
Because I was not a Jew.
Then they came for the Communist
And I did not speak out
Because I am not a Communist.
Then they came for the trade unionist
And I did not speak out
Because I am not a trade unionist.

Then they came for me
And there was no one left
To speak for me."

Over the years, people gave me reasons for not reporting; some reflected something other than cowardice:

- A teacher said she couldn't report something she didn't see. She said maybe she didn't see any abuse because she wasn't looking very hard.

- A doctor claims he saw no signs or symptoms of child sexual abuse. Had he uncovered any, he said he would have talked to the parents in order to verify his suspicions before reporting to any child protection service.

- A local businessman said he didn't think there was any sexual abuse and that Kathleen Morris was on a "witch hunt."

- A retired school administrator said he suspected some physical abuse, but not sexual abuse. He knew some parents believed in using physical force, corporal punishment, when their children were disrespectful or disobedient. He said, "Some of the families around here adhere more to Dr. Spank than Dr. Spock."

- A retired schoolteacher commented: "Even after she (Morris) told us what signs to look for, I didn't see anything that looked like child sexual abuse."

- A counselor said that perhaps the mandatory reporters were simply ignorant of the subject of child sexual abuse. He knew of no experts in the community or school system who had any education or expertise in this area.

- A church leader told me that he didn't observe any child sexual abuse firsthand, but suspected there might have been some but one does not report such stuff without real hard evidence. Also, he said most Jordan people, including himself, would try to handle any situation quietly and privately.

Some members of law enforcement:

- A cop said, "Mind your own business."

- A deputy sheriff told me after several arrests, people were "scared shitless to say anything for fear that if they did, they might get arrested, too."

- Another police officer said, "There still is an ongoing homicide investigation, and you can get your ass in a sling for interfering with a murder investigation. There is no statute of limitation on murder."

Were Jordan residents afflicted with the Genovese syndrome? It is baffling that no one reported anything on the 24 people charged (and the 35 others suspected) of abusing more than one hundred children. More appalling is the fact that today, 20 years later, many Jordan people continue their ostrich-like conduct. Many brush aside or minimize the magnitude of how that 1984 scandal affected the people in Jordan. Some who lived there in 1984, today deny that anything happened there.

> *"He who conceals his disease*
> *cannot expect to be cured."*
> – Ethiopian Proverb

Although it is quite likely that the overzealous activities of County Attorney Morris led to false accusations and false arrest, to assert that no abuse happened is to put blinders on and live in a very sick, dishonest denial of truth and realty. This scandal was not and is not a case where "silence is golden."

Undoubtedly, fear caused some people to see no evil, hear no evil and speak no evil. Fear is the curse of the world. Anxiety is fear spread thin. For many, Jordan was and is a schizophrenic place.

"To sin by silence when they should protest
makes cowards out of men."
– Abraham Lincoln

15

▼

Law Enforcement Involvement

"Who are you to judge your neighbor?"
– James 4:12

The Jordan Police

The *Jordan Independent* October 6, 1983 reported that Jordan Police Chief Alvin Erickson received a complaint from a parent on September 29, 1983 which led to the arrest of James Rud, age 26, of Lot 271, Valley Green Mobile Home Park, Jordan.

The article went on to say that Chief Erickson and police officers, Dean Johnson and Larry Norring, along with the Bureau of Criminal Apprehension (BCA), were actively investigating the cases, which involved the abuse of as many as 32 children. Chief Erickson said the male and female children were between the ages of 5 and 14.

The article asked parents to report their suspicions: "Police have requested parents who suspect that their children may have been in contact with, or who have knowledge of other children having been in contact with Rud, to call Deputy Chief Dean Johnson of the Jordan Police Department or the dispatcher."

Patrolman Norring became the scapegoat and was blamed for failure to gather incriminating evidence. On October 5, 1983, nine days after James Rud's arrest, Patrolman/investigator Norring arrived at the Rud mobile home where he observed a stack of approximately twelve videocassette tapes and a large box containing what he believed to be pornographic materials. Rud's parents were present at the time and ordered Patrolman Norring to leave. Norring failed to seize the videocassettes or other materials. When he returned the next day, the tapes and alleged pornography were gone.

Chief Erickson had been Jordan's chief for many years. On February 12, 1982, Kathleen Morris wrote to Chief Erickson thanking him for the work he had done on the investigation and trials of Cermak family. This letter of commendation was sent to Mayor Gail Andersen, Jordan's City Council, and the local newspaper, the *Jordan Independent*.

R. KATHLEEN MORRIS
SCOTT COUNTY ATTORNEY
COURT HOUSE 206
SHAKOPEE, MN 55379
(612) 445-7750, EXT. 240

February 12, 1982

Chief Alvin Erickson
Jordan Police Department
210 First Street
Jordan, MN 55353

                                        RE: Cermak

Dear Chief Erickson,

I want to thank you and your staff for all the work you did on the Cermak investigation and trials. The successful resolution of this matter required the cooperation of a number of departments and agencies and the Jordan Police Department under your leadership made essential contributions to this joint effort. As usual the Jordan Police Department responded professionally and enthusiastically when a need arose. I know the time and energy you and your personnel put into these cases created an extra burden on your budget and staff. Thank you for shouldering this burden so selflessly.

Finally, Chief, I want to thank you personally for your individual efforts and interest in the investigation and the trial.

Thank you very much.

Sincerely yours,

R. Kathleen Morris
Scott County Attorney

cc: Mayor Gail Andersen
         Jordan City Council
         Jordan Independent

Not everyone was complimentary or supportive of Chief Erickson. Many humorous stories still circulate in Jordan about his ineffectiveness and ineptitude. Perhaps some are true.

I asked Chief Erickson how much notice he received from the County Attorney or from the Sheriff's Department before County authorities showed up in Jordan to arrest a suspect and remove children from their homes. He told me he received a very short notice, and he felt the Sheriff's Department should have given him more information much sooner.

On December 10, 1983, Officer Dean Johnson was involved in an accident in Shakopee. He had been drinking and left the scene of the accident. Deputy Sheriff Don Buchan and Sgt. Ken

Reitmeier captured Officer Johnson and returned him to the scene of the accident and turned him over to Shakopee Police Officer Jerry Poole.

Reviewing a copy of the Scott County Sheriff's Department "Incident/Supplementary Report" (that I obtained from another writer who has spent many years writing a book about the Jordan child sexual abuse scandal), I was surprised.

It is a typical arrest report about an incident/accident. What is NOT typical are handwritten notes on the copy I received. "...this is a cop who thinks Morris is God." He ended up with a $250 fine and Buchan (the officer assigned to the case) was arrested on child sex abuse. Coincidence? I don't think so!

Deputy Sheriff Don Buchan wrote the incident report dated December 14, 1983. On January 25, 1984, Officer Johnson pleaded guilty to DWI charges. The *Jordan Independent* published a brief notice.

Jordan Officer pleads guilt to DWI charges

Jordan Assistant Police Chief Dean Johnson pleaded guilty Jan. 25 to charges of driving while under the influence of alcohol.

Johnson was arrested Dec. 10 in Shakopee after he struck the rear of a vehicle stopped in the intersection waiting to make a left turn. He had already made restitution for the damages to the vehicle and will pay a $250 fine and must complete counseling.

The fine was originally $700, but $450 and a five-day jail sentence have been waived on the condition that Johnson be a law-abiding citizen.

I asked Chief Erickson about his assistant police chief at that time, Dean Johnson. Erickson did not have any kind or nice things to say about Officer Johnson, that Johnson tried to undermine his efforts and stab him in the back. Today Chief Erickson is not in contact with Dean Johnson.

Like Chief Erickson, Officer Dean Johnson spoke highly of Morris. Several people told me: "He was even more in Kathleen's pocket than the chief."

It is reasonable to conclude that Officer Johnson was given a very small penalty for this offense because he was working on the Jordan child sexual abuse investigations. What would have been the jail time and monetary fine if just a regular Joe or Jane had smashed into rear of a car while drunk?

Months later, on June 4, 1984, Scott County Deputy Sheriff Donald Buchan and his wife Cindy are charged with child sexual abuse. Along with 19 others, their charges were dropped in October. The lingering, unresolved question of whether the accusations of child sexual abuse leveled against the Buchans were simply retaliation for the accident-related arrest of Officer Dean Johnson is still debated today.

The third member of the Jordan police team, Patrolman Larry Norring, a.k.a. Investigator Norring, full-time investigator, part-time Jordan cop, declined to talk to me about the investigation.

The Jordan police force, Chief Alvin Erickson, Deputy Chief Dean Johnson, and Patrolman Larry Norring, have been called many things as a result of their work on the Jordan child sexual abuse scandal of 1984. They have been referred to as: "Our three stooges, Larry, Curly and Moe; the unholy trinity; three blind mice; Huey, Louie, and Dopey; the three musketeers; Jordan's Keystone Cops"; and some more profane descriptions.

The Jordan Police force provided allegiance to and support for County Attorney Morris. No Jordan cop questioned her motives, integrity, or modus operandi. Like Morris they proceeded from the premise of "presumed guilty."

At a Jordan city council meeting early in 1984, council

member Mike Shaw introduced a resolution to suspend Mayor Gail Andersen as head of the police department. Mayor Andersen was indicted on 13 counts of misconduct as a public officer and misuse of public office, but had not yet gone to trial.

Before Shaw introduced the resolution, Mayor Andersen wanted to discuss the suspension of assistant police Chief Dean Johnson because of his recent DWI conviction.

A large crowd attended this council meeting early in 1984, some of them with questions about the James Rud case. Jordan resident, Charles Lallak asked the council why Larry Norring, a police officer licensed for part-time, was doing investigative work when Johnson, a full-time officer, had been trained in the area of sexual abuse. Lallak asked the council why they don't ask for outside help in the investigation.

Later in 1984, Charles Lallak was arrested and charged with criminal child sexual abuse—another person added to the ever-growing list.

Mayor Andersen told Police Chief Alvin Erickson that Johnson should not be doing any investigations. Councilman Ron Jabs read a letter to the council from Chief Erickson putting Norring on the case. He also read letters from some Jordan citizens commending the Jordan police department and the county attorney for their work on the sexual abuse cases. (Later, Jabs would be elected mayor of Jordan.) You have to wonder what Norring owed Morris in return? To continue the false accusations?

Patrolman/Investigator Larry Norring is quoted in *US Magazine* June 18, 1984. "Thanks to Morris and the investigators, Jordan changed. People were afraid to even be associated with Jordan. That's not true anymore. People are proud of this town now. When we're done, Jordan is probably going to be the safest place in the country to live."

In June of 1984, Larry Norring jumped on the Kathleen Morris bandwagon and proclaimed her a champion and a savior.

Chief Erickson describes Rud in *US Magazine* June 18, 1984. "He babysat for people, took the kids to ball games, movies, bowling and brought them presents. He was just a likable young man."

This makes me think of people interviewed on TV after a neighbor does some terrible deed–when they say, "He was such a nice man, never bothered anyone–until he killed his wife." For a chief of police to be quoted saying this, well....

Sheriff Deputies' Involvement

Minneapolis Star Tribune November 3, 1984, County Attorney Morris explained that she didn't push harder for a more active homicide investigation "because she was under pressure to prepare several abuse trials and had only three sheriffs' investigators to handle that 'awesome' job."

Deputies Pat Morgan, Michael Busch and Norm Pint were heavily involved while Deputies Dave Einerstson and Kenneth Reitmeier were less so.

On May 21, 2003, Sheryl Miller of the Scott County Sheriff's Office provided me with a list of names of deputies employed by the County prior to 1983 and during much of the Jordan child sexual abuse investigation of 1984. Some on this list are still employed by the Sheriff's department. Some have retired or found employment elsewhere.

The following deputies were employed prior to 1983 and are still with the Sheriff's Office:

>Dave Menden
>Dave Einertson
>George Luskey
>Merv Brenke

Terry Johnson
Bob McCue
Janice Patterson

Officers who have retired since that time are:
Don Hamilton
Bill Nevin
Mike Busch
Dave Wagner
Fred Rgnonti
Jim Manke
Dan Tietz
Pat Morgan
Dick Welch

Only a few of these officers were involved in the Jordan investigation you referred to. As these files are in the archives I cannot tell you which ones there were.

Sheryl Miller
Scott Co. Sheriff's Office

Missing from the 16-name list are two deputies who were much involved in the Scott County sex abuse scandal: Deputy Sheriff Donald Buchan and Deputy Sheriff Norm Pint.

On June 4, 1984, Scott County Deputy Sheriff Donald Buchan, 37, and his wife Cindy, 27, were charged with child sexual abuse.

Deputy Norman Pint

October 4, 1984, the *Minneapolis Star Tribune* printed an article titled: "Deputy Testifies in Buchan Case." The article reads: "Scott County Deputy Norman Pint testified that an alleged victim of Donald Buchan told him of sexual encounters between the Buchans and one of their children. Pint said that a 5-year-old friend of the Buchan children told him that both Cindy and Donald Buchan hurt one of their daughters. Pint said later this victim said Mrs. Buchan didn't hurt kids. Pint explained that *hurt* was a code word officials allowed children to use when referring to sexual abuse."

After Morris dropped the charges, the *Minneapolis Star Tribune* October 18, 1984 reported: "Chief Deputy Bill Nevin told Deputy Buchan to report back to work after four months of suspension with pay. Buchan, a 12-year veteran, was told that the Sheriff's Department would use the services of a firm that helps county employees deal with personal and work-related problems if needed."

Deputy Chief Nevin told me, "Deputy Buchan was a licensed police officer, the County Attorney dismissed charges against him; therefore, he was rightfully entitled to return to work."

When asked about how difficult it was for the accused and his accuser to work in the same department, Nevin said it was stressful.

I asked Deputy Pint if it was stressful or difficult for him when the man he testified against, Deputy Buchan, returned to duty. He replied that it might have been hard for Buchan to come back to work, but he had no problem with his prior testimony or Buchan's return to work. When I asked Pint if he thought any the people were innocent and might have been victims of false accusations, he replied, "For every person who is falsely charged, there are a least a hundred who should be in jail, but get off by some technicality, or some fancy lawyering."

I asked Pint if he could or would name any of the accused that might have been a victim of a false accusation, he responded that there was sufficient probable cause to get a judge to sign an arrest warrant.

Deputy Pint said he worked closely with County Attorney

Morris and his job was to investigate and help her build a strong case against the accused. It appears he was far more loyal to Morris than to his boss, Sheriff Doug Tietz. Pint explained to me that investigators work closely with the prosecutor trying to build a case, and the sheriff may be more involved with other law enforcement matters.

Kathleen Morris and Deputy Pint operated on the assumption of guilty until found innocent, rather than on a presumption of innocence until proven guilty. Neither County Attorney Morris nor Deputy Norm Pint has acknowledged that anyone might have been falsely accused and arrested. Neither has offered an apology to those who were found innocent, or who had charges against them dismissed.

A veteran Shakopee city cop said, "Our job is to find evidence, arrest, and help convict criminals. We don't go out looking for the innocent, the good guys. We get the bad guys."

Sgt. Kenneth Reitmeier

Sgt. Kenneth Reitmeier was in charge of the Scott County Jail during both the 1982 Cermak sex abuse trials and the Jordan cases. He had another connection with Jordan, as he had played against and for the Jordan Brewers baseball team. Deputy Reitmeier told me he was a strong supporter of Kathleen Morris and her efforts to prosecute child sexual abusers.

When asked whether he thought innocent people might have been falsely accused, he replied everyone accused claims they're innocent. He said the Cermaks claimed they were innocent, even though they were confronted with 70 photographs of the adults abusing children. He concluded that he didn't know of anyone specifically who was falsely accused in the Scott County sex scandal of 1984.

Officer Reitmeier said Morris would have had a much more

winnable case had there been photographs, or some pornographic record of the allegations. He said the physical corroborating evidence was thin, but he felt the children did not deliberately lie. He also felt more investigators and resources should have been assigned to a crime of this magnitude. Reitmeier finds no fault with Kathleen Morris' efforts or methods.

Reitmeier mentioned that Judge Mansur didn't like Kathleen Morris. Judge Mansur presided at the only case that went to trial, the trial of Robert and Lois Bentz where a jury found the Bentzes not guilty.

When asked about how he and other officers reacted to Deputy Chief Bill Nevin recalling Deputy Buchan back to work, Reitmeier replied, "Nevin avoided conflict and controversy. His bringing Buchan back and assigning him to transporting prisoners was a smart move."

Detective David Einerston

Detective David Einerston of the Scott County Sheriff's Department had worked with Morris investigating the Cermak family and James Rud.

In *City Pages,* February 8, 1984, Einerston is quoted:

"From a law enforcement point of view, the investigation of sexual abuse is made much easier by who our attorney is."

Near the end of this lengthy article, Einerston's diplomacy about his boss is mentioned. "She's not a pleasant person to be around during a case. I think she's a total workaholic, and she's very hard to work with, very demanding. She asks for and get results–and she gets the job done."

I think Det. Einerston forgot along the way that his boss in the chain of command was Sheriff Doug Tietz. A detective working for a county attorney who doesn't adhere to the legal tenant of presumption of innocence is using Gestapo-like tactics.

In a pleasant conversation with Detective Einerston, he told me that he wasn't much involved in the Jordan child abuse sex scandal. I suggested perhaps he was being too modest. I read him a part of an article printed in the *Washington Post* January 2, 1985 to remind him.

Fellow officers speak highly about Detective Einerston's expertise in the investigation and prosecution of child sexual abuse. Some say he could tell me a lot about the Jordan child sexual abuse scandal if he desired to do so. He has not offered more detail or explanation.

Deputy Pat Morgan

Deputy Pat Morgan is retired from the Scott County Sheriff's Department. Fellow officers have said he was very active in the child sexual abuse investigations and is named as an investigator in several newspaper reports.

The *Minneapolis Star Tribune* September 6, 1984, reported about Deputy Morgan's participation in the Bentzes' trial:

"The third witness was Patrick Morgan, a Scott County Sheriff's investigator who assisted in the case against the 24 Jordan adults. (Attorney) Gray aggressively questioned Morgan about specific statements six children had given him regarding sexual acts they testified the Bentzes forced them to commit. Both attorneys (Earl Gray and Barry Voss) repeatedly asked Morgan why his notes and reports did not contain references to specific statements the children gave him about sexual abuse. Morgan said that the children rarely stated specifically what occurred, but used dolls to demonstrated or wrote answers to specific questions on paper."

Deputy Morgan refused to talk with me about the Scott County child sexual abuse case. I tried to get his opinion about the possibility of any false accusations. His reply, "No comment, I have nothing to say about that."

Deputy Sheriff Michael Busch

Along with Norm Pint and Pat Morgan, Deputy Sheriff Michael Busch is cited as one of the lead investigators from the Scott County Sheriff's Department assigned to the Scott County child sexual abuse cases.

Mike Busch was born and raised in Jordan. His brother Bill was for many years the Chief of the Jordan Fire Department. I asked Mike if his being from Jordan affected his investigating Jordan citizens. He said it didn't make any difference and that he had a job to do.

Deputy Busch became somewhat famous or infamous at the trial of Robert and Lois Bentz. Attorneys Earl Gray and Barry Voss questioned Busch. The *Jordan Independent* reported on September 12, 1984:

> "Deputy Michael Busch, investigator for the Scott County Sheriff's Department, was repeatedly asked why no reports were written about a number of interviews with children.
> "In one case Busch admitted that 17 interviews had resulted in only eight reports. He was also repeatedly challenged to point out where certain specific allegations appeared in the reports that he made. He was unable to do so."

I told Deputy Busch that some of the accused told me they were not read their Miranda rights. He told me that if an officer is just having a friendly conversation with a suspect, he is not required to read that person his Miranda rights. He said if you are going to use any of the conversation in a trial, then the suspect must be read his rights.

When asked if he thought some people were falsely accused and arrested, Busch replied that sufficient and probable cause was given to a judge who then issued the arrest warrant. He emphasized that if there hadn't been probable cause, the judge would not have issued the arrest warrant.

Deputy Busch mentioned that Kathleen Morris had a special relationship with Judge John Fitzgerald that went beyond mere professional courtesy. The judge issued many of the arrest warrants.

When pressed why the Bentzes were found innocent and the others had their charges dismissed, Officer Busch said the cases were not well developed. Too many cases and too few investigators. He thinks there might have been a different result if Morris had concentrated on one or two cases rather than trying to assemble a couple dozen cases. Busch did not tell me which cases he thought were most winnable for the prosecution.

Deputy Busch commented that Sheriff Tietz and County Attorney Morris did not get along at all and this dissension, lack of communication and lack of cooperation hurt the investigation. He said Morris did a good job on the Cermak case and the photographs of adults having anal intercourse with children made for a slam-dunk guilty verdict.

Because of Morris' past success and her dominant personality, investigators listened to her and carried out her orders. Other than Sheriff Tietz, "nobody really talked back to Kathleen."

Most of the suspects who were arrested have told me they are not angry with the deputies. One said, "If I had to be arrested, I wanted it to be by the Sheriff's Department and not the Jordan police." Some sympathized with the deputies saying they understood they were just doing the dirty work for Kathleen Morris.

I believe the deputies worked hard and supported the efforts of Morris to arrest and convict child abusers. They were on an honorable mission. However, their common sense, their concept of justice and fairness and their appreciation of truth, got lost by their subservience to the powerful County Attorney. They showed no moral authority or courage to stand up and challenge her when she acted abusively, dishonestly and insanely.

A retired Deputy Sheriff told me, "Only Sheriff Tietz had the balls to stand up to Morris."

Sheriff Doug Tietz

Minneapolis Star Tribune July 3, 1986 published information about Scott County Sheriff Douglas Tietz written by an Associated Press staff writer. "Scott County Sheriff Douglas Tietz, an eight-year veteran of the Sheriff's Department, says he will not seek reelection. In making the announcement, according to KARE-TV of the Twin Cities, Tietz said only that he wants to return to private life."

At this time, Sheriff Tietz, Kathleen Morris and several other Sheriff's deputies were defendants in a $300 million lawsuit filed by persons who claim they were falsely accused and arrested in the Scott County sex cases.

Sheriff Tietz originally ran against an incumbent sheriff and was reelected for a second term. He is confident he could have won a third term. Sheriff Tietz explained that his decision not to seek reelection was in part influenced by the pending lawsuit against him. Also he mentioned, that Morris had filed for reelection the previous Tuesday. He said, "On the remote possibility that she won reelection, I wouldn't want to go through another mess with Morris as County Attorney."

Tietz and Morris were at odds during several phases of the child sex-abuse cases. Tietz said in *Minneapolis Star Tribune* November 4, 1984, "I am aware that the county attorney's office felt that our department was leaking information. The allegation is simply not true."

Rather than ordering a departmental investigation of Deputy Buchan, Sheriff Tietz asked the Bureau of Criminal Apprehension (BCA) to investigate sexual abuse accusations against Buchan. Having an outside agency investigate Deputy Buchan would eliminate suspicions of a cover-up within the Sheriff's Department. Tietz denied widespread and persistent allegations that his office leaked investigative data to defense lawyers, purportedly to undermine the case against Deputy Buchan.

Sheriff Tietz confirmed reports that he met several times with Deputy Donald Buchan after his arrest on Buchan's initiative. Sheriff Tietz, who is a born-again Christian, said he advised his deputy where to go for religious counseling, and how to obtain evidence for his defense and how to seek redress through federal authorities of what Buchan felt was a violation of his civil rights in his arrest.

Sheriff Tietz' contacts with Deputy Buchan have been criticized privately in county government, but there are no state law-enforcement standards against such a relationship. John Phillips, head of the law-enforcement program at the Alexandria, Minnesota, vocational-technical institute, said it isn't necessarily wrong for a police official to advise an arrested officer, but he is "going to have to expect some criticism" for acting as a defense attorney.

Several sources close to the investigation said Morris took over the investigation because of her strong will and dominating style, and that Tietz did not stand up to her. Tietz responded, "I don't have to inform you that Kathleen Morris is an aggressive individual. Her demands in the investigation were great and I hope that the men that I assigned to this cased were able to meet the majority of those demands."

Seeking Outside Help

Sheriff Tietz has been criticized both for calling for help from the Minnesota Bureau of Criminal Apprehension and for not asking for help from the BCA.

The BCA assisted the Jordan Police early in the investigation of child sexual abuse. The *Minneapolis Star Tribune* November 4, 1984:

> "Despite the scope and difficulty of the cases, Tietz twice failed to obtain outside help that was readily available. Earlier this year he rejected help from the Minnesota Bureau of Criminal Apprehension (BCA)."

Minneapolis Star Tribune November 3, 1984:

> "Floyd Roman, assistant superintendent of the BCA, said his agency dropped out of the investigation early this year because Tietz indicated several times that the county could handle it on its own. Even when the sheriff asked the BCA to investigate Buchan, Tietz advised that the county could take care of the rest of the investigation, Roman said."

Tietz declined to comment on why he didn't ask for help except to say that his deputies "did a fine job in the investigation and were able to meet the needs of the investigation."

Morris has been widely quoted, however, as blaming Tietz for insufficient investigation of the murder allegations. Yet her reported dominant role in the sex-abuse cases, and her last-ditch call for a more active homicide probe, raise a question of whether she was pushing earlier for an aggressive investigation.

At one point, according to psychologist Susan Phipps-Yonas, a therapist for some of the children allegedly abused, the County Attorney's office and Sheriff's investigators told her they weren't doing much on the investigation because they "didn't have anything to go on."

On October 10, 1984, Morris called a meeting of county and local authorities and asked them to actively pursue the homicide investigation. She told them that an ongoing investigation was necessary to stop a judge from turning over 126 pages of investigative notes on the homicide allegations to the attorneys for the accused.

Again Morris criticized Tietz for not thoroughly investigating murder allegations. Sheriff Tietz repeated that his investigators were doing a good an adequate job.

A former deputy sheriff who was actively involved in the Jordan investigation said, "If Doug would have been encouraged by just one of his deputies to run for reelection, he would have. His never-ending hassle with the county commissioners and Morris got pretty tiresome, and his deputies were pretty fed up with the sheriff and were relieved when he said he wouldn't run for reelection. It was time for a new sheriff."

When we look at the results, in the only case to go to trial, Robert and Lois Bentz were found innocent, and Morris dismissed the charges against 21 people she had charged with criminal sexual conduct. Attorney General Humphrey called in the BCA and the FBI to investigate the allegations of homicides related to the sex abuse cases, and they found no evidence of any murders. The new sheriff, Bill Nevin restored Deputy Buchan to full employment in the sheriff's department. It is safe to say the battle between Sheriff Tietz and County Attorney Kathleen Morris was won by Sheriff Tietz.

Sheriff Tietz was right. Calling in the BCA or other agencies would not have altered the outcome. The BCA found nothing when they did investigate, and they wouldn't have found anything if they investigated earlier.

Sheriff Tietz had several run-ins or fall-outs with the county commissioners about some of Kathleen Morris' abuses.

However, Commissioners William Koniarski, Anthony (Tony) Worm, Dick Mertz, Mark Stromwall, and Roland Boegeman were supportive of County Attorney Morris–recklessly approving any funding she requested. Rather than listening to Sheriff Tietz, they kowtowed to Morris. Sheriff Tietz has good reason to despise the 1984 County Commissioners.

A retired deputy sheriff who wants to remain anonymous said, "The Sheriff's Department in 1984 was made up of wussies and pussies. Tietz didn't let Morris crap all over him. He stood up to her, but he was the Lone Ranger. Tietz was a good sheriff, a good man."

To clarify, former County Attorney James Terwedo, who defeated Kathleen Morris in her bid for reelection in 1986, said there was a low threshold to get a warrant. He said a warrant could be issued on a signed affidavit from a police officer who suspects something. Terwedo also mentioned that the relationship between the county attorney and a judge may determine the difficulty, or lack of difficulty, in obtaining arrest warrants.

Officer Norring certainly has the right not to talk to me. However, Norring, County Attorney Kathleen Morris, Assistant County Attorney Miriam Wolf, Deputy Sheriff Pat Morgan and many others who refused to be interviewed for this book are saying a lot by their silence. What have they got to hide? What are they ashamed of?

"I can't comment on that," or "I won't comment on that," reflect the integrity or lack of integrity or obstinacy of the individual questioned.

As the law enforcement officers swarmed across Jordan and surrounding communities, knocking on doors, asking questions, arresting unsuspecting people, following up leads, speculations and accusations, accompanying child protection workers to grab children from their homes, talking to people–this investigation obviously brought fear and distrust to the community.

Often the church is a place of calm where people turn in times of trouble. How did the faith community respond?

16

▼

The Jordan Faith Community

*"Let the one among you who is without sin
be the first to throw a stone."*
– John 8:7

If you lived in Jordan in 1984, you were labeled a Catholic, a Lutheran, a Methodist, a nothing, or a non-believer. Jordan is proud of its Christian heritage. Jordan was once described as a "God-fearing town of fundamentally Roman Catholic Germans, along with some good conservative German Lutherans." Well into the 1950s, St. John the Baptist Catholic church offered a mass in German and a German language service was conducted at St. Paul's Lutheran.

From the beginning Jordan clergy were esteemed. They were trusted with the moral compass of the community and were responsible for indoctrinating and educating the children in the Christian faith.

In 1984, the four church leaders were:

- Father Thomas Carolan (Father Tom) of St. John the Baptist Catholic Church. Now at St. Judes, Warrensville, Ohio.

- Pastor Fritz Sauer (Pastor Fritz) of Immanuel United Methodist Church. Now at Advent United Methodist Church, Eagan, Minnesota.

- Pastor Paul Larson (Pastor Paul) of Hope Lutheran Church. Now at Christ the King Lutheran Church, New Brighton, Minnesota.

- Pastor Vern Voss, St. Paul's Lutheran Church. Now at Pilgrim Lutheran Church, Minneapolis, Minnesota.

Pastor Vern Voss, St. Paul's Lutheran Church

Vern Voss was the senior clergyman in town. He had pastored St. Paul's Lutheran Church, Wisconsin Synod for 14 years. Membership in 1984 was 650. His wife Kathie was active in the community and in addition to their own three kids, she provided inspiration and education to 40 more children in a nursery school she operated out of her home.

Late in May of 1984, Pastor Voss said they were victims of a "terrorist action." He received a phone call from Greg Myers' neighbor. Myers was the Jordan police officer arrested for child sexual abuse. The caller said she heard from the Myers that Pastor Voss and his wife, Kathie, were soon to be arrested and charged with criminal child sexual abuse.

Vern Voss acknowledges that he and his wife were "frightened, yes, terrified." They knew they were innocent, but rumors started circulating and more suspicious questions were being asked. In mid June, the Vosses took action. They visited County Attorney Kathleen Morris and made clear to her that the rumors about them being child abusers were baseless.

From Kathleen Morris, they obtained a written statement verifying their claims of innocence. Pastor Voss read the statement to his congregation. He asked the other clergy in town to read the statement along with his personal message to their congregations. Father Tom Carolan and Pastor Fritz Sauer read the material to their congregations. Pastor Paul Larson of Hope Lutheran did not. The weekly newspaper, the Jordan Independent, printed a letter from the Vosses carrying the message of their innocence.

Letter to the Editor, Jordan Independent, June 13, 1984

Reputations at stake due to rumor

"It is with a mixture of sadness and anger that we feel we must make this statement.

"It has repeatedly been brought to our attention this past week that a very disturbing rumor concerning us is circulating in Jordan and the surrounding communities. The rumor states that the two of us are 'under suspicion, under police surveilance, on a list of suspects, or about to be arrested and charged with sex abuse crimes.' This lie reached such proportions that we feel we must address the issue.

"We contacted the office of the County Attorney for help in dispelling this rumor. Kathleen Morris personally discounted all allegations as ridiculous and untrue! She gave us permission to quote her as such! She also suggested that if anyone had any doubts or questions about this matter, they are free to phone her directly and she would be happy to discuss it further. Her telephone number is (___).

"We feel that our reputations and our ability to continue the kind of work that we both engage in are at stake. We are saddened and, yes, also angry that anyone would start such rumors for whatever reason. We cannot look into another person's heart or mind and really know the purpose, but we do believe that it was a deliberate terrorist tactic. We would ask you to help us by using the above information to stop these malicious rumors."

– The Rev. & Mrs. Vern Voss

Although Pastor Voss and his wife were now off the suspect list, other members of St. Paul's Lutheran had not been cleared.

Four members, Greg and Jane Myers as well as Donald and Cindy Buchan, had been arrested and charged. Some members of the congregation believed the defendants were guilty and shouldn't be allowed to receive the sacraments and should be excommunicated. Other members lent their support to the Buchans and the Myers and said they were falsely accused.

To resolve this dilemma, Pastor Voss demanded the accused take an oath before God proclaiming their innocence. All four avowed their innocence and were allowed to continue as members in good standing and receive the sacraments of the church. Pastor Voss said that, had they not stated their innocence under oath, the church would have disciplined them.

Adding to the tension at St. Paul's was that Police Chief Alvin Erickson was also a member. Supporters of the accused despised Chief Erickson and accused him of being in cahoots with Kathleen Morris–to the detriment of his fellow parishioners. Supporters of the chief said he was only doing his job and by arresting fellow parishioners, he was being fair-minded and impartial.

Pastor Voss will not offer a judgment of his parishioners' guilt or innocence. In fact he will not even offer a speculation. He does some fancy equivocation and minister-talk evasion. He claims he had to remain a neutral figure and "only God can look into their hearts." He said he had to accept their oaths of innocence and if they lied, they lied to the Holy Spirit and will ultimately be judged. His Protestant theology teaches that the sole unforgivable sin is lying to the Holy Spirit. Pastor Voss offers a lame, foggy explanation for separation of church and state and matters of civil law and church law. The explanations are disingenuous.

If you are charged with child sexual abuse, you should not have to wait until you are in the hereafter to be judged.

However, even if the charges are dismissed or you are acquitted at a trial, you are condemned in the here and now. The accusation is all it takes to ruin a person and do irreparable damage to the family.

Pastor Voss has his suspicions but will not reveal who he thinks is the Judas of this mess–the source of the rumor about he and his wife. The rumor implicating the Vosses was triangular. Because of how they heard it, many assumed Greg Myers started it, maybe to discredit or confuse the entire investigation. Myers denies starting any rumors and points to Chief Erickson for blaming him. Chief Erickson said he was relating what the Vosses told him–they heard it from someone who indirectly heard it from the Myers.

Twenty Years Later: A nasty persistent rumor still surfaces from time to time. Did Pastor Voss cut a deal with Scott County Attorney Kathleen Morris in exchange for her vindicating them? It meant that he could continue his ministry, and his wife could keep her nursery school operation. Speculation is that he agreed to testify for the prosecution when the cases finally came to trial. Pastor Voss emphatically says no deal was offered and no deal was accepted. There was no quid pro quo.

The controversy surrounding Pastor Voss and his wife never ended. The question in the community remains: If Pastor Voss was able to get he and his wife off the hook, and get Kathleen Morris to absolve them of any suspicion of child sexual abuse, why could he not do the same for his parishioners.? Did he try? Did the shepherd look out for the shepherd and not the flock? If Pastor Voss accepted the oaths of the four accused members of his congregation as testimony of their innocence, and permitted them to be full participants of the sacraments, did he conclude they were innocent of the crime of child sexual abuse?

Because of Kathleen Morris' reputation for offering deals,

it is understandable how such a nasty rumor could surface and persist. The subject became moot with the dismissal of charges.

Pastor Voss has some wonderful memories of Jordan and has visited many times since 1984. He has many friends there. Pastor Voss encouraged me to write this book and agrees with me that if we are to conquer our fears, we must confront them.

"The truth shall set us free,
but initially the revelation will hurt like hell."
– Bill Wilson, Co-founder
of Alcoholics Anonymous

Like many others in the community, Pastor Voss feels some child sexual abuse happened in Jordan but that some citizens were falsely accused and arrested. He said the problem is that a child molester or pedophile is not going to admit to anyone that he is guilty of child sexual abuse. The innocent and the guilty will both passionately declare they are innocent.

Father Tom Carolan, St. John the Baptist Catholic Church

Eileen Ogintz wrote an article for the Chicago Tribune September 2, 1984 under this headline: "Sex Scandal Robs Town's Innocence." Subtitled: "Mother says parents are afraid to show their kids affection." (Photographs of St. John's Catholic grade school and Father Tom Carolan accompany the article.)

Parents were afraid to hug or kiss their children publicly. People were afraid to say anything to anybody. Paranoia about being accused and arrested permeated everyone's thinking. Fear was omnipresent.

Father Tom mentioned that his sister living in Illinois read the Chicago Tribune article and called to tell him how famous he'd become. The Jordan, Minnesota child abuse sex scandal was a national and international sensationalized news story.

From my phone conversation with Father Tom, he said that he had read the letter Pastor Voss of St. Paul's Lutheran had asked him to read. I sensed he was less than enthusiastic about reading a letter from Kathleen Morris declaring Pastor Voss and his wife innocent of any criminal sexual abuse while other members of the Lutheran church were accused, arrested and awaiting trial.

Father Tom was called by the defense to testify at the Bentz trial. He said he had met with the Bentzes in March of 1984 when they asked him to bless their house. The Bentzes were trying to sell their house to pay for lawyers. This blessing request was not unusual in this small German farming community. Priests were often called to bless many things: livestock, crops, new dairy barns, farm machinery, businesses and even sporting teams

The Bentzes also asked Father Tom to contact the Scott County Attorney's office to find out if their children were all right. Father Tom said the county officials never returned his many calls.

An elderly Lutheran lady said about Father Tom. "That Catholic Priest, he was our modern-day Dietrich Bonhoeffer. He resisted Kathleen Morris and the rest of the Scott County Gestapo. While others preachers were silent and frightened, he spoke out with courage and conviction and said Jordan was good town."

"There are things for which an uncompromising stand is worthwhile."
– Pastor Dietrich Bonhoeffer

(In 1939, Bonhoeffer returned to Germany from the safety of America to oppose Adolph Hitler.)

Father Tom told me of another disturbing incident. After the charges had been dismissed, children who had been removed and placed in foster care had not yet been returned to their parents. They were still under the control of the Child Protection Service. Parents of two children wanted to see their kids for Christmas and have some kind of celebration. They asked Father Tom to intercede on their behalf. According to Father Tom, after dealing with some caustic, cruel and insensitive county employees, especially some child protection workers, the assigned case worker relented and said the children would be allowed to spend an hour or so with the parents before Christmas, but he would have to be present. Also, a child protection worker and a policeman would have to be present.

Father Tom arrived at the house and waited for the caseworker to bring the children inside. As soon as the younger child saw his mother, he pulled away from the county employee, ran to his mother, threw his arms around her and hugged her tightly. Seeing this heart rendering, tearful, yet joyful and exuberant embrace, Father Tom said, "I knew for sure this kid had not been abused by this parent."

No Catholic Families Were Involved

No Catholic parents were accused of sexual misconduct nor were any of the children Catholic. Father Tom said he is convinced some of the allegations were false and far-fetched. He said the County Attorney's reason for dismissing the charges –an ongoing homicide investigation–was completely bogus. He commented on some investigators poking around the hillside by the Catholic cemetery looking for bodies of missing children. They didn't find any.

Father Tom said many lives were ruined and the entire

community suffered greatly. He feels that those who were falsely accused and "put through hell" should have some recourse and should be able to sue for damages. "In Jordan, justice is still undone." And as Pope Paul VI said, "If you want peace, work for justice."

Pastor Fritz Sauer, Immanuel Methodist Church

Pastor Fritz Sauer of Immanuel Methodist Church was the youngest clergyman in Jordan, serving from 1984 to 1986. At this time he was a full-time seminary student carrying a full student load and functioning as a student pastor. Most of his ministry duties focused on weddings and funerals, and established obligations, rituals and traditions.

However, he arrived in the middle of a difficult situation involving the nearby Lydia Methodist church and the Jordan church. Previously the two churches had formed an alliance to share resources. Pastor Fritz doesn't recall exactly when the two churches became yoked together in this special arrangement. He states that it was agreed that either church could opt out of the agreement and operate as a separate entity. In 1984, Lydia was the larger and wealthier congregation and elected to end the joint venture. This split with the Lydia Church put a lot of stress on the Jordan church and its youthful student-pastor. Pastor Fritz, "It was a difficult time."

Pastor Fritz said no children nor members of his congregation were involved. Although not accused, interrogated, or arrested, the Methodists were affected by the scandal, especially the young people. Pastor Fritz told of his love for the people and the wonderful time he spent with his youth group camping and exploring the Boundary Waters. He mentioned how these young people were afraid to wear their Jordan jackets. What should have been a triumphal and jubilant time for the high school students, had been turned into a time of shame and embarrassment.

Pastor Fritz said he didn't see firsthand any abuse and doesn't know if any criminal child sexual abuse actually happened. He said he got his information about the case from television, newspapers, and magazines.

After being paid a minimal salary for two years, Pastor Fritz graduated from seminary and has not revisited the area. Pastor Sauer wished me good luck and said he is eager to see the book. He said the whole community suffered and maybe my book will be a kind of helpful community therapy. We agreed: Hurt people hurt people.

> *"Truth is a demure lady, much too lady-like*
> *to knock you on the head and drag you to her cave.*
> *She is there, but people must want her and seek her out."*
> – William F. Buckley Jr.

Pastor Paul Larson, Hope Lutheran Church

Paul Larson had been the pastor at the smaller, 425-member Lutheran congregation for about six years. The scandal put him in a very difficult position. Five members of his congregation were arrested and his wife was working for Scott County Attorney Kathleen Morris. In October 1983, Kathleen Morris spoke to a large crowd at Hope Lutheran on child abuse. She said that child abuse was not unique to Jordan–and it wasn't something in the water. She said the reason it seems like there is so much abuse in Jordan was because of diligent and dedicated police work by some of Jordan's finest.

Pastor Paul, the Hope Lutheran congregation, and much of the community and the county were laudatory and supportive of County Attorney Morris. Morris' presentation at Hope Lutheran happened in 1983. Most arrests were made in 1984.

The numerous arrests caused some of Hope Lutheran's congregation and others to change their attitudes and opinions about Morris and some of the Jordan police. Pastor Paul began to have some reservations and questions.

All Lutherans are not alike. Hope Lutheran Church was referred to as the American Lutheran congregation and was not in any way connected to St. Paul's Lutheran church, Wisconsin Synod. Hope Lutheran was founded in 1973, and St. Paul's had been in Jordan since Jordan's beginning. Officially Jordan's Hope Lutheran Church was founded in 1973 and is a member of the Evangelical Lutheran Church of America.

In 1984, some misconceptions about the Jordan Lutherans were printed in several newspapers and a few periodicals. The articles tried to sensationalize some sort of schism among the Jordan Lutherans. It was erroneously reported that Hope Lutheran came into existence because some of the accused and arrested were members of St. Paul's Lutheran and some members of that congregation did not want to worship with the alleged child abusers. Another mistaken report said that accused–Jordan policeman Greg Myers and fellow member, Chief Alvin Erickson, could not worship under the same roof and one or the other would have to find refuge in the newly found Hope Lutheran congregation.

When asked whether he thought members of his congregations were guilty as charged or were falsely accused, he said he didn't know for sure then and doesn't know for sure now. He said he found it hard to believe some of the people accused could have been involved in such an atrocious crime. Yet at the same time, he didn't think a 5- or 6-year-old child could concoct such stories. "They just couldn't have made it all up."

When asked whether his wife's working for Kathleen Morris affected his thinking and judgment, he said he had been an early promoter, supporter and defender of Morris.

However, after his wife quit working for Morris and more arrests were made, he had a change of mind and heart. Pastor Paul said his wife couldn't continue working in the hostile and abusive environment of the Scott County Attorney's office. He acknowledged his wife said there was a lot of verbal abuse and even spitting upon subordinates. His wife quit when most of Morris' staff resigned en masse. Pastor Larson said Morris ran her office and much of the courthouse on fear and intimidation. When his wife finally quit, she left with trepidation as she had no new job. And people did not cross Morris without suffering dire consequences. We owe a debt of gratitude to Ester Larson and others who finally said "no" and "no more" to Kathleen Morris, quit and left that unhealthy setting.

Early on in the investigations, Pastor Larson actually went along with Morris and participated in some of her talks and presentations about child sexual abuse. Morris initially had pretty strong support in Jordan and elsewhere in Scott County.

Pastor Larson said he worked with school superintendent Ken Hanson in getting all Jordan school children to attend a presentation by the Illusion Theater. This educational production was designed to help kids understand what constitutes child abuse, what is "good touch" and what is "bad touch." Pastor Larson said he was adamant in having this program mandatory rather than a voluntary. Every kid in Jordan was better informed about child sexual abuse because of the educational efforts of the clergy and the schools.

Like many others in Jordan, Pastor Larson feels some children were sexually abused, but some of those who were accused and arrested were innocent of such charges. He says we may never know the whole truth.

"The truth is incontrovertible.
Panic may resent it; ignorance may deride it;
malice may distort it, but there it is."
– Winston Churchill

That is the key. Whether it is about pedophile priests, allegations of celebrities sexually abusing children, or a host of other unpleasant realities, people must want the truth and they must search for the truth.

Pastor Larson visits Jordan two or three times a year and has many friends there. He says it is a good and beautiful place. He supports my writing this book and encourages me to say some nice things about Jordan.

17
▼

Mandatory Reporting Laws

*"As scarce as truth is, the supply has always
been in excess of the demand."*
– Josh Billings

All 50 states have passed some form of mandatory child
abuse and neglect reporting law in order to qualify for funding
under the Child Abuse Prevention and Treatment Act
(CAPTA) (Jan. 1996 version) 42 U.S.C. 5101, et. seq. The Act,
originally passed in 1974, has been amended several times and
was most recently amended and reauthorized on October 3,
1996 by the Child Abuse Prevention and Treatment and
Adoption Act Amendment of 1996 (P.L. 104-235).

In every state, the following people are required by law to
report suspected abuse: doctors, nurses, dentists, mental health
professionals, social workers, teachers, day care workers and
law enforcement personnel. In some states clergy, foster parents, attorneys and camp counselors are also required to report
abuse. In about 18 states, any person who suspects abuse is
required to report it.

A mandated reporter in Minnesota includes:

- Health care workers: Hospital administrators, medical personnel and professionals and dental professionals

- Social service workers: Social workers group home staff and foster parents

- Mental health professionals: Psychologists, therapists and psychiatrists

- Child care workers: Home child care providers, child care center staff and babysitters

- Educators: Teachers and assistants, school administrators and school support staff

  • Law enforcement officers

  • Guardian ad litems

  • Clergy (see note)

  • Corrections management and staff

NOTE: Members of the clergy are required to report suspected child abuse or neglect unless that information is received under certain privileged circumstances. (See Minnesota Statues Section 626-556, subd. 3(a) (2) and Minnesota Statutes Section 595.02, subd. 1(c)).

The Family and Children's Service Division of Minnesota Department of Human Services published a booklet, "Reporting Child Abuse and Neglect," subtitled, "A Resource Guide for Mandated Reporters." For more information call or write:

Minnesota Department of Human Services
444 Lafayette Road North
St. Paul, MN 55155-3832

Family and Children's Services Division
651-296-2217

A mandated reporter who fails to report may be guilty of a misdemeanor, a gross misdemeanor, and under some circumstances, a felony.

Of course, one cannot report something one did not observe. In fact, Minnesota Statutes 626.556, subd. 5. states: "Malicious and reckless reports. Any person who knowingly or recklessly makes a false report under the provisions of this section shall be liable in civil suit for any actual damages suffered by the person or persons so reported and for any punitive damages set by the court or jury, plus cost and reasonable attorney fee."

The Humphrey Report mentions that mandatory reporters did not report suspicions of child sexual abuse.

18

▼

Did the Children Lie
and If So, Why?

*"It is a terrible, an inexorable law that one cannot deny the
humanity of another without diminishing one's own:
in the face of one's victim, one sees oneself."*
– James Baldwin

Socrates (c. 469-399 B.C.) advised his most famous student, Plato, against believing children or telling stories to children. He said they couldn't differentiate between allegory and
reality.

Art Linkletter, a triple Emmy award winner, now 92 years
young, interviewed 27,000 kids on his show, "Kids Say the
Darndest Things." Linkletter showed us that children can and
do come up with some preposterous stories, and tell such tales
convincingly with vivid detail. He was able to elicit stories
from kids by asking them some manipulative and leading
questions. Linkletter never told us that the child didn't believe
his own concocted fable. He never said the kid lied.

From the children questioned in the Jordan child sexual

abuse scandal, some pretty far-fetched narratives emerged. A child's imagination is boundless. Also, a child can be manipulated and coerced into believing stories and fairy tales, and to retell and enhance such yarns.

The Minneapolis Star Tribune November 15th, 1984 published an article titled "Credibility of Children Becomes Major Concern in Scott County Cases." Phillip Villaume, an attorney for a former defendant, commented, "If the FBI doesn't believe them or the BCA doesn't believe them…that goes against the credibility of the children."

Also in this article, Steve Doyle, another defense attorney said, "Some children could have been telling the truth about what they perceived to have happened, although it didn't happen at all. Frequently, especially with children, they misunderstand or misperceive what occurred."

Joe Rigert and Paul McEnroe, staff writers for the Minneapolis Star Tribune, wrote an article November 20, 1984 titled, "Boys' Admission of Lies Halted." Quote from the account: "… two boys, ages 11 and 12, admitted that they had made up stories of killings.…"

These two boys, the main and most credible sources on the homicides, began telling of possible murders in July of 1984. As the investigation continued, they would add details and then later recant some of their previous statements.

When interviewed by the Minnesota Bureau of Criminal Investigation and the FBI, they took it all back. One of the boys called the allegations "a pile of shit." The other boy said, "The story started with a little lie and grew in the telling." The boys described in specific and vivid detail how the killings took place. They talked about kids being stabbed and cut badly. They described how one victim had a sex organ amputated. They told of one boy being shot after he was badly cut.

Defense attorneys have alleged that therapists and investigators produced homicide stories by using leading questions and in repeated interviews. One of the alleged victims characterized therapist Tom Price's interview technique as being coercive and manipulative. The child said, "The psychologist provided the questions and answers."

On November 30th, 1984, the Minneapolis Star Tribune published an article titled, "Scott County Document Shows Wild Inconsistent Tales."

> "In a 126-page document, which had been kept secret for nearly five months, children tell investigators they were forced during sex parties to engage in sex with other children, forced to cut and slice them and forced to watch adults beat and kill them.
>
> "Two weeks after a 12-year-old boy began talking about homicides, he was questioned by his therapist in the presence of the sheriff's deputy who led the investigation. The boy denied any incidents regarding suspected death of any victims. After this meeting, the boy met with therapist, Thomas Price."

After this one brief meeting, and regardless that the boy had denied any knowledge of homicides, therapist Price came out and indicated that the incidents the boy originally described regarding possible deaths did indeed happen. Therapists have said that it takes time to draw out details of such painful experiences from children.

Did the child lie?
Did the therapist lie?
Did they both lie?

From a *Minneapolis Star Tribune* article December 15, 1984 titled "Two Children Recant Sex Stories: Officials Worry About Others":

> "Since the sex abuse cases were shifted from local authorities, Scott County Attorney Kathleen Morris and her investigators, to state authorities in October 1984, more unraveling has happened. Two more children who were key accusers in the sex cases have recanted on stories that implicated more than a dozen adults in sex parties and child sexual abuse."

Despite admissions of lying by children, Scott County authorities insist sexual abuse happened. "Documents in the cases include reports on more than 100 interviews in which many of the 40 alleged victims accuse their parents and other adults of sexually abusing them. They tell of gatherings or parties as setting for abuse. Some accounts are vague; others are detailed."

Did the children lie?

In an article in the *Jordan Independent* September 19, 1984, under the heading, "Jury in Deliberation Over Verdict in Bentz Child Abuse Case," Attorney Morris characterizes children as: "credible eye witnesses to a crime, besides being victims."

Lois Bentz' attorney Barry Voss said, "One alleged child victim was a liar by nature and the state took advantage of that predisposition."

Earl Gray, Robert Bentz's attorney charged County Attorney Morris of playing with the facts. He characterized each of the child witnesses as "either sick, liars, or lacking in credibility."

The *Jordan Independent reported* on November 24, 1984, "Admission of lies may be the reason investigation dropped."

The *Minneapolis Star Tribune* November 28, 1984 headlined an article, "Rud now says he lied about sex rings." The article goes on to say:

"James Rud was charged with 108 counts of first- and second-degree criminal sexual conduct. In a plea bargain with Scott County Attorney Kathleen Morris in August 1984, he pleaded guilty to 10 first-degree counts and agreed to testify against others charged in the case. Rud acknowledged to WTCN-TV that the statements he made to investigators with his plea were lies aimed at winning a lighter prison sentence. Rud said he was relieved the truth had finally come out, and he had lied when he implicated others in the investigation of two alleged child sexual abuse rings operating in Scott County.

"A Scott County deputy sheriff discussed the murder investigation with Kenneth Lanning, the FBI's top authority on child sexual abuse and child pornography. Lanning told the deputy that he was aware of seven other cases around the United States where children who had been sexually abused described mutilations and murders. Lanning acknowledged that investigators did not find any homicide victims. Lanning told the deputy there were two explanations for the murder allegations: 'that the incidents actually happened, or that when children are grossly sexually abused, there may be a possibility that they begin to fantasize as to the things which could happen that would be worse than what happened to the individual child.'"

Lanning does not flat out say that children lie, but that it is possible for them to fantasize. Kids who recanted their stories of mutilations and murders are more direct. They admit they lied.

Many alleged victims, children who have talked to me, all have said they did not tell the truth. All said they were encouraged to lie by somebody: Kathleen Morris, police, psychologist, foster parents, child protection workers, lawyers, and other children.

Did the children lie in Jordan's child sexual abuse scandal? Yes. Were they encouraged and helped to lie? Yes.

Although many of the children have admitted they lied, some people in 1984 protested that children couldn't lie about the horrible stories of child sexual abuse and homicide. In the October 18, 1984 *Denver Post*, Jordan Mayor Don Tillman and others said some of the accused may be innocent of some crimes but the children did not lie. Tillman said, "I've worked with children for 25 years now, and way down deep, once you start talking to a child and gain his confidence, very few of them lie."

The *Denver Post* article went on: "Jordan resident Wilma Schwichtenberg and others believe that Prosecutor Morris and the local police department conducted a `witch hunt' that smeared innocent people along with the guilty. They say, 'the children have been brainwashed by psychologist and investigators into believing their parents or others hurt them.'" The article did mention that many people believed the children simply lied.

An unidentified source from Scott County told the *Chicago Tribune*, "The reason I was convinced the kid was telling the truth was that he described someone dying in a way he only could if he had seen it.... He described a person growing weaker and convulsing and dying." The source said he was shaken just listening to the account.

Now twenty years later, Morris' last public comment for the record was that she believed the children and the children didn't lie. Other professionals, teachers, psychologist, and child protections workers claim that children don't lie. Some who claim children do not lie, such as Kathleen Morris, never had any children.

Children lied about sexual abuse in 1984. Children lie. Ask Art Linkletter. He will tell you "Kids say the darndest things."

19

▼

Other 1984 Scott County Cases

"Our lives begin to end the day
we become silent about things that matter."
– Rev. Martin Luther King, Jr.

While the world watched and listened to see what else would happen in Jordan, this county's prosecuting attorney had other cases on her plate. However, it appears that because she was 100 percent committed to finding all these charged members of the community guilty… she neglected the rest of her cases. Here's what happened that enraged the families involved–and should have caused people in power to do something, anything–to get this county's prosecutor back on task.

Murderer Goes Free

William Golla was found dead in his Jordan, Minnesota law office on April 4, 1982. Although he'd been shot three times by a 9mm automatic pistol, the coroner ruled that William's actual cause of death was from several blows with a blunt instrument at the base of his skull. A local cop told me that he was severely pistol-whipped. William also had been anally raped.

It was common knowledge the William and his brother Harry had arguments over settling their father's estate. William inherited the lion's share of the estate, which included a lake home and an office building in Spencer, Iowa. Crossed by the injustice, Harry had repeatedly threatened to kill his brother for screwing him out of his share. Police suspected this dispute over money was the motive for the killing. Harry was the only suspect.

Harry eluded police for nine months before being arrested in St. Paul on December 8, 1982. In February 1983, Golla was extradited to California for sentencing on an old 1971 drug conviction.

On April 14, 1983, Scott County charged Golla with second-degree murder for the death of his brother, William. He was released from the Orange County California Jail on May 1, 1983 and returned to the Scott County Jail for a trial.

On June 24, 1983, a Scott County grand jury indicted him for first-degree murder. Harry was then incarcerated in the McLeod County Jail in Glencoe, Minnesota. He spent more than 18 months in jail at Glencoe waiting for his first-degree murder trial. June 1984 a trial date for September 11 was set.

At a pre-trial hearing at the Scott County Courthouse, Assistant Scott County Attorney Pam McCabe told District Judge Martin Mansur that the trial should take about six weeks. She would be the prosecuting attorney in place of the more experienced County Attorney, Kathleen Morris, who was busy handling the Scott County child sexual abuse cases.

Well-known defense lawyer Joseph Friedberg represented accused Harry Golla. Friedberg told Judge Mansur he didn't think the trial should take very long, much shorter than the six weeks suggested by the prosecution.

Lawyer Friedberg is considered by some fellow attorneys and some judges to be in the same league with the O.J. Simpson dream team. In fact, a local judge said he is a better legal defense counsel than those who made up the dream team.

"The transcripts are full of denigrations of Mr. Golla's character. Ninety-nine percent is unmitigated hogwash. The County is mistaken if they think they can get that into the trial," Friedberg said to Judge Mansur.

Friedberg suggested the County Attorney was withholding substantial information.

Assistant County Attorney McCabe contended that all information had been made available.

Friedberg said he would not defend Golla against allegations contained in the transcript such as allegations that he attempted to murder a cat. "I'm prepared to defend against murder one!" Friedberg said.

McCabe countered and argued to Judge Mansur that such information was important to the case. "The cat incident is mentioned not because it constituted cruelty to animals, but to show how investigators knew where to look for a bullet that was found." McCabe claimed the information on the brothers' relationship as they were growing up served to support the motive for the crime.

Friedberg said Golla's defense would simply be that he didn't commit the crimes and was not guilty as accused.

At the June pre-trial hearing, Assistant Scott County Attorney McCabe, under Morris' direction, withdrew a previous plea bargain arrangement that had been offered to Golla.

Before the September 11, 1984 court date, the prosecution offered another plea bargain, reducing the charge from murder one to manslaughter. The newspaper account read:

"Harry S. Golla pleaded guilty to first-degree manslaughter in the shooting and beating death of his brother, William, a Shakopee attorney and former chairman of the school board."

Scott County Attorney Kathleen Morris said the plea bargain set Harry Golla free on September 11, 1984; the day his trial was scheduled to begin. Nobody understands why! Even attorney Friedberg was surprised. It didn't make any sense then, and it doesn't make any sense now. It's hard enough, a judge told me, to explain to the legal community, but impossible to explain to an ordinary citizen—but that's what happened!

Ann, William Golla's widow, said the family was hurt and disappointed with the release of Harry from jail. Even Scott County Sheriff, Doug Tietz, admitted he was unhappy with the lenient plea bargain.

Tietz said that investigators had done everything possible to build a solid case against Harry Golla. Nearly 400 people were interviewed. Investigative trips were made to five other states to collect evidence. The Jordan police and experts from the State Crime Bureau intensely investigated the crime scene. Thousands of hours of manpower were spent collecting evidence.

In my recent interview with Joseph Friedberg, he said he could speak now because his former client is dead. "Kathleen Morris should have tried this case. She was so obsessed with the sex cases that even a winnable murder case took a back seat," Friedberg said.

When asked about the Bob and Lois Bentz child sexual abuse trial, Friedberg said Morris was no match for Earl Gray, Carol Grant, Barry Voss and other competent defense attorneys.

Friedberg suggested Morris dropped the charges when she realized she would lose the other cases also. The excuse she gave about possible homicide investigations being the reason for dismissing all charges was unbelievable. "She did a lousy job, and I don't think she's a very good lawyer," he said.

In the fall of 1985, commission hearings were underway considering the removal of Kathleen Morris from the office of County Attorney. Specifically the Commission was reviewing Morris' mishandling of the sex abuse cases. Many thought Morris would be removed and McCabe would be appointed County Attorney. As the hearings were underway, Pamela McCabe, Judy Emmings and Peggy Flaig resigned from the Scott County Attorney's staff.

The Commission, appointed by Governor Rudy Perpich, found that Kathleen Morris committed malfeasance while holding the office of Scott County Attorney.

The Commission should have also addressed her letting a confessed murderer go free. Because even if the handling of the case may not have been malfeasance, it sure was a gross miscarriage of justice.

And, Another Murder Suspect
Goes Free: Timothy Weirke

Paul McEnroe wrote in the *Minneapolis Star Tribune* January 3, 1986 "Investigators irate over Morris' refusal to issue warrant.

"Richard Melony, 18, of Bloomington was found shot to death in a car in Lakeville, Minnesota last Thursday." (December 28, 1985).

Scott County Attorney Kathleen Morris refused to issue an arrest warrant for a 27-year-old murder suspect. Angry investigators say she is making unreasonable demands for additional evidence. Her behavior is jeopardizing the case.

Sheriff Tietz said that Morris told his deputies, Lakeville police officers and agents from the Bureau of Criminal Apprehension (BCA), that they need to come up with at least '23 additional items' in order for her to be satisfied there is enough evidence to issue an arrest warrant against the suspect identified as Timothy Weirke of Elko, Minnesota.

Observers suspect this is a continuation of the tense relationship between Morris and the Sheriff Tietz stemming from the Jordan child sexual abuse cases.

Sheriff Doug Tietz said, "We don't understand the reasons for this—we're not trying to try the case, we're just trying to get the guy arrested, somebody we should've had an arrest warrant for last Sunday."

BCA Superintendent Jack Erskine said Morris' actions were jeopardizing Weirke's arrest. BCA agents reiterated and renewed complaints and criticisms of Morris' handling of the Scott County sex abuse cases.

Erskine said authorities have a statement from Larry Getty, who says he was shot and wounded by Weirke while sitting in a car with Melony at the time of the homicide. Erskine felt that the witness statement, along with the physical evidence at the crime scene near Elko, justified a warrant.

Because County Attorney Morris refused to seek or issue an arrest warrant, Sheriff Tietz went to a Scott County judge for counsel. The judge told the Sheriff, "It was prosecutorial discretion on the part of the county attorney on whether to issue a warrant and that the judge could not."

Sheriff Tietz questioned Morris' interpretation of the law. He said Weirke should be arrested on suspicion of aggravated assault in the shooting of Getty. "We've got an eyewitness who was shot and that's now an aggravated assault–it's information enough but she still refuses to even do that."

Harry Halden, the BCA's special agent in charge of investigations, said his agents provided enough information for Morris. "We're satisfied that the standard for probable cause to arrest this person has been met, and she feels it's not been met."

The Fact and the Question:

It is strange. Morris needed little or no evidence to arrest 23 adults and charge them with criminal child sexual abuse, whereas here where you have an eyewitness to a murder and a lot of corroborating evidence, and she will not get an arrest warrant and enable the police to pick up the suspect.

Would Morris let a murderer go free because of her differences with Sheriff Tietz?

She plea-bargained with Harry Golla, after he had murdered his brother William, and he was set free. Murders can go free but anyone even "suspected" of child sexual abuse gets arrested?

Kathleen Morris again is guilty of putting personalities ahead of principles.

20

▼

They Skipped Town Because of the Jordan Hysteria

"That which the best and wisest parents
want for their own children,
the community must want for all children."
– John Dewey

While all this craziness was going on in Jordan, another family was being accused…and because they fear for the loss of their daughter as in Jordan…well, read on:

The *Minneapolis Star Tribune* reported on November 12, 2003 that a Minnetonka couple, Ed and Karri LaBois, were arrested near Salt Lake City. The couple had eluded the law for 19 years. They say they fled Minnesota in 1984 because they had been wrongfully accused of sexually abusing their 4-year-old daughter.

The *Utah Desert Morning News* on November 12, 2003 reported that Edward and Karri LaBois had been living in Utah since 1998 using assumed names of Stephen Maine Reigel and Kathrine Carri Merrill. They were arrested Monday evening,

November 10, 2003 at their home in West Valley City and booked into the Salt Lake County jail for investigation of unlawful flight to avoid prosecution.

The *Salt Lake Tribune* reported on November 12, 2003, "The two allegedly sexually assaulted their 4-year-old daughter and other small children they watched in an unlicensed day care they operated in Minnetonka, Minn., in 1984. Court records show they operated the day care for two years."

The article goes on, "According to the felony complaint filed in Minnesota, a mother found her 4-year-old daughter playing naked with a toy doctor kit in July 1984. The little girl told her mother she always played that way at her 'day care home.'"

The *Salt Lake Tribune* reported that with a court order, social workers were able to interview the LaBois' daughter at the University of Minnesota Human Sexuality Program. Police searched the Minnetonka home and reported finding pictures of naked children, undeveloped film and a book on how to take sexually explicit photographs.

Psychiatrist Dr. Sharon Satterfield, who had helped Scott County Attorney Kathleen Morris, says she still remembers Karri and Edward LaBois' car screeching out of the parking lot near the University of Minnesota on September 4, 1984. In the *Minneapolis Star Tribune* November 1, 1984, the doctor said, "I'll never forget that day. I was sure they were going for the border."

Satterfield, now a director of a state-run psychiatric service for children and adolescents in central Minnesota, said the LaBoises were dressed casually and gave a plausible story about how the children were confused about any alleged sexual contact. They sat in a waiting room during the videotaped interview with their attorney, a prosecutor and a child protection worker.

Before telling the couple of their daughter's graphic description of sex games, Satterfield put the child in a side room with her secretary. Then she told the couple the child would be removed from their home. Karri LaBois screamed, bolted past Satterfield, ran into the side room and grabbed the child and dashed outside.

Satterfield said she also interviewed a 3-year-old boy who was at couple's day care and that she believed he was sexually molested but not physically hurt so nothing was done. She said she gave the FBI a videotape of her interviews with the two children.

After the LaBoises were arrested, George Dougherty of the Salt Lake City FBI office said, "It's a good thing to have them off the street and let them face the charges against them."

Current Hennepin County Attorney Amy Klobuchar had said there is no time limit on prosecuting the 1984 charges because they were filed at the time the arrest warrants were issued. That also held true for a federal charge filed in 1984 against the couple for fleeing to avoid prosecution. Klobuchar said her office will consider filing additional charges if the evidence warrants and the stature of limitations doesn't preclude that. She makes no mention of the presumption of innocence until proven guilty.

However, on November 26, 2003 Jim Adams and Margaret Zack reported in the *Minneapolis Star Tribune* with this headline: "Prosecutors drop sex-abuse charges against couple who fled Minnesota in 1984."

After reviewing the evidence, a 1984 videotaped interview with LaBois' 4-year-old daughter, and re-interviewing witnesses, Hennepin County Attorney Amy Klobuchar said, "We conclude there is not sufficient evidence to go forward with the case against the LaBoises." Her office dropped charges of intrafamilial sexual abuse.

Klobuchar, like Morris, did not say anyone was innocent, just that they didn't have enough evidence to go forward. Prosecutors need to remind themselves of the profound American legal principle of "presumption of innocence until proven guilty."

LaBois' daughter, Aubree' Riegel, now 23, denied being abused by her parents. She said she is relieved that the charges that have followed their family for 19 years have finally been dropped.

When Edward LaBois left in 1984, he wrote a letter to his sons, then high school and college age. He explained why he fled and why he couldn't have contact with them again. He also had to leave his 83-year-old mother, who suffered from congestive heart problems and was staying at their Minnetonka home when they fled. He never heard when she died.

Karri LaBois suffered bruises when attacked by a female inmate in jail. She is angry about her treatment in jail and some distorted media reports.

When asked how he felt, Edward LaBois said, "I feel vindicated on one hand and beaten up on the other. It's like the press condemned us, and the (jail) staff executed us."

After the LaBoises were returned to Minnesota, a Hennepin County investigator visited the daughter, Aubree' Riegel in Salt Lake City. The investigator showed her the videotape from 1984. On the tape, a psychiatrist asked her leading questions, according to Riegel and Minnetonka Police Chief Joy Rikala. Reigel said that she was asked in the 1984 interview if her parents had sexually abused her and that she was given anatomically correct dolls to demonstrate it. She said abuse didn't happen at her house.

(Anatomically correct dolls were used extensively in interrogating the children in the Jordan child sexual abuse cases.)

Hennepin County Attorney Amy Klobuchar said that since 1984 techniques have been refined about what is acceptable in court and how children are questioned. Police Chief Rikala said interviews with children were less sophisticated in 1984 and that interviewers could use leading questions and sexual-abuse terminology when asking children if they had been molested. She said a defense attorney today "could make hay" out of the Reigel interview.

Amy Klobuchar said the photographs of nude children found in the LaBoises Minnetonka home after they fled were not overtly sexual, for example, a toddler in a bathtub and commented that a book about photographing erotica that also was found dealt with adults, not children.

Chief Rikala said she doesn't know whether the abuse happened or not, only that "we don't have enough evidence to prove it now." Rikala added that if Aubree' Riegel changes her mind and does recall some abuse, the charges against the LaBoises could be reinstated. The statute of limitations on the original charge was suspended because the couple fled out of state.

The LaBoises fled because 23 adults had been arrested and charged with criminal child sexual abuse in Scott County. Fear of having their daughter taken from them by some false accusation from an overzealous prosecutor drove them from Minnesota. The couple said their lives have been ruined, and they have no idea where they will find jobs or how they will live.

The consequences of the hysteria where people are presumed guilty without substantiation–extended well beyond Jordan, Minnesota.

21

▼

The Many "Victims" of This Scandal

"Whoever fights monsters should see to it that in the process he does not become a monster."
– Friedrich Nietzsche

I interviewed one man, who as a young boy in 1984 was taken from his parents and placed in foster care after his parents were arrested and charged with child sexual abuse. He said, "If lawyers are the scum of the earth, psychologist are the slime of the earth."

Talking with the people accused, I wonder:

• Were psychologists (therapists) hired to help the kids–or were they employed to help Prosecutor Kathleen Morris build a case against those she accused of committing criminal acts of child sexual abuse?

• Like Kathleen Morris, did many psychologists dismiss the notion of presumption of innocence until proven guilty?

Alleged victims have repeatedly told me psychologists tried many times to get them make false statements about their parents and others. A young man said, "My goddamn shrink kept saying that if I didn't admit my old man raped and screwed me, I would be shipped off to a shelter for abused kids or wind up in a reform school."

The *Minneapolis Star Tribune* reported on February 13, 1985: "State Attorney General Humphrey asked the Minnesota Psychological Association to examine the issue of when it is proper for therapist to act as investigators while engaged in an ongoing treatment of a child suspected of being sexually abused. He also suggested the association determine the proper relationship between therapist and prosecutors.

November 15, 1987, the *Minneapolis Star Tribune* reported on an 11-year-old boy who denied being abused for three months, but after being questioned repeatedly, said he had been abused by 19 different adults. The boy was questioned by therapists, social workers, and detectives a total of 74 times during the investigation. Later this boy was placed in a psychiatric hospital.

A former Scott County court reporter told me, "They drove the kid nuts." A psychiatrist told the parents (of a 11-year-old boy) that he suffers to this day the lingering effects of traumatic stress caused by the intense interrogation by police, psychologists, social workers and Morris. Two child psychiatrists from the University of Minnesota treated children from a few of the accused families. They wrote a report suggesting that repeated questioning of child witnesses can cause damaging anxiety for children.

The therapists, law enforcement and social workers were not really interested in the health and welfare of this child. They were helping Morris build a case against someone she had accused of child sexual abuse. Their job, their mission, was to gather evidence and confessions that would help Morris. They messed with–and messed up a lot of kids.

Dr. Jonathan Jensen, director of the University of Minnesota child psychiatry clinic and Dr. Barry Garfinkel (an authority on child learning disabilities who today serves on the Groves Resource Center board of directors) said, "In the Scott County system, the procedure of removing the child from the home for a long period of time, changing a child's identity with a new name, separation from siblings, change of religion and instruction not to reveal any identifying information about themselves produced a strong undermining of the children's personality structure."

The boy mentioned in the *Minneapolis Star Tribune* article was baptized and raised in a Lutheran Home. When he was taken from his parents and separated from his siblings, he was placed in foster care and sent to live with a Roman Catholic family and was enrolled in a Catholic School. The boy was told to use a different name to protect himself from embarrassing questions from his new classmates.

The boy blames therapist Tom Price for getting him to make false charges of sexual abuse. Price declined to be interviewed for a *Minneapolis Star Tribune* October 16, 1994 article titled "Ten Years After/The Legacy of Jordan." He said his professional ethics prevent him from discussing any of his patients. The March 1991 issue of *Mpls.St.Paul* magazine stated that Thomas Price was not a licensed psychologist; his background included a master's degree in social work and years of experience in child protection. Attorney Marc Kurzman believed that Price pressured the boy into claiming he was abused even after Price received a report from a licensed psychologist that the boy was on the verge of a nervous breakdown. Price denied any coercion even though he questioned the boy 45 times. Price said, "I was appointed by the court and my actions were reviewed many times."

Dr. Harry Hoberman, an assistant professor of psychiatry and pediatrics at the University of Minnesota, took over the care of the boy from Price shortly before the Humphrey investigation. Dr. Hoberman said, "It has taken a terrible toll in the sense that basic principles of family life were compromised; notions of truth and honesty and integrity were shattered by the way the cases were handled from the children's perspective."

Price testified in family court against granting the boy's mother visitation. It looks like the court was paying Tom Price to serve as a hired gun for the Scott County Attorney. It is easy to understand why this young man I interviewed recently would come to the conclusion that lawyers (including judges) and psychologist/therapist are scum and slime.

Other therapist copped out or opted out of interviews with me, using the same lame excuse of patient confidentiality or professional ethics. Even after I assured them of anonymity for their clients and themselves, they refused to talk. One psychologist even asked if she would be paid for granting me an interview. I told her I could not pay her for an interview but I would pick up the tab for lunch. She declined my offer, citing the confidential nature of a patient-client relationship and the possibility of legal consequences if she revealed any privileged information.

Would money have gotten me an interview? How much? Would that have been ethical or honest? Somehow paying for an interview seemed to me a lot like bribing a witness. Maybe it reflected a story I heard many years ago. "A man at a party approached an attractive young woman and asked her if she would go to bed with him for a million dollars. She hesitated for a brief moment and then replied, 'Yes, but just one time.' The man then asked her if she would go to bed with him for twenty dollars. She indigently asked, 'What do you think I am... a whore?' He said, 'We've already established that, now we're just negotiating the price.'"

"And if you are paying somebody for advice –
beware. Many therapists are looking out
for your checkbook, not you."
– Bill O'Reilly
Author, Who's Looking Out for You

22

The Power and Influence of Psychologists

"The great enemy of truth is very often not the lie, deliberate, contrived and dishonest–but the myth– persistent, persuasive and unrealistic."
– John F. Kennedy

In many famous cases, much of what happened in Jordan was explained and justified by explanations and recommendations from psychologists. For example, the Roman Catholic Church justifies transferring pedophile priest from one parish to another on the recommendations of psychologists. People are sent to prison, some even executed, while others are set free on the testimony and recommendation of psychologist, so-called mental health experts.

A couple thousand years ago when the "man from Galilee" walked about teaching, preaching and healing, he made some disparaging remarks about some people. He expressed contempt for lawyers, moneychangers, and high priests. Many contemporary prophets and peacemakers voice loathing for conniving lawyers and unscrupulous moneylenders. What about the high priests? Who are the high priests today? The most powerful people involved in the crucifixion of Jesus were the high priests. They had the power and influence to set Him free or see Him put to death.

Today's high priests are psychologists. After John Hinckley shot President Reagan, it was the psychologists who decided his fate. In Texas, a mother kills her five children, and it is the psychologists who determine whether she will be sentenced to death.

In 2002, Father Benedict J. Groeschel, C.F.R, professor of pastoral psychology at St. Joseph's Seminary in New York, wrote in his book, *From Scandal to Hope*, "Psychology and psychiatry are big words. They include many things. Among the great psychologists of history are Sts. Augustine, Bonaventure, Teresa of Avila, John of the Cross, and Ven. John Henry Cardinal Newman. Psychology simply means the study of the functioning of the human mind. Some of the great psychologists of modern times have made some big mistakes, especially Sigmund Freud."

Freud's methods as a psychoanalyst ranged from unorthodox to unethical: He tried to explain psyche mathematically, ate dinner while seeing patients, and conducted five-minute sessions while billing for a full hour.

I have found no one in the Scott County court system who questioned the bills submitted by the psychologist hired by the county. A Scott County Commissioner told me they were ordered by a judge to pay all bills from the psychologist (but can't remember which judge).

Anyone with the slightest degree of objectivity and a little more than cash-register honesty can see that the psychologists involved in the Jordan child sexual abuse scandal made some huge mistakes in methods of inquiry and erroneous conclusions.

My conclusion is that they were well paid by the County to make faulty conclusions–and they complied with the expressed or implied request of Prosecutor Kathleen Morris.

"A neurotic is a man who builds a castle in the air.
A psychotic is a man who lives in it.
A psychiatrist is the man who collects the rent. "
                                            – Jerome

Fr. Groeschel, a prolific writer recognized by Catholics everywhere, said he realized that when a scandal occurs, about two percent of what is said in the media is true. Some Scott County residents today speak out and assert the Jordan scandal was one big lie concocted by County Attorney Morris with the help of psychologists.

Jesus warned His disciples: "Scandals will necessarily come and make people fall; but woe to the one who brought it about."   – Luke 17:1

I know that some psychologists lie. Some psychologist will check the Diagnostic and Statistical Manual (DSM) manual against the prospective patient's insurance coverage and then diagnose the illness that will reimburse them the most money. The first DSM came out in 1952, followed by a revision in 1968; the DSM4JJ appeared in 1980, and was followed by its own revision–the DSM-JIJR in 1988. In 1994, the DSM-IV was some 900 pages long, covering 374 mental disorders. This is a tool for larceny. Its use is dishonest but probably legal.

From my interviews with several of the alleged victims, their parents and other adults, I know some of the psychologists used by the prosecution lied to and about children, parents and others involved in the Jordan scandal.

Dr. Bill Backus, psychiatrist and well-known Christian

author of *Telling Yourself the Truth*, had this to say:

> The therapist can facilitate, in the way of a midwife at a birth, the recovery of legitimate traumatic repressed memories, some of which have to do with sexual or physical abuse. These, I have no doubt, are legitimate. This has happened to every therapist. What concerns me, however, is the possibility of a therapist actually planting his or her presuppositions and suspicions into the mind of the client.
>
> I have seen people who've had this happen to them where the therapist says, 'Your symptoms sound like you've been abused when you were a child. What can you tell me about that?' The client denies it, but the therapist won't take no for an answer. That's an illegitimate tactic, because the therapist is a powerful person, and many clients are extremely impressionable, particularly where there's high emotion. Our minds are capable of repression and they are also capable of receiving suggestions.
>
> It appears to me that stories of ritual abuse, stories of any kind of abuse or trauma that happens to be popular on the daytime serials ought to be looked at with caution because they could be the result of suggestion.

Dr. Backus politely describes the possibility of therapist planting their presuppositions and suspicions into the client's mind. In the Scott County sex abuse cases, mind bending, mind manipulation, and planting falsehoods was not just a possibility, it was a probability.

From my research and extensive interviewing, I (as do several of the children who received therapy) know some of the psychologists being paid by the County were dishonest. A young man who asked anonymity told me, "she lied to me... she's a lying bastard... she said she wanted to help me and my mom and dad, but she just wanted put them in jail. I told her I was never abused. She didn't believe me. She said I was lying. Look, I'm over 30 years old now, and I tell you I learned from that bitch not to ever trust any of them son-of-a-bitch psycho-bastards."

"The unconscious by definition is what you
are not conscious of.
But the analysts already know what's in it–
they should, because they put it all in beforehand."
– Author Saul Bellow

"Psychoanalysis is the disease it purports to cure."
– Viennese satirist Karl Kraus (1874-1936)

The soap opera that played out as the Jordan abuse scandal should have been looked at with caution because it could have been the result of suggestion. There was plenty of rumor, suspicion, suggestion, innuendo–but an absence of any hard, tangible evidence or corroborating testimony from mandatory reporters.

23

▼

Medical Examinations

As reported in the *Shakopee Valley News* August 15, 1984, Cindy Buchan asked Kathleen Morris for advice, and whether she should be concerned that her children may have been abused. Morris told her "Bring them to me."

Cindy Buchan brought her children to Kathleen Morris. The oldest child, age 4, was the only one interviewed by investigators who had decided the 1- and 2-year-old Buchan children were too young to talk.

Cindy Buchan said that her daughter played with anatomically correct dolls while the investigators watched and asked questions. She said she was asked to leave the office.

After the interview, the investigators told Buchan that they didn't think her daughter had been abused. But Morris told her to take her daughter to a doctor for a physical examination.

Dr. Barry A. Bershow with Burnsville Family Physicians determined that "no physical findings can be linked to sexual or other forms of child abuse."

The *Minneapolis Star Tribune* reported August 13, 1984, "Medical examinations of the four children the Buchans are accused of abusing show no evidence of sexual contact according to court documents. Those examinations were done by Dr. Barry Bershow, a doctor hired by the county to do many examinations of children suspected of being abused."

The *Minneapolis Star Tribune* September 6, 1984 reported, "Yesterday's last witness was a physician, Dr. Barry Bershow, a family practitioner from Burnsville, who testified that one witness, a 9-year-old girl who stated that Robert Bentz had vaginal and anal intercourse with her, appeared to have an undamaged vagina and anus. He added that sexual abuse still could have occurred.

It is important to point out that Dr. Bershow was hired and paid by the same Board of Commissioners who approved unlimited spending by Morris. It is logical to speculate that he was another expert, another hired gun employed to help County Attorney Morris build the prosecution case against the accused. His clever hedge remark, "that although he didn't find any evidence of sexual abuse in his examination, abuse still might have happened," can be interpreted to mean that he isn't going to give any clear-cut honest appraisal that may call into question allegations of child sexual abuse made by Morris.

Also, such ambiguity would keep him on the payroll. Some questions tax payers should want to have answered are:

- How much did the County pay Dr. Bershow for his examinations and expert testimony?
- How expensive was this hired gun?
- Could any of the poor defendants afford to hire a competing hired gun?

E. Michael Jones writes in *Fidelity* magazine February 1985 about another doctor employed by Scott County: "In a Nightline segment broadcast on October 15, 1984, Dr. Carolyn Levitt, a pediatrician employed by Scott County to examine some of the children, denied the allegation that the psychologist and other professionals were financially motivated. (Read the entire article in Chapter 42.)

More disturbing though than any amount of money they may have earned was Dr. Carolyn Levitt's description of her method of interrogation. "One thing a physician can do which no one else can do," she told Nightline correspondent James Walker, "is we can use the child's body, and I do that because I'm a female physician and I feel comfortable doing that. I actually put my finger in a little girl's vagina and ask her, 'Is this what they did to you, and do you think it went in that far, and did it bleed?'" Levitt concludes: "I have no doubt that these children were abused."

After hearing about her methods, it's hard to disagree. The real question for me, though, is: Who is doing the abusing?

Dr. Levitt has been paid a lot of money over a long period of time testifying as a witness for the prosecution. She doesn't work for free. Regardless of her published sentiments, she is financially motivated and well paid with taxpayer dollars.

Adam Pitluk of Court TV explained how Dr. Levitt (expert witness in Jordan case) testified for the prosecution in former Green Bay Packer, Mark Chmura's trial for sexual assault. The alleged victim, a 17-year-old named Allison, claimed she was sexually assaulted by Chmura at her after-prom party. The prosecution said that Dr. Levitt was an expert and had done more than 4,000 pelvic examinations.

Dr. Levitt, testified for the prosecution that although she never examined Allison, she had done enough examinations to know that Allison could have been assaulted.

Mark Chmura was found innocent. A thorough medical examination showed that Allison's hymen had not been disturbed. Regardless, Mark Chmura was finished as a professional football player for the Packers. Even if you are found innocent of the accusations of sexual abuse, your employer may not want you around any more. Mark Chmura lost his job.

Dr. Levitt is still providing expert testimony for a price. She is the Medical Director for the Midwest Children's Resource Center, 347 North Smith, Suite 401, St. Paul, MN 55102.

Dr. Paul Stahler, who had by 1984 been practicing medicine in Jordan for 35 years, is quoted in the *Chicago Tribune* September 2, 1984, "I was shocked." Stahler said, explaining that many of the suspects and their children were his patients. "There was nothing to make me suspect it." Dr. Stahler added, "This little city was traumatized. Now people don't know what to think."

Some medical experts who helped Morris build her cases against the accused child abusers have questioned Dr. Stahler's competence. Dr. Levitt mentioned Dr. Stahler lacked training and expertise to do examinations for child sexual abuse.

Dr. Stahler has known the accused parents and children as patients for years. He has credibility because he was not hired by the County to testify for the prosecution.

Who should be trusted? The physician hired by the County who's an expert in the field or the small-town country doctor concerned with the health and well being of his patients.

Dr. Stahler has since retired and still lives in the community.

24

Who Is Kathleen Morris... and How Did She Get to Such a Place of Power in Scott County?

Kathleen Morris became a critical factor in this scandal. She was the driving prosecution that pressed criminal charges, ordered the removal of the children from their homes, and shook the town. Her flamboyant style set her apart as a brazen attorney with a whip–a whip with an itchy hand. She seemed to relish each stroke of the power she wielded–and demanded, and it gave additional strength to her position as our first female county prosecutor.

No one in town sat on the fence about Morris. They both hated and feared her and her style, or they supported her. There seemed to be no gray area, and there were lots of opinions about her.

Rumors and hearsay were part of daily talks at our barbershops, saloons and salons. She was the office water-cooler talk every day and the fodder for secret grumblings in many households affected by the criminal charges.

Kathleen Morris' real name is Rita Kathleen Morris. She felt her values were fixed from her small-town roots in Harrisburg, Illinois where she attended a Southern Methodist church. "You didn't drink or smoke, or wear make-up. You didn't dance or play cards. You didn't have sex before marriage, and you didn't take the name of the Lord in vain," she said about her upbringing.

She's the daughter of a Harrisburg, Illinois elementary school principal and a kindergarten teacher. After graduating from Southern Illinois University, Morris spent time in a commune and was a member of the Yippie Party, an anti-establishment group that was involved in many peace demonstrations of the late 1960s and early '70s.

Morris originally followed in her parents' path as she taught high school for several years at Cerro Gordo, Illinois, a town of fewer than 2,000 people.

While teaching, some people questioned her morality. At Cerro Gordo when she was teaching high school, there were rumors she was allowing sex and drug parties for some football players at her residence.

Sam Brandenburg, school board member said, "Morris is anti-everything. She was a product of Kent State and the '60s. She's the kind of person who would take hold of something and jump off the deep end."

Mark (Smitty) Smith, one of Morris' students said, "Sure we'd stop and say hi, but she never bought us beer. A few of us would be drinking beer and driving around and we'd stop there, but her apartment was never a place to go and drink."

Morris provided a sophomore football star a place to stay in her apartment because he had problems at home.

Dr. W.H. Shackelford, former president of the school

board, said there was a lot of gossip, but no proof of any unlawful sex going on. The school board told Morris they thought the living arrangement she provided for the football player was inappropriate. Morris was unbending, unwilling to compromise. Morris told the board there was no sexual impropriety; she was not in love with him and was not sleeping with him.

Dr. Shackelford said he was not surprised that Minnesotans might question the way she conducted the Scott County sexual abuse cases. "I think it is all entwined with her personality. She got into the ego part of it, and got over her head and couldn't change her perception."

After being confronted by the school board, Morris refused to change her ways. At the end of the school year she wrote a letter saying only, "I quit."

Some former residents of Cerro Gordo say Morris might say she quit, but she wasn't going to be rehired and, in fact, she was fired.

Attorneys for some former defendants in the Scott County cases indicated they would use Morris' background in Cerro Gordo to allege a pattern of irresponsible behavior. They had hoped to win million dollar lawsuits for violation of rights. (They did sue in 1985, but lost.)

In Morris' own words in the *Minneapolis Star Tribune* January 3, 1984. Morris was at this time 38 years old and contends that prosecuting the sex cases made her more worldly.

"I was kissed the first time when I was a senior in high school on the Wednesday before Thanksgiving, and I cried and cried and cried. I had been going steady with this guy for two years." She went on to say, "I was 28 and a virgin when I got married the summer of my freshman year at law school."

In 1973, Morris came to Minnesota to study law at

Scott County Attorney Kathleen Morris with the
anatomically correct dolls used with the children.

© United Press International.
Photo appeared in the Washington Post January 2, 1985.
Used with permission from Corbis Professional Licensing.

Hamline University, St Paul, Minnesota. The young attorney was hired as Assistant Scott County Attorney in 1976 and started making waves–and enemies. "I've always been a mouth and I didn't lie down and play dead," she said.

First Important Case...

In late 1977, Morris prosecuted a man accused of sodomizing his sister-in-law, a juvenile. The man was convicted, but appealed on a variety of grounds including several items of prosecutorial misconduct.

Gary Hanson, a former special assistant attorney general, was assigned to write the brief defending the prosecution. Hanson said that while the instances of misconduct by Morris were quite minor, they were so clear and numerous that he couldn't convince the court to uphold the conviction. He described them as "excesses of zeal that caused her to cross the line quite a few times."

For the only time during his eight years with the Minnesota Attorney General's office, Hanson said he decided the state should not argue with the appeal but admit its error and agree to a new trial. Kathleen Morris demonstrated misconduct early on in her legal career, a pattern that would repeat in the Jordan scandal.

Morris said she later sought a second trial of the case, but the victim was unwilling.

In 1978, Morris was working for Scott County Attorney Dennis Moriarty and was prosecuting drug charges against high school students. She told the *Minneapolis Star Tribune* that she had smoked marijuana socially in college and that she favored legalizing its use. She and County Attorney Moriarty disagreed over her honest opinions and she resigned. Later, in 1978, after Moriarty did not seek reelection, Morris ran for County Attorney and won. Moriarty has often said that he regrets that he ever hired Kathleen Morris, and that it was one of his worst decisions.

In 1979, two years out of law school, Morris became Minnesota's first female county attorney. During her first term, she prosecuted Jim and John Cermak of Prior Lake, Minnesota of having abused their own and other children. The brothers' wives and parents followed them to jail on similar convictions.

Morris, 38, said in *US Magazine* June 18, 1984 about the Cermak case: "All I heard was I was carrying it too far. 'Why did you have to arrest the mothers? After all they're women!' When I arrested grandma and grandpa, the big line was, 'If the great grandparents were still alive, you'd arrest them.'"

Morris exclaimed, "Your dang right I would have! If they were sexually abusing kids, that's exactly what I would have done."

Failure to convict the Bentzes and the dismissal of charges against 21 other defendants dethroned Morris

The *Jordan Independent* December 26, 1984 wrote "Scott County Attorney Morris was formally reprimanded last Thursday by District Judge Martin Mansur for allowing child witnesses to stay together in a motel last summer."

In *Minneapolis Star Tribune Sunday Magazine* September 6, 1987, Norm Coleman, Minnesota Solicitor General, who as the state's Assistant Attorney General, supervised the state/federal investigation into the Scott County cases comments:

"The reality is that she made some terrible mistakes. She handled cases in ways that hurt a lot of children.

When you look at the files, look at the (Lois and Robert) Bentz case. In the course of the trial those children were   subjected to some very withering examination. She never once objected. If you look at the fact, those kids were interviewed 30, 40 times. Anyone who had the perspective of protecting kids, those were the ones who were most disappointed in what she did.

What it really comes down to is questions of competence and questions of integrity. And those are things that she suffered from. The reality is there are a lot of good, concerned prosecutors who aren't being attacked because they're out front on child abuse...

When you read the Morris Commission report, you get the questions of integrity coming out... At times she simply wasn't honest with the press, with the public, with the commission. Those are damning."

Norm Coleman, now a U.S. Senator from Minnesota, stands on his record–that what he said a couple decades ago he meant, and it is true today. He said, "Kathleen Morris was incompetent and dishonest."

In the *Minneapolis Star Tribune* October 19, 1984, Kathleen Morris said her primary goal in sex offender cases is not to win convictions or send offenders to prison—it is more important to get treatment for the child victims and the perpetrators. "But I would like to just put a sign of their houses that says: "Pervert Lives Here.""

The writer continues, "A statement like that, and the person who made it—cocky, colorful, committed and willing to go beyond the normal bounds of the prosecutor's role—evoke strong reactions, favorable and unfavorable."

After Morris removed herself from the sexual abuse trials, she said in *Minneapolis Star Tribune* September 27, 1984, "When I am in some way hurting the process, then it is time not to remain involved. I don't want to hurt the process. I don't want to hurt the children. The children are the ones who have been sexually abused. What I am concerned about is that we are trying to protect children. When people try to make me the issue more important than protecting children, then I should not be involved."

Clarence Kaiser, owner of Clancy's Bar and Restaurant, served as chairperson of the Kathleen Morris for Scott County Attorney Committee in 1978 when Morris first ran for political office. Kaiser did not chair her reelection campaign. He said there were a lot of people in Jordan for her, but also some strongly opposed to her. He said he didn't want to alienate any of his customers, so he had to remain neutral.

One day after Morris was decisively defeated in 1986 in her attempt for a third term, she had government files removed from her office. These files contained information about the Jordan cases, over which Morris was being sued in federal court. Richard Beens, who was defending Scott County in the sexual abuse cases, said that someone from Morris' office did remove the files relating to the Jordan cases, and delivered them to Attorney James Martin at his Edina law office. Martin was representing Morris in cases where she was being sued in federal court.

County Administrator Joseph Ries said the county retains control over the files, and he would seek a court order to have the files returned if necessary. The question remains: Why would Morris and her lawyer remove the files from the Scott County courthouse? Certainly these two lawyers knew it was wrong.

Did they sanitize the files? Under threat of a court order the files were returned, but no one knows if they were all returned and intact.

Many local people were quoted with their opinions in *Jordan Independent* newspaper.

In the *Minneapolis Star Tribune* November 6, 1986, Eldred Hoover said: "Maybe she wasn't wrong, but she didn't go about it right. I'm sure it cost her the election."

Diane Hennig, a hostess at Wampach's restaurant in Shakopee said she believes that powerful forces in the county wanted Morris ousted and went about discrediting her. She felt Morris had helped many people. Henning said, "She was a scapegoat, and now we are all going to have to suffer."

Margaret Duke said many people don't appreciate Morris' contributions to the understanding of sexual abuse. She said, "I feel that for a fact she woke up the whole United States that we do have child abuse. A group of the county's affluent and powerful attorneys didn't like the sometimes-abrasive Morris because she was a woman. Morris could have found the resources to fight them."

"Sources have said that Morris acted as an investigator as well as the County Attorney, that therapists acted like cops and cops acted like therapists, that social workers went along on a search party warrant."

In the *Minneapolis Star Tribune* October 6, 1987, it said, "The U.S. Supreme Court Monday let stand an appeals court ruling that Scott County Attorney Kathleen Morris cannot be sued for her conduct in the Jordan sexual abuse cases."

After Losing Re-election…

Minneapolis Star Tribune, December 19, 1986 reported that Kathleen Morris will become a part-time public defender after she leaves office in January. At her request, District Judge Michael Young appointed her to one of the 12 rotating monthly slots that he assigns to local lawyers. She will serve as a court-appointed lawyer for people making their first appearances in court on misdemeanor charges. Morris will serve in July and will be paid at the regular rate of $40 an hour (as reported in *Minneapolis Star Tribune* October 19, 1986). One of Morris' assistants, Miriam Wolf, who is resigning from the Scott County attorney's office, also requested a public defender position and will serve in February.

One must wonder if the fact that Norm Coleman said lawyer Kathleen Morris was dishonest and incompetent, why would Judge Young appoint her as a public defender? After the Scott County sexual abuse cases fiasco, would you want her to be your court-appointed lawyer?

Minnesota Supreme Court Chief Justice, Kathleen Blatz is

on record praising Minnesota's public defenders. Several of the falsely accused in the Scott County sex abuse case were assigned court-appointed public defenders. Several complained about lack of interest or competence exhibited by some public defenders. It may boil down to what could you expect for $40 an hour.

Certainly Kathleen Morris deserves some praise for convicting the incestuous Cermak family, and convicting child sexual abuser, James Rud. She made us all aware that child sexual abuse is a reality. We cannot hide from this ugly truth.

Morris likewise deserves a lot of criticism for her mishandling of the Scott County cases. To those she falsely accused, she owes restitution. To the children who may have been returned to an abusive environment, she cannot undo the harm and heartache she caused.

Does Kathleen Morris warrant our sympathy, compassion and praise–or our anger, contempt and scorn?

The lesson learned from the court's decision: It is possible to be falsely accused and arrested, stand trial and be found innocent, or have charges dismissed, and not be able to recover your losses from your accuser or the government body that financed the actions of your accuser.

Kathleen Morris was ruthless in her pursuit and apprehension of suspected child abusers. Perhaps we should be as ruthless in our opposition to injustice–and also to false accusations.

"Kathleen Morris' intense interest in sexual abuse created a climate of anxiety unique to Scott Count, Minnesota—one that intensified the ultimate eruption. She's the trigger that set off everything else."
– Michael Haeuser, Chief Librarian (and author)
Gustavus Adolphus College, St. Peter, Minnesota

In the December 24-31, 1984 *People* magazine, Joseph Friedberg, well-known Minneapolis lawyer believes Morris' zeal was directly responsible for the Jordan fiasco. He says, "She is a sincere person, but a bad lawyer because she becomes too involved. Somewhere along the line she sacrifices due process."

Attorney Stephen Doyle said to the *Minneapolis Star Tribune* on December 3, 1984, "Kathleen is strong and aggressive and commands attention, and she is a difficult person about whom to be neutral." Originally he was the lawyer for one of the accused. After the charges were dismissed, Doyle represented Morris against her removal from office.

Somehow I find it inconceivable, at least dubious, that Kathleen Morris–dope smoking, yippie commune dweller, activist/radical–was virginal and sexually inactive. How did this sexually naive person emerge as America's leading prosecutorial authority on child sexual abuse? When I visited the County Attorney's office in 1984, anatomically correct dolls were scattered about, many positioned to depict sexual acts.

Morris was reelected in 1982 with 59 percent of the vote. In 1986, two years after the debacle, James Terwedo, a grass-green young attorney, trounced her 2-1 in her bid for reelection and a third term. Morris commented on the election in the *Minneapolis Star Tribune* Sunday Magazine on September 6, 1987: "The sad thing is it didn't matter who they ran. They could have run a duck against me in the election, and the duck would have won."

Morris after the Cermak trial and during most of the Jordan 1984 scandal was kowtowed to by her supporters and sycophants. According to Patrick Finnegan, "The brown-nosing, ass-kissing police, county commissioners, social workers, judges, psychologist, reporters, lawyers, clerks, crazy feminists, and clergy enabled Kathleen to think she could walk on water. All she really did was trample over the rights of many innocent people."

Attorney Earl Gray in the *Jordan Independent*, September 19, 1984, is quoted accusing Morris of playing with the facts. He says Morris has a terrible thirst of the ego. Before the jury, he accused Kathleen Morris of being a little god.

Marc Kurzman, an attorney for Greg Myers, tried to get Judge Fitzgerald dismissed from the case because "the judge is prejudiced in favor of Scott County Kathleen Morris." The relationship between Judge Fitzgerald engendered much gossip and speculation in 1984. Today, many people familiar with the case still offer comments about an improper sexual relationship between Morris and Judge Fitzgerald. James Terwedo, Morris' successor as County Attorney says he does not think there was anything-sexual going on with Morris and Fitzgerald. He says he sees it more like father figure helping by offering advice and counsel to a daughter or a protégé. Terwedo did say the Morris-Fitzgerald behavior and friendship might have looked like something beyond just a professional relationship.

Thomas Vasaly, representing the Lawyers Professional Responsibility Board, said Morris violated Minnesota's ethical code for lawyers. He contended that a special commission appointed by Governor Perpich found Morris guilty of malfeasance and that was proof of ethical violations.

Malfeasance: When an official consciously does an illegal act or a wrongful act which infringes upon the rights of another to his/her damage, and the act is outside the scope of the official's authority.

Judge Fitzgerald furnished an affidavit to hearing referee Judge James Preece of Bemidji stating that Kathleen Morris had done nothing improper.

Some courthouse employees told me about a book making the rounds among employees, *The Mask of Sanity*. A terrified clerk, who does not want to be identified, said just after the trial, "Read the book. Kathleen is crazy, and she is driving the rest of us crazy."

Dr. Ralph Underwager told me, "If anyone is a sociopath or psychopath in sex abuse cases, it is County Attorney Morris. She is the Pied Piper." The story of the Pied Piper is part of the lore of Hamline University, where Kathleen got her law degree. "She certainly was leading the rats," he added.

Det. Dave Einertson, with the Scott County Sheriff's department, worked with Morris on both the Cermak and Rud cases. He said in the *Twin City Reader*, February 8-14, 1984, "She's not a pleasant person to be around during a case, he said, then conceded," I think she's a total workaholic, and she's very hard to work with, very demanding."

The credit for exposing child sexual abuse in Jordan goes to Kathleen Morris. In June 18, 1984 *US Magazine*, Richard Seely, who directs the intensive treatment program for sexual aggressives at St. Peter's Minnesota State Security Hospital says, "She's put up with an awful lot of social pressure to get that abuse stopped. She's done so at great personal risk."

A child victim is quoted in *US Magazine* June 18, 1984, "That's the woman who listens to kids."

Tom Price, a psychotherapist who worked with Kathleen Morris said, "She would die before she would let you beat her. She has an intensity that's incredible."

Morris says that seeing kids safer keeps her going.

Today, Kathleen Morris is divorced without children.

Today, Attorney Kathleen Morris practices law with her former law clerk in downtown Shakopee, Scott County.
— Author's collection

25

▼

When the Wall
Started to Crumble...

*"I am as isolated as you could wish me to be.
The word has been given out to abandon me,
and a void is forming around me."*
– Sigmund Freud

In the dark days of 1984, when it seemed that the world had turned against her, Kathleen Morris made several copies of the above Sigmund Freud quotation. She framed the quote and placed copies at her desk, by her bedside and on her refrigerator. Morris says she received the quote from a psychologist she didn't know.

The September 6, 1987 *Minneapolis Star Tribune Sunday Magazine* said Morris was:

"Sometimes vulgar, but always quotable. Morris became the media darling: Gutsy. Charismatic. Driven, if difficult. A pioneer in the cause of protecting children from sexual abuse..."

The article went on:

"From the Shakopee sheriff's office to the Scott County
Board, people backed away from her with moral indignation.
Lawyers who had found Morris conduct unprofessional earlier
talked more openly about it. And the media, once so captivat-
ed by Morris turned on her, examining her methods, her
motives, even her abilities as a lawyer.... Former defendants in
the Jordan cases sued her and Scott County for more than
$500 million.... Four of five of her assistant county attorneys
(Pamela McCabe, Judy Emmings, Peggy Flaig, and Mary
Yunker) on her staff quit, charging that Morris was a petty
tyrant without scruples."

Pamela McCabe who worked for Morris for five years
from 1980 through 1985, the year following the dismissal of
the criminal suits said, "She (Morris) frightens me. There was
a long period of time that I wouldn't go into Scott County
without my cross on."

Peggy Flaig explained her resignation to the County
Commissioners: "It is not so much an office where legal work
is performed as it is a temple for a cult of personality. There is
no such a thing as a 'difference of opinion' in the office; failure to agree on the most trivial matter is construed as disloyal-
ty and results in childish 'punishments.'

Judy Emmings wrote to the commissioners how Morris
stood outside the doors of attorneys who were out of favor,
loudly announcing that new stationery was to be ordered without any of their names on the letterhead. Emmings concluded
her letter to the commissioners: "In the library of life's experiences, I will shelve this thin volume somewhere between
Caligula and The Emperor's New Clothes.

Attorney Mary Yunker joined Morris' staff in the chaotic
period before the commission hearings and witnessed an incident that convinced her that something was seriously wrong.

From the *Minneapolis Star Tribune* Sunday Magazine September 6, 1987:

"It was May 1985. Yunker was in Morris' office discussing a case, and Miriam Wolf came in. Morris was attending a seminar the next day in downtown Minneapolis and asked Wolf for the quickest route in. Soon Morris and Wolf began debating whether downtown streets or avenues run north or south. The argument just kept escalating. And Kathleen kept getting angrier and angrier that Miriam wouldn't change her opinion and agree, Yunker recalls. Kathleen said, 'Miriam, you're wrong and you know you're wrong!'

"With that, Yunker heard a gurgling noise in the back of Morris' throat and watched as Morris spit on Wolf. She remembers the gob of saliva collecting on Wolf's chest and dribbling down her shirt. For maybe 30 seconds, Yunker and Wolf stared in disbelief at Morris.

"Then to my complete astonishment, Kathleen made noises in the back of her throat and spit again on Miriam. Miriam was obviously embarrassed... I said, 'Kathleen! For heaven's sake.'

"Kathleen realized at this point that she had gone beyond any acceptable conduct. And she laughed and said, 'Oh, I spit on Miriam all the time. Don't I, Miriam?' And Miriam didn't say anything. Kathleen repeated in a more demanding tone, 'Don't I, Miriam?' And Miriam said yes.'

"Embarrassed, Yunker left for her own office. Not four minutes later, she heard Kathleen coming down the office   corridor, saying loudly to secretaries along the way: 'Mary's new here. She doesn't understand what close, loving relationships we have with each other. But she'll learn.'

"During the commission hearings, Yunker cited the spitting episode to the commission as evidence of Morris' abusive behavior to her staff. Morris says hastening to explain that spitting has become one of those silly, idiosyncratic jokes among her friends and Yunker has misinterpreted it.

"So (the commission) called Miriam and (Doris Wilker, a close friend and social worker on the Scott County cases.) And they said, 'God, we do that to each other all the time. It's one of our jokes. That's the spitting incident. Oh yeah, we still do that. One of our big things is you see a group of us saying, 'Now don't anybody spit...' It sounds crazy. 'No spitting. No hitting. No whining.'"

What would happen today if a boss spit on a subordinate? In 1984, the AIDS virus was discovered and people were made aware that bodily fluids such as saliva could spread this deadly virus. Morris had to be one mean sick woman to spit on people in 1985, and she had to have been surrounded by some sick women that allowed her to get away with such behavior.

Morris does not apologize for what she did in the Scott County cases. She said her only regret is trusting State Attorney General Skip Humphrey. She said, "He lied to me. And he lied to the people on my staff. And he lied to the public... and now we've got kids home. And talk about being hurt. My God. You think you can believe the attorney general. What a joke.

"It never dawned on me that to be a senator is more important than to just make sure kids aren't hurt anymore. And it was."

26

Who Controlled
the County's Money?

"Nothing is hidden that will not be disclosed."
– Luke 8:17

Top Dogs of Scott County

Jordan had long been a tightly knit community built around a history of tough pioneers and hard-working farmers. Everyone knew everyone and it was a supportive community for raising your cattle, soybeans, or children. Community members had a mutual respect for each other and trust of the community in its entirety. People were good neighbors and helped each other out.

Depending on your perspective, many people feel the county attorney position is the top of the totem in the community. But it's actually the elected county commissioners who reign at the top of organizational chart.

1984 Scott County Commissioners were:

District 1: William Koniarski
District 2: Anthony (Tony) Worm

District 3: Dick Mertz

District 4: Mark Stromwall

District 5: Roland Boegeman (d.1987)

In 1984, these respectable citizens openly professed their Christian beliefs and their desire to serve the County with honest and honorable intent. That was the same year that the Scott County Commissioners stood behind their good intentions and approved an expenditure to give Morris funds to investigate suspicions and allegations of child sexual abuse in Scott County.

Adding Insult to Injury...

October 22, 1985: Scott County Commissioner's Record, "as recorded."

"NOW, THEREFORE, BE IT RESOLVED, that the Scott County Board of commissioners hereby determines that it is neither in the public interest nor in accord with the law to pay the legal fees and expenses incurred by R. Kathleen Morris for her representation by Stephen Doyle in the investigation and hearings of said Removal Commission."

"BE IF FURTHER RESOLVED, THAT Stephen Doyle's claim against Scott County for $162,427.89 is hereby denied."

"WHEREAS, said Removal Commission conducted a thorough investigation and held lengthy hearings, and;

WHEREAS, said Removal Commission summarized its Findings as follows:"

"We have found that Kathleen Morris did not respect the rights of the accused when she violated Rule 9.01 of the Minnesota Rules of Criminal Procedure. We have found that she did not deal openly and honestly with the trial judge when she falsely stated that the defendants had not asked for notes when they had. She did not deal honestly with the trial judge when she failed to disclose that the children were housed together. Kathleen Morris did not respect the rights of the accused nor did she deal openly and honestly with the trial judge when she violated the sequestration order and said she had not. We have found that Kathleen Morris did not see that the guilty were prosecuted when she dismissed the twenty-one pending sex abuse cases. She misled the public when she told the media that the children were not subject to dozens of investigative interviews when they were. Finally, the Commission has found that Kathleen Morris was unnecessarily abusive to her staff and associates."

This Scott County Board of Commissioners initially had whole-heartedly supported Kathleen Morris and approved any funds she requested for her inquisition. Now that support was gone!

Money

If you want to dance,
You got to pay the fiddler.
Admission: $1.00 - one dollar
– Sign at entry-way to the
1950's Kasper's Dance Hall

Money plays an important role in our judicial proceedings. Is there one justice for the rich–and a different justice for the poor?

Are O.J. Simpson, Kobe Bryant, Michael Jackson, Martha Stewart and a host of other wealthy people accused of crimes treated by our justice system the same way the poor, the working poor and the middle class are treated? There were no wealthy people accused in the Jordan Child abuse sex scandal.

If Morris had not been authorized to spend large sums of taxpayer money to investigate alleged child sexual abuse, to arrest and incarcerate suspected child abusers, and to bring to trial the accused, the scandal may never have happened. Certainly, with less money available, the scope and magnitude of the scandal would have been smaller.

Dennis Moriarty, Morris' predecessor as Scott County Attorney, the man who hired her to work in Scott County and had been her former boss, said this in the *Minneapolis Star*

Tribune October 19, 1984, "Presumably she spent a million bucks (on the Jordan sex cases), and I don't see where she accomplished anything. Was there 15 minutes of thought that went into any of her decisions, or was it just a matter of making the next news deadline?"

In this same article, Scott County Administrator Joe Ries estimated that the abuse cases cost the county about $450,000.

In truth, the total 1984 budget of Scott County was $20,053,520. According to Mary Petrick, Administrative Assistant/Budget and Gary Shelton, Deputy County Administrator, $1,546,644.27 was spent on the Jordan cases–or almost 10 percent of the total operating budget.

Over several years and from many sources, I tried to get the more specific detail on these expenditures. I would like to know the names of psychologist, the special investigators, the outside lawyers, the foster care providers and others who made money off this. I have been stymied in my search with a variety of excuses such as: "We don't have any archives of expenses from that far back. Only authorized personnel would be able to look at those records. Those records are sealed. Because of lawyer client privilege, that information isn't available. Because children were involved all this information is strictly confidential. There is a gag order not to talk about this. The Doctor/patient confidentiality rule prohibits us from identifying by name doctors, nurses, psychologist and other professionals. You would have to get a court order to get any specific information about people who worked with the victims. You would have to check with Child Protection Services about getting any names of persons."

Suffice to say, excuses for not giving me frank and candid replies and truthful data are legion.

What Does All This Cost Scott County Residents?

The investigation became the crowbar to open a chasm of distrust and uncertainties amid the mounting allegations of child abuse. People began to wonder things about their neighbors that they never would have thought without the prompt. Whispers followed those accused–guilty or not. And the whispers became so loud that it burned the ears and reputations of all those not just named in the event, but those that had the misfortune to be near the events or circumstances named.

But it didn't stop there. Innocents were jeered and ridiculed. Neighbors who lived, worked and shopped next to each other for years, were now shunned and blackballed by some of the closest friends they'd had throughout their lives. The trauma left them scarred then–and scarred now. And Jordan would never be the same community again.

On June 27, 2003, I received the following letter providing a general breakdown of the total cost of **$1,546,644.27.**

SCOTT COUNTY GOVERNMENT CENTER
Budget & Strategic Planning

200 Fourth Avenue West
Shakopee, MN 55379 - 1220
(952) 496-8386 . Fax (952) 496 8382
http://www.co.scott.mn.us

June 27, 2003
Mr. Tom Dubbe
Shakopee, Minnesota

Dear Mr. Dubbe:

I have gathered the following information you requested on the Jordan cases. Scott County recorded costs by project in the following areas:

Human Services	$795,517.41
Legal	655,559.42
Sheriff	95,567.44
Total costs	$1,546,644.27

The above information should assist you in writing the history of Jordan.

Sincerely,

Mary Petrick
Administrative Assistant/Budget
Cc: Gary Shelton, Deputy County Administrator

On September 17, 2003, Gary Shelton sent me the below correspondence adding some specifics and amending some numbers.

SCOTT COUNTY SERVICES DIVISION
GOVERNMENT CENTER

215200 FOURTH AVENUE WEST
SHAKOPEE, MN 55079
(952) 496-8105   Fax (952) 496-8180   Web www.co.scott.mn.us
Gary Shelton, Deputy County Administrator   gshe/tonco.scott.mn.us

September 17, 2003
Mr. Tom Dubbe
Shakopee, MN 55379

Dear Mr. Dubbe:

Enclosed is the information that you requested in your letter of July 15, 2003.

This information is pertaining to the expenses in the Jordan cases in the areas of Human Services, Legal and Sheriff. After reviewing the specific expense categories, I realized that there were some that obviously did not apply to this case. Therefore, you may notice some slight differences in the totals of these lists compared to the totals tat were sent to you earlier.

This information is broken down into specific expense categories, but we do not have the vendor information. This is the extent of the information that is available.

Gary L. Shelton
Deputy County Administrator
Enclosures (3)

Detailed Expenses
Human Services Expenses for Project H1

Supplies/Direct Materials	$ 211.70
Contract Payments Direct to Services	348,052.90
Counseling Services	27,140.75
Child/Adult Shelter	182.00
Child/Adult Foster Care	44,130.20
Rule 5/Facility Emotionally Handicapped	1,222.02
Clothing	169.00
Meals	40.77
Group Home	182.00
Administrative Salaries/Wages	7,177.35
Professional & Technical Salaries/Wages	188,096.51
Professional Contracts	360.00

Clerical Salaries/Wages	1,472.35
Other Salaries/Wages	10.98
Meals Expenses	3,935.11
Mileage Allowance	57,285.12
Parking Fee	1,055.06
Mileage Rough Roads	24.08
Mileage Allowance	833.44
Mileage Allow/Client	47.44
Other Reimbursement	111.01
Consultant Services	1,934.71
Other Services	7,307.76
Program Activity Supplies	19.23
Audio Visual Supplies	36.84
Telephone and Telegraph	15.67

Total: **$791,054.00**

Legal Expenses for Project L 6

Contract Payments	$ 7,050.05
Juror Per Diem	6,035.25
Juror Meals	558.80
Witness Per Diem	3,776.12
Psychological Testing/Treatment	3,272.50
Juror Mileage	1,987.00
Witness Mileage	133.92
Professional & Technical Salaries/Wages	20,381.73
Professional Contract	234,610.93
Clerical Salaries/Wages	4,641.27
Air Fare	1,274.20
Meals	9,780.29
Mileage Allowance	2041.19

Parking	13.80
Mileage Reimbursement	88.20
General Supplies and Expenses	745.58
Copy Machine Reproduction	1,122.51
Book Expenses	7.90
Misc. Expenses	274.00
Total:	**$297,795.24**

He concludes that they do not have vendor information and what they have given me is all that is available. Whatever the precise accounting may be, it was a lot of money for Kathleen Morris to do what she did.

Just how did she get these funds? Who approved such expenditures? Why?

Kathleen Morris got the funds by requesting such monies from the Scott County Board of Commissioners–the final decision makers (named earlier).

Some of the Commissioners have explained to me why they approved her request. Some explanations seemed coherent and logical. Some answers were evasive and nonsensical.

Commissioner Worm said they had no choice. Law required them (by Minnesota statue and orders from a judge) to allocate and appropriate the necessary funds for the investigation of child sexual abuse. Also, he mentioned that because of Morris' previous success in prosecuting the Cermak of child sex abuse, he felt she "was on to something" and the County had an obligation to adequately fund her investigation.

Commissioner Dick Mertz, who has been called by his follow commissioners "the money man" of the board, said initially they had to approve the request by Morris to adequately fund the investigation. The law required approving the budget submitted by the County Attorney. After the charges were dismissed, Commissioner Mertz, along with Commissioner Koniarski, wanted to cut back almost immediately some of expenses incurred by the County Attorney. The board had authorized the hiring of three lawyers, a law clerk and secretary to work on the cases. An estimated $663,543 was requested for the 1985 budget for five county departments that had some role in handling the cases. In 1984, after the charges were dismissed, Commissioner Koniarski says he was not completely behind Morris on her request for more funds but feared the board may be powerless to refuse funds. Also, he mentioned that the board must pay any and all bills accrued by the prosecutor.

Most recent comment from Commissioner Koniarski in 2003, "It was a long time ago. Things were different. I cannot answer the questions you are asking. We were under a gag order not to discuss the cases."

27

▼

People's Thoughts on Kathleen Morris

"The man who never alters his opinion is like standing water, and breeds reptiles of the mind."
– William Blake

Fern Sepler-King Speaks Out...

Fern Sepler-King, a sexual abuse specialist from the Minnesota Department of Welfare, disputed Morris' accusations that Humphrey sacrificed the children's welfare for his own political aspirations. Sepler-King early on had been one of Morris' biggest fans. She admired how Morris would use sex and sexuality effectively to persuade a jury. King said of Morris: "She seems to relish detail. She knew what worked. She knew what struck horror in people's minds."

Although Sepler-King supported Morris in her efforts to arrest and convict child sexual abusers, she mentions precisely when she started to have some reservations about Kathleen Morris.

In the September 6, 1987 *Minneapolis Star Tribune Sunday Magazine.*

"It was Nov. 3, 1982–the day after Morris was reelected county attorney–and people dealing with the budding issue of sexual abuse were brought together for a conference in Brainerd, Minnesota.

"Morris was in her heyday. Prosecution of the Cermaks was on everyone's lips. Anatomically correct dolls were being mass-produced because Kathleen Morris used them to such great effect in court. Word was, she aimed to become Minnesota's first woman attorney general. Nobody had heard of Jordan yet.

"This time Morris was one of a panel of experts. But she took over, continually interrupting others. It became a one-woman show.

"Then the conference broke into small groups to discuss the handling of real sexual-abuse cases. Unbeknownst to participants, Sepler-King slipped in a bogus case where a non-custodial parent had coached the child to claim abuse where none existed. Morris' group got the hoax case.

"Again, Morris took over: 'I'd charge the case,' she told the group members. 'I'd remove the kids. You've got to believe the kids.'

"Morris was so sure she was right, that even Sepler-King was intimidated. Finally Sepler-King broke in and said the sexual abuse never occurred in that situation. But by then, group members were so absorbed in discussion of the Cermack case that no one seemed to grasp what she was saying.

"All attention focused on Kathleen Morris. Even as far back as 1982, Morris was guilty of presuming people guilty even if they were innocent.

"Sepler-King concluded, 'Let's not forget through all of this that Kathleen is a politician. She could light an audience on fire...'"

By 1986, the Jordan scandal was history, and so was the after glow of national media attention and Morris' carte blanche power that split and financially destroyed families, ruined reputations, burdened the town, and impacted the children for years to come–only to dismiss charges against the twenty-one alleged offenders.

Others Comment...

*"I think Kathleen has a great deal of difficulty
understanding adverse judgments made by other
people of her. She is bound and gagged by the clarity
of her own standards–how life should be lived and how
people should relate to each other."*
– Stephen Doyle, Kathleen's former husband

*"She just wanted to be right. She had a penchant
for being right. She just always enjoyed being right,
even if she had to twist things around to make her right
and the other person wrong."*
– Darlene Goodson Duning, who lived with
the Morrises after her mother died

"It's like Nazi Germany. Good law is being misused."
– Gail Andersen, former mayor of Jordan, who
was prosecuted by Morris' office

*"The county attorney is a vindictive, power-hungry
lady who has a grudge against Jordan."*
– Local realtor, Anna Sandy

*"What Kathleen Morris has done to our town is terrible.
I think they'll hang her from the yardarm
for her improprieties and get her to resign."*
– Jordan realtor, Gerald Sandy as quoted in People
Magazine, December 24-31, 1984

Lawyers for the Bentzes portrayed Morris as "a sick person"
who brainwashed her young witnesses to concoct the Bentz case
and then rewarded them with gifts when they cooperated.

*"They are brainwashing kids. Kathleen Morris wants
numbers and she doesn't care who they are."*
–Robert Bentz, who stood trial with his wife, Lois Bentz

A Letter to the Editor in the November 1984 *Minneapolis Star Tribune:*

The Jordan Case
"There is something going on in Jordan. A case with such potential should not be ruined by Kathleen Morris' inexperience and emotionalism. Her one-woman crusade could destroy great strides that have been made thus far.

"She was wise to remove herself from several cases and should refrain from involvement in any in the future. Her loss of perspective is reflected in her comment, 'I'm sick to death of things like the presumption of innocence. Thomas Jefferson laid the groundwork for our legal system by stating that it is better to let a thousand guilty men go free than for one innocent man to suffer. If Morris does not agree, she is free to practice law in the Soviet Union. In the meantime, let's get someone in there who can find the facts without dragging down everyone else in the process."

                                 – Terry Joseph, Bloomington, Minnesota

Minneapolis Star Tribune October 21,1984:

"Morris attributes much of the hostility of the legal community toward her to men's inability to handle the presence of a woman in a position of authority, and her refusal to genuflect to the 'Old Boy Network.'

"After the Bentzes were acquitted, she made three remarks to reporters that startled some people in the legal community.

"First, she implicitly criticized the jury, saying the verdict shows society doesn't believe children. The legal profession strongly disapproves of trial lawyers publicly criticizing verdicts.

"Second, she said she planned to tell the child witnesses that the Bentzes were acquitted because the jury was mad at Morris, not because the jury didn't believe their testimony. She had been criticized during the trial for manipulating the kids and now it seemed she planned to lie to them. (She confirmed that later saying: "Yes, I lied to them.")

"Third, she went so far as to question a principal tenet of the American legal system—the government has the burden of proof of proving that a citizen accused of a crime is guilty. According to a transcript later prepared for the Minnesota State Bar Association (which got a "whale of a lot of calls from lawyers" about it, a spokesman said), Morris said: 'I'm sick to death of things like the presumption of innocence.'"

"She was a bitch who wanted to be a son of a bitch."
– Wally Stang, former Jordan Fire Chief

I wonder why her peers, The Lawyers Professional Responsibility Board, didn't chastise her?

28

The Judge...
and Kathleen Morris

*"Justice is often determined by the
personality of the judge."*
–Judge Andrew Napolitano, FOX News expert

Was Judge John Moonan Fitzgerald having a sexual relationship with Morris?

During a lengthy telephone interview with the judge, he
raised the issue. He supposed I was going to ask him about the
rumors circulating around the courthouse about he and Morris
having some sort of sexual relations. I told him I was primarily concerned with the Jordan child sexual abuse cases that
were dropped. He insisted we get the sex matter out of the way
before we talk about the cases.

Judge Fitzgerald said there were some gossips and jack-
asses in the courthouse who just didn't like him. "After more
than 30 years of sentencing people around here, you make
some enemies, and some cowards will try to slander you with
rumor and gossip." He continued, "None of the cowards would

ever say anything to my face, but I knew people were talking behind my back."

After a pause, he continued, "If you don't believe me, here I'll let you talk to my wife Mary. She's been married to me for more than 50 years, and she'll tell you there was no truth to any of rumors about me and Kathleen Morris."

(In 1951, Fitzgerald married Mary Mach of New Prague. He had joined an uncle's law firm. An active DFLer, he was elected to the state House in 1957. Five years later, Governor Karl Rolvaag appointed him a district judge in the First District, which includes Dakota, Scott, Carver and four adjoining counties.)

I told him again I wanted to talk only about the Jordan case.

Judge John Moonan Fitzgerald

A large version of this portrait hangs on the second floor of the Scott County Courthouse in Shakopee.

Photograph courtesy of Greg Rademacher, photographer, 166670 Franklin Trail, Prior Lake, Minnesota 55373

Judge Fitzgerald is a polarizing person. He has his admirers and supporters, his detractors and enemies.

Court Clerk Darlene Menke said, "I've seen people wet their pants and faint and everything else in front of him. He could pick up real quick when somebody needed to have their attention brought forward."

Mrs. Menke would not comment on the rumors about any sexual hanky panky by Morris or Fitzgerald, although he did have a reputation for sexual impropriety that would never be allowed in the year 2005. She admired his get-tough action on fathers who failed to make child support payments. Defendants squirmed under his stern gaze and vicious tongue-lashings.

"If they don't support their children they go to jail until they agree to do so, Fitzgerald said, "I tell them, `I paid for my six kids; why should I have to support yours, too?'" He noted that those jailed often quickly produced large sums of overdue support money.

Sandy Keith, former Minnesota Chief Justice who grew up across the street from Fitzgerald in Rochester, Minnesota, had this to say about "Fitz." "He has the Irish wit and tradition. He was giving me hell the other day about my sins of omission and commission, which he considers to be rather lengthy."

Margaret Born, another of the 13 Scott County courthouse clerks who each received a Christmas poinsettia from the judge said, "He is very forthright. He'll tell you exactly what he thinks."

On his way to the Scott County Courthouse from his home in New Prague, Judge Fitzgerald would stop nearly every morning for the 7:45 mass at St. John the Baptist Church in Jordan. Reverend Brennan Schmieg said, "He always starts the hymns. They all join in once he takes off. You can tell when he's not there." Deputy Sheriff Kenneth Reitmier said, "He has a tremendous voice. He sings like an angel."

Many Jordan citizens admired Judge Fitzgerald and considered him almost saintly. Juvinaus Pauly, co-proprietor of the Scott County Oil Company in Jordan was impressed by Fitzgerald's attending daily mass.

On January 20, 1993, Judge Fitzgerald turned 70. He was at that time the state's longest-serving active judge. The impish judge said, "I'm not looking forward to retirement." During his nearly 30 years on the District Court bench, he wrangled with many lawyers. He enjoys telling about past skirmishes in and out of court. He is a storyteller.

Rick Mattox, the chief public defender for the First Judicial District, is quoted in the *Minneapolis Star Tribune* January 3, 1993, "He is known as a fair judge and a scrupulous enforcer of proper court attire, decorum and punctuality. He nailed me a couple of times, once for having my hand in my pocket. He demanded more from us: that we prepare our cases thoroughly and treat witnesses properly and fairly.... He made us better lawyers."

Many attorneys who appeared in Judge Fitzgerald's courtroom tell incredible tales of his abusive behavior. He would glare at them and tell them to correct their posture, and even ask when they last shined their shoes. A bailiff said, "He scared the shit out of a lot of people, and he liked doing it."

Several lawyers asked to have another judge try their cases. Attorney Marc Kurzman representing accused Greg Meyers is quoted in the *Shakopee Valley News* September 19, 1984 requesting Judge Fitzgerald to remove himself from the case. Kurzman said, "The judge is prejudiced in favor of Scott County Attorney Kathleen Morris. Kurzman's colleague, Carol Grant presented evidence that Fitzgerald's son was given a lighter sentence for drunken driving and obstructing justice because Kathleen Morris was the prosecutor on the case. Grant and Kurzman mailed a photocopy of the plea bargain struck between Fitzgerald's son and Kathleen Morris to the courthouse. The deal for a light sentence for Judge Fitzgerald's son enhanced and enlivened suspicions and rumors of sexual misconduct by Kathleen Morris and Judge Fitzgerald. The suspicion lingers."

Fitzgerald's supporters and admirers vehemently defend him against any such allegations that he interceded on his son's behalf.

The Myers' trial date was moved from October 1 to November 5, 1984, a change his attorneys said would unnecessarily hurt their client. Fitzgerald reassigned the October 1, 1984 court date to suspects Don and Cindy Buchan. Was this decision another favor to Kathleen Morris in exchange for something else?

The judge mentioned to me that after the Jordan sex abuse cases were over and Kathleen Morris opened her own law firm, she handled divorce cases before him. He said that he ruled in her favor every time because she was better prepared and a better lawyer.

On June 16, 1988, the *Catholic Bulletin* printed an article about the Archdiocesan Pastoral Council. The Pastoral Council was established in 1972. It was still in its infancy when Archbishop Roach succeeded Archbishop Leo C. Bryne in 1975 and made the Council more accessible and visible. The *Catholic Bulletin* published the roster for the 1988-89 Pastoral Council and among the new appointees was "John Fitzgerald, District Court Judge, First Judicial District, New Prague."

Being a Catholic of conviction and not merely of convention, I penned a letter to Archbishop Roach on June 23, 1988, expressing my displeasure with his appointing John Fitzgerald to the Pastoral Council. This is what followed:

1. On June 30th, I received a letter from Archbishop Roach telling me that Judge Fitzgerald was highly recommended by his parish priest and was a good member of the Pastoral Council.

2. On August 8, 1988, I wrote Archbishop Roach again concerning his appointment of Judge Fitzgerald. I told Archbishop Roach that the recommendations of a parish priest might in itself be suspect because of stories of priests sexually abusing children. I invited Archbishop to listen to many others mistreated by Judge Fitzgerald.

3. In September (after many phone calls, leaving messages with various gatekeepers), I finally got connected to a voice identified as Archbishop Roach. When I told him I was calling about Judge Fitzgerald, he said that matter had been settled–that Judge Fitzgerald had an excellent history of service to the Church and was highly recommended by other church leaders. (I then asked him who these leaders were, and what credentials they had, and whether they had asked anyone in Jordan about the judge, especially the people who had been falsely accused.)

4. Archbishop Roach said he sensed my anger and hostility and I should pray for forgiveness. He said he would pray for me–and he had another appointment. I wondered if he might have meant forgiveness for himself or maybe Judge Fitzgerald. But then I realized that the church and the court relied on the opinions of the psychologist, hence Judge Fitzgerald and Archbishop Roach were at least as justified and innocent as Pontius Pilot.

My feeling is that the child abuse scandal of 1984 would not have happened without the unholy alliance of Kathleen Morris and Judge Fitzgerald.

29

▼

McCarthyism Revisited in Jordan in 1984

*"Just be what you are and speak from your
guts and heart–it's all a man has."*
– Hubert Humphrey

On February 9, 1950, Senator Joseph McCarthy, a Republican from Wisconsin, claimed to have a list of 205 people in the State Department who were members of the American Communist Party. The possibility of Communist subversion caused some people to lose their jobs when they admitted to have been Communist Party members. To save their skins, accused Communist Party members had to expose other members of the party during the McCarthy investigations. The ensued witch hunt and anti-communist hysteria was known as McCarthyism.

Playwright Arthur Miller saw parallels between the McCarthy witch hunts of the 1950s and the Salem witch hunts of 1692. He wrote his play "The Crucible" in the context of the Salem witch trials, but everyone understood is was a metaphor for the McCarthy hearings. The play shows many innocent people being accused of crimes they did not commit. Throughout history and in Jordan in 1984, society has been blinded by similar occurrences or "witch hunts."

The work of Senator McCarthy and Scott County Attorney Kathleen Morris share a disturbing fact. Both compiled list of suspects simply based on prior associations with others who were accused. On June 8, 1984, Morris published a list of 46 names of people she said were "Implicated Persons...who have sexually abused children." Guilt by association rather than by hard corroborating evidence was the rule.

Three years after writing "The Crucible" in 1956, Miller was called before the House Un-American Activities Committee. He refused to name people he allegedly saw at a Communist writers' meeting a decade before and was convicted of contempt. However, he appealed this verdict and later won.

In 1956, Miller married actress Marilyn Monroe. After divorcing Monroe, Miller wed Ingelborg Morath. She died in 2002. Arthur Miller died of congestive heart failure on February 10, 2005 at his home in Roxbury, Connecticut. He was 89 years old.

Miller said the question to be asked about "The Crucible" is: "What should be done to keep the innocent from being accused and presumed guilty?"

Many Americans felt afraid to speak out about the human rights abuses and false accusations during the McCarthy hearings. Many Jordan citizens were afraid to speak out about the unjust actions of Scott County Kathleen Morris during the Jordan child sexual abuse investigation. Fear doesn't travel well. It can warp judgment and diminish memory's truth.

The interrogations in the Salem witch trials, the McCarthy hearings, and the Scott County sex abuse cases are eerily compared to Stalin's Russia, Pinochet's Chile, Mao's China and other cruel and unjust regimes.

The stories of false accusations, false arrests, wrongful convictions, violations of human rights, and loss of liberty must be told and retold often and forcefully.

The Salem witch trials, the McCarthy witch hunt, and the Jordan witch hunt are true frightening stories about the failures of our justice system to protect the innocent. Miller's question must be asked–and answered:

"What should be done to keep the innocent from being accused and presumed guilty?"

30

▼

Satanism in Jordan

"A problem ignored is a crisis invited."
– Henry Kissinger

John W. Decamp wrote a book, *The Franklin Cover-up*: *Child Abuse, Satanism, and Murder in Nebraska*. The first edition printed May 1992, the second August 1992 and the third, February 1994. A second edition was first printed in December 1996 with a second printing in 2001.

Decamp reveals in this book how Paul Bonacci, a witness and child abuse victim, recollects his involvement in the "notorious pedophilia and ritualistic abuse case in Jordan, Minnesota."

Decamp mentions that in 1983 and 1984, Scott County Minnesota prosecutor Kathleen Morris investigated and began prosecuting a ring of child molesters centered in the town of Jordan. He cites the *Minneapolis Star Tribune*: "The case involves the largest adult juvenile sex ring in Minnesota history."

The author writes that child victims in Jordan testified about satanic rituals and the filming of children in sex acts. He claims the children told of witnessing three ritualistic murders. On page

235 he quotes *People* magazine, October 22, 1984: "The village harbored rings of adult sex abusers who incestuously victimized their own children and other children during ritualistic sex parties involving sadism and bestiality. Some children described a bizarre variation of hide-and-seek in which children who were 'found' were taken in a bedroom and abused."

Decamp says that child-care workers and psychologist found the children highly credible. Psychologist Michael Shea treated some of the children and told *People* magazine: "Children are not able to fantasize in such graphic detail about sexual acts which are outside their experience. And they certainly cannot be coerced or bribed or brainwashed into making statements about their parents."

Continuing this line of reasoning, Decamp wrote about psychologist Dr. Susan Phipp-Yonas. She interviewed some of the children and believed their reports and stories. She told the *Minneapolis Star Tribune*: "It is just not the details that make them convincing, but the (emotional) effect behind their stories. They're extraordinarily upset when they recount these things. They'd have to be world-class actors to be so convincing if it wasn't true."

Phipps-Yonas and Decamp speculate that since the children talked about large sums of money being exchanged, organized crime was likely involved.

John Decamp attacks Minnesota Attorney General Skip Humphrey and his 29-page report, "Scott County investigations." DeCamp is critical that the cases were closed for "insufficient evidence." After the cases were dismissed, Minnesota Governor Rudy Perpich appointed a Commission to investigate Scott County Attorney Kathleen Morris. Decamp says that Skip Humphrey named one of his political cronies, lawyer Kelton Gage, as "independent counsel" to present evidence against Morris.

In 1991, Decamp claims that Paul Bonacci, a victim of child sexual abuse and Satanism in Nebraska identified by name and from pictures, some of the individuals Morris had investigated in Jordan. In a recorded transcript, Bonacci recalls going to James Rud's trailer home at the Valley Green Trailer Park in Jordan. Bonacci said other adults, and specifically Bob and Lois Bentz were abusing kids. Upon further questioning, Bonacci wrote a list of names of other child abusers in Jordan. He said children were tortured and forced to play a game called "hide-and-seek-basketball."

DeCamp's book paints Jordan as a haven for drug abuse, pornography, child sexual abuse, gangs, satanic cults, political cover-ups and political corruption. He presents a compelling case for a linkage between the Jordan child sexual abuse scandal and the subject of *The Franklin Cover-up: Child Abuse, Satanism, and Murder in Nebraska*.

John W. Decamp is a lawyer for victim-witness Paul Bonacci in the Franklin case. He has the distinction of being the most praised and the most attacked Nebraska state senator as named by the *Omaha World Herald*. The paper said he was the most powerful and effective senator between 1976 and 1986 in the Nebraska Legislature. Now the *Omaha World Herald* frequently attacks him for fighting against drug dealers and child abusers.

Decamp shows us a logical parallel between *The Franklin Cover-up* and the Jordan Minnesota cover-up. The corruption of governmental institutions and the press is evident. Maybe what happened in Jordan isn't an aberration. Maybe, State Attorney General Skip Humphrey and Governor Rudy Perpich, for political considerations, successfully obscured or covered up the truth of the Jordan scandal. There still are a lot of unanswered questions.

Perhaps if the judges in the Scott County cases hadn't been so blatant and prolific in issuing "gag orders," more truth would have come forth in 1984, and the cover-up ended. The Jordan cover-up is ongoing today.

31

▼

Mayor Gail Andersen

"Have regard for your name, since it will outlive you...
The days of a good life are numbered,
but a good name lasts forever."
– Sirach 41:12

The following commentary was published in *The Jordan Independent* (date uncertain):

Former mayor Gail Andersen lives in Jordan and is an active senior citizen. She has strong feelings about the Jordan child sexual abuse scandal and willingly shares her opinions. In 1984 while still mayor, Gail Andersen wrote a commentary on the Jordan child sexual abuse sandal.

Viewpoint/Gail Andersen

Child Abuse in New Form

Legal system goes too far in Jordan?

The paper's flamboyant articles on sexual abuse of children need some response.

As mayor of Jordan, which is now regarded by the media as the "child abuse center of the state," I have been close to the problem in Scott County. Some of the tragedies taking place behind the scenes because of the merciless tactics of some public officials, supposedly intended to protect our abused children, are appalling!

Yes, actual sexual abuse exists. Every effort must be made to seek out the unfortunate children who are its victims and to give them help and understanding.

But, because this particular problem is "in style" now and politically popular, are we going too far? Are we being caught up in a Salem-witch hunt-type hysteria, where innocent people may also suffer?

Jordan-area children have been seized from their homes without warning by ambitious law enforcement people and placed in foster homes. Parents who have been ordinary good citizens, with no previous offense records, are arrested and jailed, sometimes for the benefit of television reporters who somehow get tipped-off ahead of time on pending arrests.

These arrests sometimes are based on statements interpreted by police investigators after interviews on intimate   sexual matters with a few children, some under 10 years old.

The seized children are told they will have a "new mama and daddy." All contact with grieving parents is forbidden–not even a phone call, card, letter or visit from a friend, relative or religious adviser to let them know their parents still love them and have not abandoned them.

Laws meant to protect children in emergencies from extreme abuse are being used to take protesting children from caring parents, sometimes on flimsy charges. These parents are labeled criminals through guilt by association with known child molesters with previous records. Mug shots of these parents, unshaven, disheveled, sometimes in jail garb, are broadcast repeatedly over TV.

Is this not also a form of "child abuse," to have one's own parents exposed publicly, especially if they may be innocent?

Some of these seized children are now being questioned intensively by county officials. Their answers, as interpreted by their questioners, are used to incriminate friends, neighbors and relatives. The Russians know that even an adult, if isolated and relentlessly questioned, can, without physical torture, be made to say untruths. How about bewildered children, torn away from their homes and familiar surroundings?

Some Jordan area people have become afraid to speak up in protest, fearful of police reprisals. I have experienced this myself. Some live in fear that they will be arrested, added to the "Sex Ring" score, and their children abducted by county officials.

Some adults who insist they are innocent face lifetime in prison sentences and public shame. They are asked to plea bargain for lighter sentences and perhaps to testify against others in the same predicament.

What a choice that would be—plead guilty to something you have not done, or face life imprisonment.

Thus, the "Jordan Sex Ring" grows.

I have seen reputations ruined, homes lost to pay for bail and defense attorneys. Families are broken up, jobs lost, parents, grandparents and relatives driven close to mental collapse, close even to suicide.

As for these innocent children kidnapped by the county and now in foster homes, only the future can tell what emotional scars will be left when and if they are returned to their homes.

Yes, we all want to protect those children who are truly sexually abused. I cannot say who is innocent or guilty. But in less extreme cases, where guilt is not actually proven, aren't there more compassionate, less drastic methods?

Cannot these borderline suspects be put under observation, or advised of suspicions and undergo further questioning before being arrested for the benefit of TV and the newspaper, their lives and families destroyed?

If it is found they are doing wrong, but are not extremely dangerous, can't they receive counseling or treatment, with an effort to keep the family together, as is done with alcoholics, drug abusers and the like?

How do we help a child by stigmatizing him for having an imprisoned "criminal" as a parent, and putting him in foster homes the rest of his childhood?

As a mother and grandmother, as well as a public official, I say there must be better ways.

– Gail Andersen is the mayor of Jordan, Minn.

Author's Note: Mayor Andersen was originally charged with 5 counts of disorderly conduct and 8 counts of misconduct of a public officer. The original 13 charges stemmed from three incidents that happened in Jordan in1982. She was found guilty on 2 of 4 counts.

The Mayor's Legal Troubles

In his *Politics,* Aristotle said, "Man is a political animal." His claim was that we realize proper ends only through political engagement and action.

NOTE: In August of 1983, charges were dismissed when a judge found they were not specific enough. Later, the Scott County grand jury reconsidered the case, and again indicted Mayor Gail Andersen.

February 6, 1984 Jordan City Council meeting:

- Before Mayor Andersen stands trial, the Jordan City Council votes 4-1 to suspend the mayor as head of the police department.

- Before Councilman Shaw introduced his resolution, Mayor Andersen wanted to discuss the suspension of Jordan Deputy Police Chief Dean Johnson. Mayor Andersen said Jordan should not have Johnson on the force because of his recent conviction on a DWI offense.

- Council members Mike Shaw and Del Oltmans objected to any discussion about Officer Johnson or his DWI and voted to table the discussion.

- Councilman Mike Shaw introduced the removal resolution, claiming the police department could not operate efficiently with indictments against her.

- City Attorney Barry Meyer said that according to the city charter, the council has the duty to regulate the duties of officers and could legally suspend them.

- Councilman Steve Betchwars cast the only vote against the resolution.

- A large crowd attended the council meeting, some of them with questions about the investigation of the James Rud case.

- Mayor Andersen commented that she had previously told Jordan Police Chief Alvin Erickson that Johnson, not Norring, should be doing the investigating.

- Councilman Ron Jabs read a letter from Chief Erickson putting Norring on the case. Councilman Steve Betchwars said Chief Erickson was not telling the truth. He said County Attorney Kathleen Morris requested to keep Norring on as investigator to keep the continuity since he began the investigation.

- Councilman Ron Jabs read letters from Jordan citizens commending the Jordan Police department and County Attorney Morris for their work on the sexual abuse cases.

- District Court Judge Thomas Lacy issued a temporary restraining order preventing the Jordan City Council from removing Mayor Andersen as head of the police department.

- District Court Judge Martin Mansur dissolved the temporary restraining order. Mayor Gail Andersen wa suspended as head of the Jordan Police Department.

- Mayor Andersen's defense attorney, Dennis Moriarty, said the only reason the council took away her position as head of the police department was to embarrass her for her upcoming trial to be held in nearby Carver County.

February 28, 1984:

Mayor Andersen's jury trial opened at the Carver County courthouse in Chaska, Minnesota with Judge John Fitzgerald presiding.

Mayor Gail Andersen went to trial to defend herself against a 13-count indictment issued by a Scott County grand jury.

October 1982:

1. Andersen allegedly accused a Jordan couple of selling narcotics, suggested that they move out of town and berated them for receiving public assistance. The couple complained to the Jordan Police Department and City Council.

2. Andersen reportedly berated two city council members and a police officer, asking them to leave a grocery store.

3. Andersen allegedly asked two council members to leave the police department building.

March 9, 1984:

After two days of deliberating, the jury found Mayor Andersen guilty of two of the criminal counts presented by Scott County Attorney Kathleen Morris.

- Her conviction became official when Judge Fitzgerald sentenced her on two gross misdemeanor charges to two years probation and a $750 fine.

- Kathleen Morris' assistant, Gehl Tucker of the Scott County Attorney's office asked the court to give Andersen a $3,000 fine and a two-year probation on each of the two counts against her. He said that at a pre-trial meeting, Mayor Andersen had shown no remorse.

- Andersen's attorney, Dennis Moriarty asked Judge Fitzgerald to keep in mind Mayor Andersen's age, 66, her long life of community service, her lack of previous criminal involvement and that her motive was benevolent. (She was only trying to "get rid of drugs in the community.")

- Judge Fitzgerald said he was fully aware of the political opposition Andersen faced from the Jordan City Council and that her motives were well intended. In passing sentence, he described her actions as "unfortunate instances that never should have occurred, Fitzgerald went on: "Because public officials have certain power, they must exercise that power wisely. The ends don't justify the means… the road to hell is paved with good intentions. It is no justification."

- Upon leaving the courtroom, reporters asked Andersen if she wanted to say anything in her defense. She replied. "I feel this boils down to a political vendetta against me." She approached two reporters outside of the courthouse and reminded them that she was found innocent on 13 of the original 15 charges against her. And she said she was innocent of the other two as well.

- Mayor Andersen said she would appeal the conviction and the sentence.

Follow-up:
- Just hours after Andersen was sentenced, the Jordan City Council called a special meeting and cited a state statute that allows for the removal of an elected official if he is convicted of any infamous act or for violation of his official oath.

- Voting 3-0 for the resolution to remove Andersen from her elected office of mayor were council members Ron Jabs, Harry Johnson and Rosemary Lucius.

- Former Jordan City Councilman, Johnny Johnson, strongly objected to the resolution. "I have never seen anything as rotten or terrible as this. It reminds me of

Nazi Germany in World War II. Let's give them a fair
trial and hang them in the morning."

• Gail Andersen got a temporary restraining order and
  retained her position as mayor. In June 1984, Jordan City
  Council attorney, Barry Meyer faced off against
  Andersen's attorney, Dennis Moriarty before Judge
  Martin Mansur to argue the merits of the restraining
  order.

• Judge Mansur said it was his opinion that Andersen's
  gross misdemeanor conviction could not be defined as an
  "infamous crime" because it did not lead to confinement
  in a state prison.

• Andersen said it should be the voters who decide her fate
  and not the city council. She criticized the council for
  taking action before her appeal was heard.

• Councilman Ron Jabs said, "We have a mayor who has
  been convicted of crimes, and we have an obligation to
  follow Minnesota laws.

November 6, 1984:

Don Tillman was elected mayor of Jordan with a heavy
voter turnout. Tillman received 733 votes; Gail Andersen, 354;
and Michael Sullivan, 186.

Interesting thoughts that might suggest "payback" to the
mayor from the County Attorney Morris.

1. Gail Andersen criticized Kathleen Morris' handling of
   the Jordan sexual abuse cases.

2. Police Chief Erickson received commendations from
   Morris.

3. Judge Fitzgerald, who had a beyond normal professional
   relationship with Kathleen Morris, sentenced Gail
   Andersen.

4.   Jordan policeman Larry Norring, who failed to get evidence from Rud's trailer home, is kept on the investigative team at the request of Morris.

5.   The Jordan City Council refused to fire Jordan policeman Dean Johnson after he is convicted of DWI. Johnson was given a reduced sentence at the recommendation of Kathleen Morris. Johnson continued to investigate the sex abuse cases for Morris.

6.   Dennis Moriarty had originally hired Kathleen Morris when he was Scott County Attorney. He became defense council for Gail Andersen.

7.   Councilman Ron Jabs voted to remove Andersen from the office of mayor. Years later Jabs became mayor and likes the job.

8.   Judge Martin Mansur dissolves the temporary restraining order issued by Judge Lacy that prevented the city council from removing Mayor Andersen as head of the Jordan Police department. Later, Judge Mansur presided at the one and only sex abuse case to go to trial, the trial of Robert and Lois Bentz.

The removal of Mayor Andersen from office was pretty smelly. Lawyers, judges, policemen and city council members played some dirty politics.

Mayor Andersen wrote the following letter to the editor in response to her conviction.

Jordan Mayor Responds to Conviction

Jordan's Mayor is now a convicted "criminal," after over 40 years of adulthood. Her worst offenses previously were occasional traffic tickets.

On Friday, March 9, after two days of deliberating, the jury decided I was guilty of two of the 13 criminal counts presented by Scott County Attorney Kathleen Morris.

What did I do? Rob a bank? Kill someone? Inflict physical injury? Was I guilty of kidnapping, rape, fraud, larceny? No!

My first crime was a private conversation with Barbara Sames of Jordan, after witnessing suspicious goings-on in our park where drug deals reputedly take place. As a concerned mother and grandmother, I told her I felt it was wrong for anyone to make drugs available to young people, and ruin their lives. I did not necessarily accuse her, but objected to just anyone who trafficked in drugs.

I "got involved," as we are supposed to do. This is what happened to me as a result.

Mrs. Sames and about five relatives protested at a Jordan City Council meeting, thus causing the matter to become public. It was referred to Jordan Police Investigator Dean Johnson.

My second crime for which I was convicted was a conversation in Jordan's Red Owl with Johnson while he was grocery shopping, witnessed by our other Investigator, Larry Norring.

As the "Investigation of the Mayor" was making headlines, I reasoned with Johnson that we were spending too much time and money on trivial matters. As his efforts seemed against me only, I suggested he investigate the Sames, too.

This was distorted in court by Johnson and Norring that I, as mayor, had used my authority to "order" the investigation stopped, and threatened consequences if it wasn't. I had nothing to hide. The investigation was not stopped. I made no attempts to stop. My previous recommendation that Johnson not be on Jordan's police force was based on numerous other things I felt he had done wrong.

After over a month of "investigating," Johnson didn't produce much information on me, and nothing on the Sames. He then took it to County Attorney Kathleen Morris.

The nine additional criminal counts brought against me were based on complaints by Councilman Bill Brooks and Harry Johnson.

As neither was employed full time they spent much time coffeeing and socializing with the police, and sitting in police headquarters. I, as head of the Police Department, according to our City Charter, felt excessive socializing could prejudice their Council decisions.

These criminal counts were based on two conversations with Brooks and Johnson expressing my concern. No abusive language. No one physically touched. I was the one who walked away first in both occasions.

These counts were dismissed by the judge before even reaching the jury for decision. This, after over a year spent gathering information, weeks spent interviewing witnesses, volumes of typewritten official reports, much legal maneuvering, headlines in newspapers, TV coverage and my being indicted by Scott County's grand jury twice! All at taxpayers' expense!

Alice in Wonderland had some strange experiences in that rabbit hole. So have I in the City of Jordan, County of Scott, State of Minnesota.

Barbara Sames' husband, Tom, one of my accusers, never appeared in court. Why?

The court was told that during a pretrial hearing Dean Johnson stated that I had ordered a police badge for myself and red flashers for my car, implying that I meant to take on the duties of a licensed police officer.

Actually, when Chief Erickson ordered other badges, he included one for me that said "Mayor." I never "ordered" it, but was pleased at his thoughtfulness. I don't wear it or flaunt it, but keep it in my purse. The red flashers are pure Dean Johnson fiction.

Under our city charter, I believe the mayor serves like the administrator of a hospital, who doesn't perform surgical operations or try to do the job of a registered nurse, but sees that the right people are hired, the finances are handled correctly and things run smoothly.

But under the question-and-answer procedure of our courts, I was never able to say any of this. Only "yes" or "no" to questions.

In the same pre-trial hearing, Johnson stated that I "had a screw loose" and "wasn't wrapped tight." This about an elected official and his superior in rank. He now continues to investigate other Jordan people. In 1983 Jordan's police department spent $20,000 over budget.

Councilman Shaw, a Jordan High School teacher, when asked if there is a drug problem in our schools, answered "No."

In addition to all the time and money spent on two grand juries, the trial itself lasted nine days. Paid from public funds were 12 jurors, the bailiff, court clerk, court reporter, judge, county attorney's prosecutor and his assistant and use of Carver County court facilities.

My legal expenses, loss of time from work and damage to my reputation are staggering. All this for four private conversations!

Is there still Freedom of Speech in Scott County? Who will be next?

— Gail Andersen, Mayor of Jordan

32
▼

Plea Bargains

*"An unrectified case of injustice
has a terrible way of lingering, restlessly,
in the social atmosphere like an unfinished equation."*
– Mary McCarthy

The *Washington Post* on January 2, 1985 printed an article titled "Child Abuse Mystery Stuns Midwest Town," subtitled, "Charges of Sexual Attacks, Murder, Riddled 15-Month Case in Minnesota.

In August of 1984, prosecutors became worried. The first trial, that of Bob and Lois Bentz was to begin on August 27th. One prosecutor said, "She [Morris] wanted an adult witness real bad."

Morris and her fellow prosecutors discussed the possibility of plea bargains with several defendants in return for testimony against others. The only defendant to accept Morris' offer was James Rud, who also had the most to lose. With his two previous convictions for sexual child abuse–one in Virginia, the other in Minnesota–and given the 110 counts against him, Rud could have been imprisoned until he was 75.

Rud took the offer, under which he would have to serve only six years in prison. One state prosecutor said, "For her to offer Rud the deal she did, she had to be very desperate."

In a 113-page verbatim transcript, Rud implicated himself and 15 of the 24 defendants and recounted 10 instances in which other adults abused children.

In October, after Morris had dropped charges against 21 of the accused, and Attorney General Skip Humphrey III took over the sex-abuse cases, Rud told investigators from the FBI and the BCA that "the statement he had given three months earlier was a tapestry of lies."

Rud said he had no knowledge of child sexual abuse by the other adults he had implicated. He said, "I worked on my own. Put yourself in my shoes. Think of 40 years behind bars. You'd probably do anything to get out of that."

A March 1991 *Mpls.St.Paul* magazine article titled, "The Scars of Scott County," describes another plea bargain. According to both BCA agents and attorney Marc Kurzman, in early June, Kathleen Morris approached accused police officer Greg Myers with an incredible offer: If Myers would plead guilty to a reduced misdemeanor charge and incriminate any of the adults charged with abuse, his children would be returned to him immediately. Scott County would pay his moving expenses to another location and would assist him in establishing a new identity.

Attorney Kurzman tried to convince Myers this was as good an offer as he could expect out of the system. Myers told his lawyer that he was a police officer and he believed in the justice system. Myers rejected the offer, and lawyer Kurzman concluded that he had an innocent client.

I interviewed one of the accused men (on the condition I would not use his name) who said he almost made a deal.

Holding his thumb and index finger almost together he said, "I came that close to admitting to something I didn't do. Morris said I would do no jail time and my kids would be returned from foster care immediately if I would confess to sexually abusing a child–and give her names of other abusers. Initially I had told her I hadn't molested any kids, and I didn't know of any others who had either.

"Morris and one of her investigators then started telling me horror stories about what happens to a child molester in prison. They told me over and over that child molesters were on the bottom of the totem pole in the prison population. The cop said that 'a little man like me would get the shit kicked out of himself, get raped and corn-holed, and more than likely killed.' Another investigator told a story of a pedophile priest who was sent up for molesting a young boy. He said the priest was dead within a week.

"When Kathleen reiterated the deal with no jail time, I almost agreed, but then I couldn't see myself telling my child and my wife that I lied just to stay out of jail. Morris told me I would regret not cooperating."

33

Rud's Statement– His Confession

"The truth is seldom pure and never simple."
– Oscar Wilde

When I originally came upon James John Rud's multiple statements, I didn't intend to include them in this book. After the numerous hours transcribing and personnel hours spent recording James Rud's statements, he recanted his words and claimed his testimony never happened.

Yet the length and its minute detail of the incidents cannot be disregarded. It's too hard to imagine a fictional story with the accuracy of explaining the visuals moment by moment; Rud's feelings; what was said, by whom; the children's responses to the activities; and how the subtle seduction was mastered with a promised trip to K-mart. I leave this up to you to decide whether you believe these words happened, especially when he begins with the incrimination of his own parents, Rosemary and Alvin Rud (who he refers to as Alfred).

Rud's statements included detailed recollections of numerous sexual encounters with children and other adults, probably with the promise that his 110 criminal counts would be lightened. Instead, without a trial, he received a sentence of 40 years in prison in exchange for his plea bargain.

Rud's testimony would enrage any reader by the horrifying child sexual abuse. Please do not read the details if you don't feel ready to handle the graphic details. I include them because these statements fueled the prosecution's reactive response to quickly act upon the reports of alleged criminal sexual abuse charges. Children were taken abruptly from their home with little, or no investigation, and parents charged with sexual misconduct with little, or no corroborating evidence.

I am not condoning a rush to arrest any adult for the sexual offense of a child without a solid case against them. However, his detailed testimony certainly explains how Scott County prosecuting attorney, Kathleen Morris, Jordan Police and Scott County Deputies were eager to arrest and prosecute suspects.

The #### is where the children's names are protected–and is how the documents were sent to me from the court. To help you understand what these #### represent, remember the mother who made the first complaint had an 8- and 10-year-old girl that she said were the victims.

This part of the confession covers Rud's involvement his parents and another adult and four children under the age of 13.

This is typed exactly as I received it except for the formatting into more readable paragraphs.

VOLUNTARY STATEMENT (Official)

Statement is being taken from James John Rud, DOB 3-23-57. Present also are Michael Busch, Michael O'Gorman and Pat Morgan. The date is 8-14-84, the time is 9:05 AM.

MORGAN: Jim, for the record, state your full name and date of birth, please.

RUD: James John Rud, 3-23-57.

MORGAN: Jim, do you understand why you are here tonight, to give us a statement regarding your sexual activity with children and adults?

RUD: Yes.

MORGAN: Do you recall any sexual activity involving yourself and your parents regarding children?

RUD: Yes.

MORGAN:: Can you tell me about one incident that you recall?

RUD: Yes. It was between me, my mom, and dad, ##### and ##### ##### and I think #####

MORGAN:: Can you identify which of these people are adults and which are children, please?

RUD: The adults are myself, Alfred (sic) and Rosemary Rud and #####

MORGAN: ##### are all...

RUD: Children.

MORGAN: Can you estimate ##### and ##### age for me, please?

RUD: ##### years old.

MORGAN: ##### age?

RUD: She would have been #####

MORGAN: And ##### age?

RUD: #####.

MORGAN: Can you tell me in your own words what happened

with these people?

RUD: Okay, I had ##### myself, and the kids, which would have been ##### and ##### ##### and ##### in the car with me to take ##### shopping at K-mart. When we got toward Shakopee, I said I want to stop by my parents' house so ##### said that was okay.

The reason why I wanted to stop by my parents' house was to have my parents get better acquainted with #####. So we got to my parent's house and my dad was outside in the shed area in the yard. My mom I assumed was inside at this time. I told ##### she could go in the house since it was already open and she didn't have to knock or anything. So she went in.

The kids stayed outside at this time and I went towards the shed to talk to my dad for a while. He had asked me who I had brought over and I told him it was a real good friend of mine. I'm not positive how the rest of the conversation was. It was pretty much how's my work going and general information like that.

During this time I assumed that ##### met my Mom as she was already in the house and they were having a conversation. I don't know what it was about. About 15   minutes after I arrived or around that time I went into the house and my dad followed me in. He went to get a beer and I went to get a Pepsi. If I recall, my dad went into the living room where ###### and my mom were. After I got my Pepsi I introduced my dad to ######## and we sat down for a while. I think I recall telling my parents that ###### was separated or something to that sort. I'm not positive on what I had told them. About this time ###### had come in 'cause she knew my brothers had an Atari Game. Is this the right story, I may be mixed up. Yeah it's the right one. ###### said she wanted to play the Atari and I said okay. So I took ###### to the back bedroom to my   brother's bedroom where the Atari was at this time and I set the Atari up and started showing her how to play the game, giving her instructions on what to do and that sort. So after I showed her how to do it, we started playing a game. I think it was Donkey Kong. I'm not sure if it was or not. Ten minutes into the game or so, I had unbuttoned and unzipped #####'s pants.

During this time, I started fondling her inside her clothes on the outside of her vaginal area. I started necking with her face, cheeks, that general area of the body while I was fondling her with one of my hands. This lasted maybe five minutes, maybe a little longer. My feelings toward that was I was turned on by it.

Even though she wasn't naked I was still turned on by it. Shortly after, within ten or whatever minutes, I heard the trailer door open and shut. I didn't know who it was and I didn't know that was going on out in the living room. I just assumed that they were getting acquainted. I heard ######'s voice asking where ######. I don't know who had told her where we were, but the next thing I know I heard a knock on the door, the bedroom door, and it was ######, ###### and she noticed that we were playing the Atari game and she wanted to join in. I said, "Okay." I proceeded to show her how to play the game also. I was sitting on the bed with ###### on one side and ###### on the other. Since I was already involved with both girls before I knew it was easy for me to pretty much get what I want so while ###### was learning how to play the game, I had unbuttoned her pants and unzipped them. Once she got into understanding the way the game was played, I started fondling both of them outside their vaginal area. I remember having intercourse with my finger on ######. I'm not sure how long it lasted for. I remember I wanted to have one of the girls by myself even though they were both there so I think I took ###### off to the side after a certain amount of time while she was playing the game. I laid her on the bed alongside me. I had taken her pants down to about her ankles. I didn't take them off. During this time I unzipped mine and took mine down to about just about my knees so that means I would have been naked from the waist down except for the pants along the knees. I proceeded to have, I would say, outside intercourse with her where I would put my penis between her legs but not attempting to penetrate. This went on until I was just about ready to ejaculate and I pulled away from her because I felt ashamed or guilty of ejaculating on her. Then I proceeded to neck with her, give her kisses on the lips and along the neck area, attempting to work my way down to the vaginal area.

I made it down there and I started licking her vaginal area. All the while ###### was still playing the Atari game. I'm sure she was watching at times. To the best of my   knowledge I don't recall her saying anything to us. I remember asking ###### every once in awhile if it felt good, if she wanted me to stop or not do some-thing to let me know and to let me know if I was hurting her. She said it felt okay and yes, she would let me know if I hurt her. So at this point, I didn't want ###### to feel left out. I didn't want her to get mad at me for putting her off to the side, so I told ###### to go ahead and pretty much do what she wanted and she want-ed ###### to play the Atari game and I took ###### and laid her on the bed.

I recall fondling her on the bed and remember getting my finger inside her vaginal area a very short distance. She complained of a little bit of pain, so I didn't want to go any further. After I had done that I decided that I wanted to lick her so I proceeded to go down her vaginal area with my tongue. I was kind of curious on why nobody else showed up at this time or why nobody was looking for me or wondering where we were at. I just figured somebody would walk in on us. This only lasted a short time with ######. Maybe at the most ten, fifteen minutes.

I didn't want to take my chances. I really wanted to play Atari too, in fact. So all three of us ###### was already dressed so me and ###### got dressed. I'm not sure what happened after that. I remember playing Atari for a little while and then I left the room. When I got toward the kitchen area, I saw that my parents were sitting on the couch and ###### was on the floor. The way it looked to me was that dad was coming on real heavy with my mom and if I recall, ###### were sitting with ###### on the floor, both of them. I couldn't exactly see what ###### was up to at this point. She was in sort of a blind spot for me.

I went a little further in and noticed ###### had ###### on the floor. ###### had their pants down. I want to correct myself. When I came out of the bedroom, my dad was on the couch with ###### and my mother was on the floor with ######. What I saw when I come out of there was ###### had her panties on and her bra and my mom, all I saw was her back, but to what I saw she was still dressed. I couldn't see her front at this time. I went further towards the living room. I saw that ###### had their pants down, my dad's hand looked like he was fingering her. It was inside of her underwear, so to me it looked like he was fingering her and I think he, no I don't think, he gave her some kisses along the cheek and neck area. I sort of acted a little bewildered but not too surprised. I didn't think my mom and dad and ###### would get along this well. I'm not sure, I can't remember how I got started in it. I think I took one of ######. One of the girls I took, which is ###### want to make sure I correct myself for a minute. When I saw my mom, she was nude from the waist up.

When I saw my mom, ###### was sucking on my mom's boob and my mom was fondling ###### so at this point I took ######. I went over and sat on a chair and I felt like I'm not going to be left out so I thought I'd join in with everyone else so I dropped my pants to my knees and while I was sitting there I proceeded to have ###### give me a blow job while at the same time I started to fondle her vaginal area. I glanced over and I saw ###### and my dad, or ###### excuse me, and my dad having, I think my dad was having her ###### give him a blowjob. I wasn't too worried about what my mom and dad were doing at this time. This might have gone on for ten, maybe fifteen minutes.

I remember ###### coming out of the bedroom. I'm sure they saw what was going on but they never said anything at least until later on when I was alone with them. they headed straight for outside. I remember telling them to stick around the area because we were going to be leaving pretty soon. I was just telling you that ###### went outside and I told them to stay in the general area because we, me and ###### and ###### were going to leave pretty soon. I glanced over and I think I remember saying something to my dad about we got to get going pretty soon. I didn't say right away. He sort of nodded his head and said, "Ah huh."

During the time when I said that to him he was, him and ###### were moving around. I think he was attempting to get on top of ###### to have intercourse and then I glanced over to where my mom was and mom was licking ##### 's vaginal area. So about that time I had ###### stop giving me a blowjob and I proceeded to lick her vaginal area. I sort of brought her, I switched places with her so she could be on the chair and I would be on the floor kneeling in front of her. When I finished with that, I wanted to finger her before I decided to leave the house, so I spread her legs a little more and I put my little finger into her vagina just a short distance up until she told me that it was starting to hurt. So I backed off. I told her that it would be okay, that I wouldn't hurt her, but I assured her that everything would be okay. I sort of comforted her in a manner of letting her know where we're going afterwards, which would be K-Mart. I think I told her that if she complained, she would have to stay in the car or something, and she didn't complain.

So when I was finished, I noticed that ###### and dad were just finishing up intercourse and in the process of getting dressed. Then I looked over, wanted to know how my mom was doing. I looked over and wanted to know where or what my mom was doing cause I didn't hear any noise and I noticed that she was just helping ###### get dressed and I figured this was pretty close, about the time we were about ready to go, so I remember seeing dad and ###### start dressing and told ###### she could go ahead and get dressed and while she was getting dressed, I was in the process of getting dressed, too. By this time everybody was, the girls were out, I remember my mom just finishing buttoning her blouse. During this time my mom went outside with ######. I had another Pepsi out of the refrigerator, dad got another beer. ######, me and him went outside also. He went toward the shed area to proceed to finish up what he had started earlier. There was a little conversation afterwards, but I don't remember getting into any physical contact or sexual conversation after this.

MORGAN: Okay, Jim. When did this happen?

RUD: Sometime around June of '83.

MORGAN: Do you recall the time of day it began and what time it ended approximately?

RUD: I'd say early afternoon, I don't know, the weekend at least.

MORGAN: Where did this occur, can you tell me the address?

RUD: Lot 20 Mobile Manor.

MORGAN: That is?

RUD: My parents' house.

MORGAN: That's just outside of Shakopee?

RUD: Yes.

MORGAN: Prior to this incident were you sexually active with ####?

RUD: Yes.

MORGAN: Were you sexually active with ##### and ##### prior to this incident?

RUD: Yes.

MORGAN: In talking about the incident with ##### you said you had outside intercourse. Have you in fact had penetration with your penis into ##### vagina?

RUD: Yes.

MORGAN: Prior to this, and after this incident?

RUD: Yes.

MORGAN: Have you had penetration with your penis into ##### also?

RUD: Yes.

MORGAN: Prior to this and after this incident?

RUD: Yes.

MORGAN: You also told us that during this incident ##### said that it was okay, it didn't hurt that much. Were there occasions when you have hurt children physically and have them protest while you are making that penetration with your penis or finger?

RUD: Yes.

This excerpt is from pages 1-5 of Rud's 15-page testimony from August 14, 1984.

If this abbreviated confession (page 1 to 5) sickened you, imagine what other gory and graphic details he spilled in the 113-page testimony on August 14, 1984. I've read every page and was repeatedly repulsed.

After hours and hours of law enforcement investigators' time and that of the county staff, Rud recanted his confession on October 15, 1984.

34
▼

Rud Confesses in August, Recants in October

- Rud's original plea offer from County Attorney Morris was for treatment and no jail time.

- The court wouldn't allow her to make such a deal so it was amended.

- He would plead guilty to 10 of the 110 counts made against him, and in return would receive a jail sentence of no more than 72 months.

- Rud acknowledged he had committed some criminal sexual acts and agreed to the plea bargain.

- In a series of interviews that begin early August 1984, Rud gave the police a 113-page statement confessing numerous admissions of child sexual abuse.

- Robert and Lois Bentz were acquitted of all sexual abuse charges on September 19, 1984.

- Donald and Cindy Buchan were scheduled for trial on October 15, 1984.

- October 15, 1984, Rud recanted the 113-page confession to FBI Special Agent Bobby W. Erwin and BCA Special Agent Patrick L. Shannon.

- With the understanding that his plea bargain with County Attorney Morris would not change, he agreed to tell the FBI the truth.

- He believed the FBI suspected his confession was false.

- The FBI relayed this information to County Attorney Morris.

Kathleen Morris was enraged!

Rud contends the false confession was coerced by illegal pressure applied by police and County Attorney Kathleen Morris. He says they supplied him with the details they wanted him to confess. During the many interrogations, he would tell the investigators that the stories and allegations were untrue. They persisted and kept accusing him of being involved with many children and adults at many parties where heinous sexual crimes against children were committed.

Face to Face with James Rud:
How All the Accusations Came About...

Rud describes how he and his lawyer, public defender, William Christianson were called to Morris' office. Morris demanded that he stick to his original confession. She wanted him to tell the FBI that his recantation was false. Rud said he told Morris that he would not tell lies for her anymore and the original confession was manipulated and coerced. It was not true, and he would not take back his recantation.

When I interviewed Rud at the Moose Lake Correctional Facility on February 9, 2005, he elaborated, "Kathleen was really pissed. She wanted me to lie for her. I continued to refuse. She cursed me and called me a fucker and said that I would never get out of jail unless I cooperated. My lawyer never said a word, never objected to her swearing at me and shouting obscenities at me."

James Rud said that all during the many hours of questioning by several police and Kathleen Morris, his lawyer was not present. He said his lawyer simply told him he was old enough to answer their questions and that if he got into a real jam, he could call him at his Red Wing office.

In my conversations with him, Rud contends his lawyer incompetently defended him. To complete a 113-page confession comprised of several police interrogations over a period of several days without a lawyer seems outrageous to me.

Rud believes some of his legal rights were violated. He hopes some lawyer will take up his case on a pro-bono basis. Also, he would like to get some help from a legal aid agency. He wants somebody to investigate his case.

After Rud refused to do what Morris wanted, the plea bargain was voided and he was sentenced to 40 years in prison. James contends that the original plea bargain should have been honored or Judge Mansur should have allowed him to withdraw his guilty plea. Rud commented that he believed Judge Mansur was not an impartial judge and intended to sentence him the maximum 40 years without hearing any evidence.

James Rud said that if he could go back to the beginning, he would plead not guilty and go to trial–and take his chances with a jury.

Rud offers additional information:

- His parents or other relatives never sexually abused him.

- He was not an abused child.

- One of the most painful parts of the false 113-page confession was accusing his parents of child sexual abuse.

- In a proposed letter (I have from Rud) to the children he abused, Rud states that he is truly sorry for robbing them of their innocent childhood. He acknowledges that he knew what he did was wrong.

- He writes that immediately after committing the sexual abuse, he would feel guilt, pain and shame. But still, he continued to abuse.

- He is very sorry that these children were taken away from their families and friends. He concludes his draft letter, "I hope that sometime in the future I can personally tell you how sorry I am, but until that time I must work at bettering myself so I can enter society a changed man."

Rud is currently in a four-phase treatment program for sexual offenders. Since his incarceration, he has taken higher education classes through Saint Cloud State University. James needs to complete only five more classes to receive an Associate of Arts degree. Also, he has been certified to drive a forklift. He completed 1400 hours as a custom cabinetmaker, and he has learned basic computer skills.

He is somewhat apprehensive about being released from prison and finding employment. If he completes his present sentence, he will have spent 26 years in prison and will be 52 years old. He is hopeful and optimistic that he will find a job and a community that will accept him living there. He is scheduled to appear before the parole board to be considered for release in September 2009.

Over the years, several writers and other media people talked with James about writing a book, doing a TV documentary or making a movie. Rud mentioned that John DeCamp, author of The *Franklin Cover-up*: *Child Abuse, Satanism, and*

Murder in Nebraska, visited and asked about satanic cults and sex and pornographic rings operating in Jordan. James said he told DeCamp that he was unaware of any cults or rituals or the production or sale or distribution of any pornography in Jordan. Rud stated that he never took any nude pictures of any children and the police never found any when they searched his house or his parents' house. DeCamp didn't return and Rud concludes he didn't find any porn pictures. James said the writers and the TV and movie people never offered him any money. Perhaps they lost interest when they realized there were no murders or sex rings.

Rud said he is sorry for all the trouble the falsely accused had to bear and the losses they suffered. He hopes to personally apologize to all the accused.

In that February 2005 interview at the Moose Lake Correctional Facility, Rud told me he personally knew only three of the accused. A few he might have met on the street at some time. Most of the accused he did not know and had never met. Rud repeated his statement that he never witnessed any of the accused having sex with children. He asserts that he knew nothing about any kids being murdered. He said, "Look I got the maximum sentence, there is no reason for me to lie today."

James Rud wrote in a letter, "To the Children I Abused," February 5, 2005 (as yet unsent), "I would like in the future to talk with parents' groups in what to look for in an abuser such as myself."

35

21 Adults Had the Charges Dismissed Today!

"I am not afraid of storms
for I am learning how to sail my ship."
– Louisa May Alcott

Starting in October, and over the next nine months, 24 adults were arrested and charged. October 15, 1984 brought dismissal to 21 people charged (reprinted verbatim).

State of Minnesota   District Court
County of Scott   First Judicial District
(The official stamp: Received October 15, 1984, Clerk of Courts, Scott County, Minn.)

STATE DISMISSAL OF
COMPLAINT, PURSUANT
TO RULE 30.01
COURT FILE NO. 8   4-xxx

State of Minnesota
PLAINTIFF   VS.   DEFENDANT

Christine Brown
Jim Brown
Tom Brown
Helen Brown
Donald Buchan
Cindy Buchan
Scott Germundson
Marlene Germundson
Judith Kath
Charles Lallak
Carol Lallak
Irene Meisinger
Terry Morgenson
Greg Myers
Jane Myers
Duane Rank
Delia Rank
Robert Rawson
Coralene Rawson
Alvin Rud
Rosemary Rud

(Individually named each one of the 21 falsely accused)

- -

The State of Minnesota hereby dismisses the Complaint in the above-named case for the following reasons:

The court in another related case has recently ordered the release of documents which had previously been withheld by that court because of their serious and confidential nature and because they concerned an active criminal investigation of great magnitude. The recent action of the Court has prompted a further evaluation by persons involved with the child victims such as guardians, police, social workers, therapists and foster parents as to the child victim's ability to testify in further criminal proceedings. In a prior related trial, the treatment of the children had such a debilitating impact on them that their ability to withstand any further criminal proceedings is in doubt. It has become increasingly clear that many of the children would be unable to testify in any further criminal proceedings without great emotional distress or trauma.

The release of these sensitive documents which relate to another ongoing criminal investigation of a serious and sensitive nature will no doubt be an issue in this criminal proceeding. Prejudice would likely result to this ongoing investigation by release of this information at this time.

The protection of children and the need to safeguard them from further victimization are the State's most important objectives. It has become obvious that at this time these objectives can best be served by proceeding in another legal forum which may be more effective in furthering the State's desire to protect children.

The evaluation of the consequences of further participation in the criminal proceedings by the child witnesses has led to the determination that to continue to pursue criminal charges at this time would not be in the best interests of the victims or further the interests of justice.

The State is compelled to assume its public responsibility to exercise its sound discretionary authority and dismiss the criminal charges in this matter.

Dated: OCTOBER 15, 1984   R. KATHLEEN MORRIS
SCOTT COUNTY
ATTORNEY

R. Kathleen Morris
Attorney for Plaintiff
Scott County Courthouse
Shakopee, MN 55379
(612) 445-7750

Letter to the Editor, *Jordan Independent Centennial Issue*
September 26, 1984:

Where would you begin to pick up the pieces?

On Thursday, September 20th, the headlines announced the verdict in the Robert and Lois Bentz suspected child abuse sex ring trial, which was held in Jordan, Minnesota.

Imagine yourselves sitting there weeping, holding hands in the courtroom, while you hear them read off "NOT GUILTY" on all 12 counts, and where would you begin to pick up the pieces and start over?

This case has made three points very clear to those who read the article, and I believe we should all pay close attention to the lesson being taught.

1) Be extremely careful about spreading rumors you hear about others, and continue to pass along not knowing the facts.

2) Be thankful that we still have a court of law in this country that believes in presenting the truth in order to provide us with "A FAIR TRIAL."

3) Finally, as a result of this trial, we should have become a little more open minded, and at least question the truth as well as the falsities being presented.

Didn't we within our own minds have these people convicted before the case ever went to trial? And all because of what the news media brainwashed us with!

It's my belief that if the Bentzs had been found even 1 percent guilty and there had been any solid evidence to have backed up the claims being made, they would have at least been convicted on ONE count.

I often wonder as to how many people today are being falsely imprisoned on such charges where the evidence that was presented appeared as being somewhat more believable.

Some psychologists tell us we should believe what children have to say more often, such as the doctor who was trying to build a case against the Bentzs.

It's almost as if they are telling us it's not possible for youngsters to make such false claims against a parent.

Why, I read just the other day where a 14 year old boy back East threw kerosene over his parents bed while they slept and then torched the blankets critically injuring his father and killing his mother.

Or, how about the 16-year-old in California who stabbed her 35-year-old mother to death for not accepting her boyfriend.

With scores upon scores of young people across the country continually committing such acts of violence against parents, wouldn't it be just as easy for them to say that their parents sexually abused them?

After all, it's one way of getting even and at the same time, drawing national attention to themselves.

When you grow up not feeling loved or recognized by a parent (which is far too often the case these days) how do we know what extreme anyone might just go to in order to gain that necessary exposure!

– Jimmy Luhm
Saginaw, Minnesota

36

▼

County Attorneys
Play God

*"Do not find fault before you investigate;
examine first, and then criticize."*
– Sirach 11:17

A retired Scott County judge told me that the County Attorney has awesome power. They can charge or not charge someone with a crime. They sometimes play God and behave like they are all powerful. Did Kathleen Morris go beyond the duties of a Minnesota County Attorney in the massive arrests made during the Jordan child sexual abuse scandal of 1984?

Duties of the County Attorney
Minnesota Statute § 388.051

In each of Minnesota's 87 counties, a county attorney is elected to handle numerous criminal and civil legal responsibilities. Following is a brief description of the duties of the county attorney and the county attorney's relationship to the county board.

Civil Advice

The county attorney is the legal advisor for the county board of commissioners, county officials and county departments. The county attorney is not authorized to provide civil legal advice to private citizens in his or her capacity as county attorney. As the legal advisor for the county, the county attorney serves in a role that is similar to that of an in-house corporate counsel. The county attorney provides legal advice to the county board and county departments in areas involving waste management, defending challenges to property tax values, representing the Human Services Department on welfare appeals, enforcing county environmental and health ordinances, and forfeiting property used in connection with criminal activity, Additionally, the county attorney's office assists the county in buying property; negotiating leases and contracts; and in defending against personal injury, workers compensation, employment, civil rights and other law suits.

Adult Prosecution

The county attorney primarily prosecutes felony crimes (crimes which carry a maximum penalty of more than one year in prison) which occur within a county. Examples of these crimes include murder, sexual assault, drug offenses, serious property offenses, and child abuse. Misdemeanors and gross misdemeanors (crimes which carry a maximum penalty of less than one year) are the primary responsibility of city attorneys in some metropolitan and greater Minnesota areas, but may also be prosecuted by county attorneys. Prosecution may involve reviewing the investigation of law enforcement officers, filing criminal complaints, presenting cases before a grand jury, representing the state in court hearings and trial, and making sentencing recommendations.

Juvenile Prosecution

The county attorney is the prosecutor in all cases involving juvenile offenders. These range from curfew violations to the most serious felony criminal behavior. County attorneys may also oversee diversion programs which allow juvenile offenders to receive consequences involving minor offenses without going to court. These programs are intended to hold the juvenile accountable and often include an educational component to reduce repeat offenses. Due to public safety concerns, for more serious offenses the county attorney may ask the Court to certify a juvenile to stand trial as an adult. Upon conviction, the juvenile could then receive all potential adult sanctions, including a prison sentence.

Victim/Witness Assistance

County attorneys provide assistance and support to the victims and witnesses who play a vital role in the criminal justice system. They advise crime victims of their legal rights and status of their case, and will request restitution for losses suffered.

Family Services

The county attorney initiates CHIPS (Child in Need of Protection or Services) petitions to protect abused or neglected children in the county. The county attorney starts legal proceedings to protect the health and safety of vulnerable adults within the county when they are in need of assistance. The county attorney also files involuntary commitment actions to provide necessary treatment for individuals who are mentally ill, chemically dependent, or mentally retarded. When a family is receiving public assistance, the county attorney brings actions to obtain or enforce child support obligations, or to establish the paternity of a child, in order to obtain reimburse-

ment for assistance and other costs to the taxpayers. Parents
not receiving federal or state monetary assistance may also
apply for and receive these child support enforcement or paternity establishment services from the county attorney at minimal cost.

Assistants to the County Attorney

The county attorney could not perform the many duties
required without assistant county attorneys. The county attorney must supervise these assistants, establish policies and
guidelines to be used by them, and perform necessary admin-
istration to insure that the duties and responsibilities of the
office are properly completed.

Pursuing Improvement & Prevention

The county attorney plays an important role in seeking
new laws to strengthen law enforcement, criminal justice,
child protection, victim's rights, and other areas. The county
attorney also participates in efforts to prevent or reduce crime
in the local communities and statewide.

The Minnesota County Attorneys Association
100 Empire Drive Suite 200, St. Paul MN 55103
Phone 651-641-1600
Fax 651-641-1666

37
▼

Alice in Wonderland Was Right... It Gets "Weirder and Weirder"

"Truth is a demure lady, much too ladylike to knock you on the head and drag you to her cave. She is there, but the people must want her and seek her out."
– William F. Buckley Jr.

On June 8, 1984 after almost two dozen Scott County residents had been arrested and charged with child sexual abuse, Morris penned a letter with a list of individuals. It referred to the alleged "as persons who have sexually abused children."

The list was mailed to:
- Alvin Erickson, Jordan Police Chief
- Doug Tietz, Scott County Sheriff
- Norm Pint, Pat Morgan and Mike Busch, Deputy Sheriffs
- Larry Norring, Jordan Police Officer

- Paul Gerber and Pat Shannon, BCA officers

Gossip in the courthouse spread quickly about the list.
- Who is on the list?
- How many people are listed?
- How did they get on the list?
- How was it compiled?
- Who will be arrested next?

Rumors spread. Speculation, terror and panic swept through the community.

Along with the list of names, Morris stated that "It appeared that over 100 children have been victimized ...." She encouraged quick action and stated that many of the individuals she had listed have children in their custody who have reportedly been abused.

Small-town gossip spreads like wild fire. Ever-growing stories quickly popped up everywhere. The rumor mill said at least 500 people were on her list. Some even said most of the townsfolk were suspected and on that list.

A former Jordan elementary teacher told me that the fear of being on that list of suspects caused some people to quickly move from the community.

A retired local farmer said of Morris, "If you get on her bad side and on her shit list, you're all done. You're ruined. Your reputation is shot."

I believe Morris knew she could intimidate an entire town by releasing such a list of alleged suspects. I could find nothing that indicated the people she listed had been investigated and found innocent. Perhaps she put out more lists of suspects, even she was naive to the power of these allegations. But just making the list terrorized and ruined lives–without a trial to convict or clear an innocent person's name.

Morris must have completely believed her source. She ignored her legal oath that those charged were presumed innocent until proven guilty. She had no presumption of their innocence. So zealous and misdirected was her fight and righteous claim that even when a jury found defendants innocent, she attacked the system or the jury for their verdict as in the Bentzes trial.

Morris' list of alleged offenders left more innocent people with ruined reputations. Those victims wronged by the defamation should have been able to successfully sue Morris and the County for destroying them. At the very least, she should apologize. But she never has.

R. KATHLEEN MORRIS
SCOTT COUNTY ATTORNEY
COURT HOUSE 206
SHAKOPEE, MN 55379
(612) 445-7750, EXT. 240

Assistants
  Miriam Jeanne Wolf
  Pamela Ann McCabe
  Richard S. Virnig
  R. Gehl Tucker
  Patricia M. Bliss
  Kevin W. Daily
  Law Clerk
  Nancy Platto

June 8, 1984

  Chief Alvin Erickson
  Jordan Police Department
  Sheriff Doug Tietz
  Scott County Sheriff's Department

RE: Implicated Persons

Dear Chief Erickson and Sheriff Tietz,

We are aware of information from police reports, officers, other investigators, witnesses, psychologists, social workers and guardians that the victims and others involved in the current series of criminal sexual conduct cases, in Scott County have implicated the following list of individuals as persons who have sexually abused children:

Larry and Bonnie Eiden
George Gould
Sharon Nelson
Ginger and Bruce Sly
David Sly
Shorty and Jeannette Wirk
Toni Walsh
Bob Fossen
Bob Fossen Jr.
Curt and Julie Fossen
Terry and Linda Beuch
Bob and Kathy Hart
Pat Weliski
Marjorie Jellinick
Barbara Borgen
Kathy Olson
Terry Schultz
Dan and Wanda Magers
Jim and Diane King
Rose Anderson
Sheri Konapechi
Diane and Don Wiemer
Lisa Armatrout's father
Bob Brown
Lorenz Robert's father
Tess Hakarine

Mark Lehman
Matt Lehman
Kim Peppel
Man in Buchan neighborhood
Fred Peppel (dead we believe)
One-armed man
Bear (dog)
Casper (cat)
(one blacked out name)

We will gladly provide you with all the information we have relative to these matters if it will aid your investigation. Of course you are aware of the urgency in investigating these matters. It appears that over 100 children may have been and are being victimized in these reported incidents. Many of these individuals have children in their custody who have reportedly been abused. Therefore, these reports should be investigated as soon as possible to protect these and other children.

Please let me know as soon as these cases are ready to be charged. If I can be of further assistance, please call.

Sincerely yours,
R. KATHLEEN MORRIS
SCOTT COUNTY ATTORNEY

R. Kathleen Morris
RKM:pmw
Cc: Larry Norring
         Paul Gerber
         Pat Shannon
         Pat Morgan
         Mike Busch

38
▼

"Truth does not come cheap.
It makes demands and it also burns."
– Cardinal Joseph Ratzinger

REPORT ON
SCOTT COUNTY
INVESTIGATIONS

HUBERT H. HUMPHREY III
ATTORNEY GENERAL

February 12, 1985

TABLE OF CONTENTS

Introduction

On October 15, 1984, R. Kathleen Morris, the Scott County Attorney dismissed charges against twenty-one citizens accused of child sexual abuse in Scott County.

In dismissing those cases, the County Attorney made reference to a court-ordered release of documents in a case concerning "an active criminal investigation of great magnitude." The County Attorney went on to say that prejudice would likely result to this ongoing investigation by release of this information at this time." This "investigation of great magnitude" referred to allegations of homicide made three months earlier by some child victims in the sex abuse cases.

The County Attorney also noted the need to protect and safeguard the children from further victimization. She indicated this could best be done by these cases proceeding in family court rather than a criminal setting. Finally, she noted that it had become increasingly clear that many children would not be able to testify in the criminal proceedings without great emotional distress or trauma. She concluded that it would not be in the best interest of the victims and the further interest of justice to continue with these criminal proceedings.

During the week of October 15, 1984, the Minnesota Bureau of Criminal Apprehension (BCA) and the Federal Bureau of Investigation (FBI) began investigating the alleged homicides, pornography and child abuse in Scott County. On October 17, 1984, Hubert H. Humphrey III, Minnesota Attorney General, sent a letter to the Scott County Attorney, urging that she provide a more detailed public explanation of why the criminal charges had been dropped against the twenty-one defendants. On October 19, 1984, the Scott County Attorney requested that the Minnesota Attorney General assume responsibility for the pending family court matters and any criminal charges which might arise out of the FBI/BCA criminal investigation of the alleged sex abuse, pornography and homicide cases.

During the course of that investigation, over a dozen state and federal investigative agents focused on what happened in Scott County. Many of these agents had substantial experience in investigating child sexual abuse and pornography. The main case agents and others from the BCA had successfully overseen the Children's Theater sexual abuse investigation.

The FBI effort was overseen by the supervising agent in the FBI St. Paul office. Among the FBI personnel working on this case was the agent responsible for training other agents and law enforcement personnel in the Midwest region in child sexual abuse investigations. The jurisdictional focus of the FBI effort was on allegations of homicide and pornography.

Metropolitan area county attorneys, including Dakota County Attorney, Robert Carolan, Hennepin County Attorney, Thomas Johnson, and Ramsey County Attorney, Tom Foley, also provided assistance by assigning staff attorneys to handle the child neglect and dependency cases arising out of the sex abuse allegations. In addition, eight attorneys and four criminal investigators from the State Attorney General's Office participated in this effort.

At the conclusion of their investigation, the FBI/BCA agents submitted their investigative findings to Attorney General Humphrey. Those findings are as follows:

1. There is no credible evidence to support allegations of murder which arose during the sexual abuse investigation.

2. There is insufficient evidence to justify the filing of any new sex abuse charges.

Those findings were unanimously supported by each investigator working on these cases.

It should be emphasized that some children in Scott County were sexually abused. One individual has already been convicted as a result of a guilty plea. Other offenders received immunity and are undergoing treatment. In one instance the abuse occurred outside the period of the statute of limitations. In another instance a woman admitted sexually abusing her son but the Scott County Attorney decided not to file charges. In that case there were no indications of any connection with a sex ring or other adults. With respect to all other allegations of abuse, however, it is impossible to determine whether such abuse actually occurred, and if it did, who may have done these acts. The reasons for this impossibility are set forth in this report.

Before detailing these concerns, a statement must be made regarding the nature of the charges. Sexual abuse of children is horrible and shocking behavior which our society, until recent years, has too often hidden or ignored. Recently, however, hundreds of child sexual abuse cases have been aggressively and sensitively pursued each year by Minnesota prosecutors. This has been possible because, in properly handled cases, children can be credible trial witnesses. For the most part, the delicate balance between the interests of children and the rights of accused individuals has been properly struck.

In the Scott County cases, however, something clearly went awry. This is not to suggest that the objectives of Scott County authorities were improper. There is no evidence that the Scott County authorities were motivated by anything other than concern for the protection of children. That concern is shared by the Attorney General and by everyone involved in the investigation. That legitimate concern, however, must be balanced against the rights of accused individuals. That balance can be best maintained when such cases are investigated and handled in a manner which results in the development of credible evidence. The best way to protect children is to conduct investigations in a responsible manner, in a way that will lead to discovery of what really happened and lead to convictions, if justified by the evidence. It is in this regard that the Scott County cases floundered.

This report summarizes the basis for the findings of the investigation. It is not intended to provide a chronological review of all the evidence in these cases. Nor does it comment on guilt or innocence or any specific individuals.

Included in this report is a section entitled

"Recommendations for Action." These recommendations have been developed as a result of one Attorney General's state-wide survey of the handling of child abuse and from our experience with the Scott County cases. These recommendations provide the opportunity to develop a positive conclusion from the Scott County cases.

In an effort to protect the children involved from further public exposure, neither names nor initials of any children are mentioned in this report. Similarly, none of the former defendants, except James Rud, who is the only individual convicted of a crime in these cases, has been identified.

Homicide Investigation

On November 14, 1984, the Attorney General, the Federal Bureau of Investigation and the State Bureau of Criminal Apprehension announced that based on all available information, there was no substantiated evidence supporting allegations of murders in the Scott County sexual abuse probe. Before reaching that conclusion, FBI and BCA agents had spoken with the Scott County Attorney, staff from her office, investigators and staff from the Scott County Sheriff's Department and the Jordan and Shakopee Police Departments. Therapists and school personnel who had worked with the children who made the allegations were also interviewed. In addition, investigators consulted with psychologists not involved in the case, including one from the FBI behavioral sciences unit at Quantico, Virginia. This individual was also familiar with similar investigations around the country. Inquiries were made of the following sources: The National Crime Information Center (NCIC), FBI, FBI records, Minnesota Criminal Justice Information Systems (CJIS), Minnesota Motor Vehicle and Driver Services (DVS), Minneapolis Credit Bureau, and the

Scott County Jail. Long distance telephone tolls and subscriber checks and inquiries were obtained. The U.S. Postal Inspector and the U.S. Customs Service were contacted to determine if any of the accused appeared in their files in reference to child pornography. Background investigations were commenced on suspected perpetrators. The final step in the process was interviews with the children themselves.

Those interviews with the children resulted in three individuals recanting their earlier allegations of killings. Four other children who had been identified by Scott County authorities as having given statements regarding homicides stated they had never actually witnessed any killings. The only child to continue talking about murders gave investigators three entirely different versions of what she claimed happened, all within the course of one interview session. In sum, by November 14, 1984, there was no credible evidence to believe homicides had occurred.

The first interview with a twelve-year-old boy, who had provided the most graphic details of homicides, took place on November 2, 1984. During the interview the child described in detail seven children being stabbed, mutilated and/or shot during the spring and summer of 1983. This contrasted with his statements in July 1984 to Scott County investigators. At that time he had described three homicides. He also indicated at that time that at least fourteen adults and eleven children observed one child being mutilates and killed.

When interviewed in November 1984, he indicated that five bodies had been disposed of in the Minnesota River. He described how a caravan of cars had gone to the Lawrence Campgrounds and that the group involved in the homicide walked across a walkway bridge. This description of the caravan of cars traveling through the streets of a small

Minnesota town on a summer's eve caused investigators to question the feasibility of the allegations in that no witnesses had ever reported seeing such a caravan of cars. The youth went on to describe the disposal of one of the bodies. He stated that the group involved in the homicides carried a body to the park, while armed with flashlights. He stated that it was so dark outside that one child stumbled off the bridge and was retrieved from the water. He said the bodies of the alleged homicide victims were disposed of in the river.

On November 3, 1984, BCA agents accompanied this boy, his guardian ad litem and therapist to the area where the child said bodies had been dumped. He stated that some of the bodies had been placed in an inflatable boat, paddled out and dumped in the middle of the river.

Shortly before a November 6 interview with this boy, state/federal agents spoke with a park ranger, who has kept a diary noting the depth of the river and certain occurrences there in 1983. The park ranger indicates that in March of 1983 the river had flooded over its banks and had swept away the walkway bridge, which was not replaced until late summer of that year. He stated that during much of the spring and early summer of 1983 the trails or paths which are located next to the river had been impassable because the river had flooded those areas. This was the same time period during which, according to the boy, bodies were carried along the paths and over the bridge. The physical impossibility of such events during that period raised severe doubts as to the boy's credibility.

On November 6, 1984, the agents met with this boy in the presence of his therapist. Again he spoke of bodies being disposed of at the campground site. Agents asked the boy if he still recalled bodies being placed in inflatable boats which were then rowed to the middle of the river where the bodies were dumped. This was asked because agents had been informed by law enforcement personnel familiar with the river that currents would have pulled any inflatable boat downstream, making it unlikely that a boat could have been rowed to the middle and back. The child began to change his story about where the boat took the bodies. The agents told him that the walkway bridge was not in place when he said a body was carried across it. At that point he broke down and cried. He admitted that he had lied and stated that there were no murders. He stated that he was still telling the truth about the sex abuse but that he had invented the murder stories because he didn't want to go home.

The agents also interviewed another child who had made allegations of homicide. When interviewed in July by Scott County investigators, this individual told of three or four killings. He told of victims being shot and stabbed, and of one being drowned in a neighbor's pool. He described one of the victims as a drummer in a rock and roll band, who was playing at a party when he (the drummer) was killed. When told that the purpose of the agents' interview was to discuss the alleged homicides, this child immediately stated that he had lied about the cutting and the torture and death of any victims. He stated that the idea of the homicides came into his head when Scott County investigators questioned him about a black or mulatto boy who may have been cut or tortured. He said he got the idea of ritualistic torturing from a television program he had seen. He stated that he lied about the murders because he wanted to please the investigators.

On November 6, 1984, state/federal agents met with a nine-year-old girl who had made allegations of murder in July 1984. In July she had stated that her father shot and killed an 8-year-old black boy in the kitchen of their home. She did not describe any other children being present, nor any mutilations or sexual abuse accompanying the killings. The residence where she stated killings took place was not the site of any of the alleged sex parties or ritual killings described by any other witness.

When she met with state and federal agents in November 1984, she immediately recanted all allegations of homicide. She states that the reason she made up the story about someone being killed was because her "very good friend" told her to say these things. This friend was the child who first made mention of killings in July 1984.

The child who first mentioned killings is a twelve-year-old female, who met with Scott County investigators after she had talked to her therapist about homicides. This child had been sexually abused by James Rud over an extended period of time. By July 1984, this child had been interviewed no less than twenty-three times about the sex abuse allegations. She had accused eleven adults of sexually abusing herself or other children.

When questioned individually about homicides, she told Scott County investigators that she had seen a person stick the broken stein of a wine glass into the vagina of a baby girl, then stab the baby in the chest and bury it. She stated the child's mother was told that day that the baby was dead.

She also told of a woman in her thirties who had been sexual with her and then was killed by the same person. A third victim she described was a young mulatto boy killed after having sex with her.

When this witness met with state/federal investigators in November 1984, she vividly described very different homicides. She again told of a baby being killed–this time with its head partly cut off. She stated that the child's mother had dropped the baby off at her friend's house, where her friend's father was going to baby sit. She stated that her friend's father killed the child because he could not tolerate the baby.

She spoke of a three-year-old black boy being stabbed. This child was killed, she states, because it had gotten into her friend's father's shed and started a fire. She stated that this aggravated her friend's father so he killed the child with a pocket knife and buried the child in his backyard.

The next victim she described was a four-year-old boy who, she states, started a fire in the street and was then stabbed in the heart by her friend's father because he stated that the child deserved punishment.

The fourth alleged victim was an eleven-year-old boy for whom the girl said she was babysitting, even though she was only ten at the time. She stated that this child had taken some pills from a cabinet and got intoxicated from them. She stated that her friend's father revived him and then killed him with a knife.

She told investigators that all those killings took place on the very same day. She also made no mention of the woman in her thirties she has said was killed during her July 1984, statement.

During the interview the girl was at ease and extremely talkative. In each case she talked about the victims being cut and stabbed. She was asked by the agents if there was any shooting involved and she said "no." One of the agents then pointed out to her that earlier police reports showed individuals being shot. She then described the four homicides again and this time changed her story, stating that all the individuals had been shot rather than stabbed. Her therapist then asked a question, and the child said that the individuals had been stabbed rather than shot. Because of the demeanor of this child and as a result of the shifts in her story within a relatively short period of time, it became clear to investigators that this child was simply not believable as to these stories.

Three other children who had been described in police reports as having discussed alleged homicides were questioned. They told state/federal investigators that they had not observed homicides but rather talked of people being hurt. Therapists informed these investigators of a fourth child who said that he had never used the word "murdered" but rather "hurt." State and federal investigators attempted to interview this particular child. The child indicated that he would only be willing to talk to the agents through puppets. He indicated that he would nod the head of one of the puppets yes or no. At some point in the interview the agents asked him if he had seen any kids that were killed. This child shook the puppet's head "no." When questioned by his therapist as to whether he has spoken last summer with a Scott County detective about homicides, the child indicated, through the puppets, that he did not remember that conversation.

When state/federal agents first began investigating the alleged homicides, they planned a search of the Minnesota River. Investigators consulted with pathologists to determine what, if any, evidence of a body would still exist after being in a river for an extended period of time. They spoke to the Army Corps of Engineers to determine if any evidence, assuming it existed, could be discovered through such a search. They spoke with law enforcement representatives from other Minnesota counties who have had experience with river search operations. They were informed that the possibility of finding such evidence was extremely slim. However, it was felt that every reasonable investigative effort should be made. Plans were made to begin the river search in early November 1984. Bad weather forced a postponement of that search. It was at this time that investigators discovered that the walkway bridge has been washed away months earlier and children began recanting allegations of murder. As it became clear that there was no credible evidence of murders, the river search was canceled. In the absence of any credible evidence, both the FBI and BCA felt it would be inappropriate to risk injury or potential loss of life in a river search.

In addition to planning a search of the river, investigators had prepared search warrants based on the original statements of the children. However, as the stories collapses and as the physical impossibilities of the original allegations piled up, it was concluded that there was no probable cause to justify the filing of any search warrants.

Sexual Abuse Investigations

After concluding that there were no homicides, state and federal authorities turned their focus to the allegations of sexual abuse and pornography. They began to reconstruct the investigation made by Scott County authorities, continued to interview child victims, therapists, and do background investigations and interviews of the former defendants. Their investigation included contacts with law enforcement authorities in New York, Alaska, Utah, Kansas, Iowa, Washington, D.C., Georgia, Missouri, California, and Texas.

The original investigation by Scott County authorities failed to produce a single photograph containing child pornography, despite the fact that numerous children had mentioned that photographs had been taken during some of the alleged sex parties. By the time of the BCA/FBI entry into these cases in October 1984, the only evidence of pornography and sexual abuse of children by the accused adults rested principally on the statements of the children. However, as a result of the original investigative process, many of the child witnesses were simply unable to provide credible testimony. In a number of instances, therapists advised state/federal investigators that certain key child witnesses would be unable to testify credibly in any further court proceedings.

The current absence of credible testimony and the lack of significant corroboration lead to the inevitable conclusion that no new criminal charges are warranted. The credibility problems result from repeated questioning, a lack of reports and cross-germination of allegations. The opportunity to obtain corroborating evidence, on the other hand, was largely lost forever by the filing of the original criminal charges in Scott County before the completion of thorough investigations. These concerns are set forth more fully below.

Repeated Questioning and Lack of Reports

The central problem with which state and federal investigators were confronted when conducting their investigation was that many of the children had been questioned about sex abuse a large number at times. A therapist's report in February 1984, notes one child who had already been interviewed by nine individuals about the alleged abuse. The mother of another child indicated that her daughter had been interviewed at least thirty and possibly as many as fifty times by law enforcement or Scott county authorities. A number of other children also were repeatedly interviewed.

Repeated interviewing and discussions about abuse undermine the credibility of witnesses. It can cause confusion in both adults and children. With children it raises the additional concern of suggestibility. According to experts, children may interpret repeated interviews as demands for more or different information than they have already given. In one Scott County case a trial court judge refused to allow into evidence the testimony of a nine-year-old who made some incriminating statements against his parents after being "interrogated" by his foster parents about the abuse. The judge noted that this child had steadfastly denied any criminal sexual conduct on the part of his parents until he had been placed with new foster parents, who questioned him extensively.

The repetitive pattern of questioning often occurred in circumstances which threatened the integrity of the children's responses. In many cases children were removed from their hones and isolated from all family contact for prolonged periods, even though the children denied having been sexually abused. In some instances, the children did not "admit" that their parents had abused them until several months of such separation, marked by continuous questioning about abuse. In the most extreme cases, these children were also told that reunification with their families would be facilitated by "admissions" of sex abuse by their parents and other adults.

The problem of over-interrogation was compounded by a lack of reports. For example, Scott County investigators' notes show that one nine-year-old girl was interviewed by law enforcement authorities approximately twenty times and yet there were only four written reports concerning those interviews. In addition, her meetings with the County Attorney are undocumented. That pattern was not at all unusual. Investigators' notes show that another child was interviewed by law enforcement officers over twenty times and yet there are reports from less than half of those interviews. In addition, on at least a half dozen occasions she met with the County Attorney, again with no reports on these meetings.

The County Attorney played a major role in interviewing and meeting with the children during the course of the investigation and in preparation for trial. In some instances, when children were picked up and taken from their parents' homes to be placed in foster care, they would first be brought directly to the County Attorney's office, In addition, the County Attorney or her staff would meet with and receive information from children about alleged abuse which would serve as a basis for a criminal complaint before law enforcement personnel actually spoke to the children about the new allegations. Again, the files contain little reference to those meetings.

The absence of reports with investigative personnel and the County Attorney makes it difficult to determine whether an individual has been consistent in making allegations. It makes it difficult or impossible to determine when and under what conditions claims of sexual abuse were made. It is standard procedure for law enforcement personnel to make out reports, particularly in instances where a witness says something of importance to the case, such as an accusatory statement. The lack of reports undermines the credibility of witnesses at trial by subjecting them to claims of recent fabrication.

State/federal investigators were faced with the lack of reports both in regard to allegations of sexual abuse and to statements about homicides. Although some children who made the homicide allegations spoke with investigators about murders in July 1984, at the direction of the county Attorney reports concerning those interviews were not prepared until October 1984, shortly before the criminal charges were dismissed.

The pattern of repeated questioning and the lack of reports permeated all levels of the original investigation. In addition to being interviewed by law enforcement and the County Attorney, the children often discussed sexual abuse with therapists, in some cases on a weekly basis. In some instances even foster parents and the drivers who took them to interviews questioned them about abuse.

As children continued to be interviewed the list of accused citizens grew. In a number of cases, it was only after weeks or months of questioning that children would "admit" their parents abused them.

In working with child sex abuse it is not unusual for children to initially deny being abused. In subsequent interviews they may finally admit what happened. However, the Scott County cases raise the issue of how long and how often one can continue to question children about abuse before running the risk of false accusation.

The children who told the homicide stories had been questioned repeatedly, over an extended period of time, about sex abuse. Some had initially denied being sexually abused by their parents until questioned over a period of months. In some instances, over a period of time, the allegations of sexual abuse turned to stories of mutilations, and eventually homicide.

The Scott County experience has demonstrated that in some instances prolonged interrogation of children may result in confusion between fact and fantasy. This conclusion was specifically drawn by the therapist of one alleged victim. The therapist believes that the repeated interrogation of this child has rendered him psychologically incapable of distinguishing among what actually happened, what he has previously described, and what has been told by others.

Cross-Germination of Allegations

In addition to the problems of repeated interviewing and

lack of reports, another concern which undermined the credibility of witnesses in these cases is "cross germination." In some instances witnesses were informed what other witnesses had stated. Sometimes, two children would be interviewed together. Some examples are set forth below.

In one case a twenty-one-year-old female described being interviewed by the Scott County Attorney when her 11-year-old sister was also in the same office. She stated that her eleven-year-old sister first described the abuse that she (the 11-year-old) had allegedly endured. After hearing that story, the twenty-one year old claims she was then asked what information she had concerning the same individual in question.

An eighteen-year-old who admitted to abusing children was questioned about abuse by adults. He claims to have been provided with allegations of abuse made by another child concerning adults whom he knew. He stated that he was then asked to report on what abuse he observed concerning those adults.

The parents of a 12-year-old child indicated that their daughter was questioned by law enforcement, then told what another child had said, and then questioned again.

In some instances young children were brought together and interviewed to discuss the allegations of abuse. In one instance this occurred during a therapy session in which a child was told that his sibling had made allegations against a parent. He was then asked to describe what has happened to him. On another occasion, during the one case that went to trial, child witnesses were provided with the same motel accommodations, ate meals together, and were otherwise permitted to have contact with each other.

The statement by James Rud also demonstrates the

problem with cross-germination. In August 19, Rud gave a statement implicating eighteen adults in sexually abusing children. He later recanted that accusatory statement. Rud claimed to have obtained and reviewed copies of police reports regarding other defendants before he gave a statement implicating these individuals in the sexual abuse of children. It is interesting to note that in Rud's 113-page statement the only individuals identified by him were those whose names had been in the police reports, and all but one of whom has already been charged with a crime, The one not charged was a close acquaintance of a number of the defendants.

Finally, it should be noted that there is nothing per se improper about joint interviews of children. Some child sexual abuse investigators indicate that on rare occasions one may conduct a joint interview to limit the number of times a child will be questioned. However, in these cases the problem of cross-germination exacerbated the severe credibility problems already created by excessive interviewing of the children and the absence of reports to document the allegations made by the children.

Absence of Corroborating Evidence

Corroborating evidence is evidence which confirms the verbal allegations of a crime victim. While corroboration is rarely an absolute legal requirement in a criminal case, it is always of the utmost importance. Absent corroboration, a criminal case boils down to a debate between the accuser and the accused. It is difficult for prosecutors to prevail in such cases.

Corroborating evidence is particularly critical to both the accuser and the accused in child sex abuse cases. In the interests of the accuser, corroboration is of immeasurable value to the credibility of a victim who may be impeached due to youth, or limited memory, or limited ability to communicate. In the interest of the accused, the search for corroboration protects individuals against unjust prosecution.

Corroboration for an allegation of child sex abuse comes in many forms. It may be in the form of physical instruments or evidence of abuse; or concurring accounts by other witnesses; or even incriminating statements by the suspect or another adult. In any event, all of these possibilities should normally be well explored prior to the filing of criminal charges. Afterwards, evidence of either guilt or innocence is far more difficult to gather.

A major problem with the Scott County cases is that a thorough search for corroboration was generally not completed prior to the arrests. As a result, the cases rested almost exclusively upon me credibility of the children, credibility which was severely compromised. Most every opportunity to gather credible corroboration was consequently lost forever, long before the BCA/FBI investigation began.

Representatives of the Scott County Attorney said their office felt obliged to arrest suspects and remove children from homes with great dispatch whenever a new adult was identified as an abuser. In many instances, this resulted in persons being charged with abusing children, at a time when these children had either denied the abuse or had not even been interviewed

For example, neighbors of two former defendants described a meeting with the defendants following their arrest to discuss and review the complaint. During the meeting the neighbors learned for the first time that their own child was an alleged abuse victim of those very defendants. At that time, neither the children of the accused, nor the neighbors' child, had been questioned by authorities.

In several other instances, parents were arrested and charged with abusing their own children, even though those children denied the abuse through several weeks of interrogation and separation from their parents.

Likewise, the suspects themselves, their spouses, or friends, were seldom, if ever, interviewed prior to being charged. Thorough background investigations, prior to criminal accusations being brought, were not done.

Finally, the haste with which charges were brought often precluded a search for corroborating physical evidence. Surveillance techniques were not utilized. Search warrants were rarely obtained. In a number of instances there were allegations of individuals being involved in photographing victims. No warrant to search for those photographs was obtained at the time those individuals were arrested

In the very few instances where searches were utilized, they were not always thorough. In the case of James Rud, on October 5, 1983, nine days after Rud's arrest, a Jordan police investigator arrived at the Rud trailer where he observed a stack of approximately twelve video cassette tapes and a large box containing what he believed to be pornographic materials. Rud's parents were present at the time and ordered the officer to leave. The investigator failed to seize the video cassettes or other materials. When he returned the next morning, the tapes and alleged pornography were gone.

The Scott County Attorney sought to compensate for an absence of corroborating evidence by inducing some defendants to testify against others She indicated that the standard plea offer in these cases was for the defendant to plead guilty, undergo psychological evaluation and treatment. Most often, she indicated, treatment meant at an in-house program at St. Peter State Hospital. The defendant would receive a stay of imposition, meaning it they completed their probation without incident, they would end up with a misdemeanor rather than felony record.

Former defendants also indicate that they were promised agreements which would provide them with no jail time, treatment and probation in exchange for their testimony. In one instance, a few days before the County Attorney dropped all criminal charges in these cases, two defendants were allegedly offered the dismissal of all charges if they would provide information about the alleged homicides. The defendants were also allegedly told that if they did not provide the information, the prosecution of the sex abuse charges would go forward. Their attorneys state that they recommended that their clients accept the offer if they had any information to give. The defendants refused the offer, indicating they simply had no knowledge of any homicides.

In sum, with the single exception described below, none of the efforts to obtain incriminating evidence of sex abuse from the defendants or from other potential adult witnesses produced any fruit whatsoever.

The only defendant who accepted the County Attorney's offer of leniency in exchange for testimony was James Rud. James Rud is a confessed child abuser. He described in detail sexually abusing numerous children through cajoling, forced persuasion and violence. He faced charges of one hundred and eight counts of sexual abuse. If convicted on all counts, he faced the possibility of over 40 years in prison. The agreement offered by the County Attorney initially called for no jail time, but rather treatment at St. Peter State Hospital. That agreement was rejected by the trial court and replaced by one in which Rud would plead guilty to ten counts of abuse, and be sentenced on one. Sentences on the other nine counts would be delayed until after Rud completed his initial sentence and testified truthfully at trials of other defendants. Ninety-eight counts were dropped.

Rud gave a 113-page statement in which he implicated eighteen of the twenty-four defendants. He testified at the trial of two defendants accused of abuse. He was, however, unable to identity one of the accused. The jury was soon instructed to disregard his testimony because of legal issues regarding the propriety of the plea agreement.

In early November 1984, Rud met with state/federal agents on at least two occasions. He was given polygraph examinations, one of which was inconclusive and a second one which he failed. He had also met with attorneys representing the Attorney General's Office who were handling the family court cases, in preparation for their hearings. These attorneys noted that Rud's testimony was "troubling" because in a number of instances he could give no reasonable account of why he was at a particular party where he claimed to have observed adults sexually abusing children.

On November 20, 1984, Rud again met with state/federal agents who informed him that he failed the second polygraph test. He then recanted his earlier statement about other adults being involved in mild sex abuse. He denied ever attending any sex parties or that there was a "sex ring." He gave investigators the names of sixteen children, ranging in ages from five to twelve, male and female, whom he had sexually abused in 1981-83. He indicated that he knew several of the former Scott County defendants, but had no knowledge of their sexually abusing any children.

Rud claims that he felt pressured to fabricate the involvement of other adults in order to please the County Attorney and assure himself of a lighter sentence. Rud's public admission that he lied resulted in his losing the benefit of the plea arrangement originally offered by the Scott County Attorney. On January 18, 1985 Rud was sentenced to forty years in prison. The sentencing court noted that Rud's statement rendered him ineffectual as a witness in any further proceedings

Corroborating testimony for the sex abuse trials was also sought from older juveniles, who themselves admitted sexual involvement with child victims. The County Attorney gave these older juveniles immunity from prosecution as adults in exchange for testimony regarding other alleged abusers.

Most notable among these was an 18-year-old who in January 1984, admitted sexually abusing his nine-year-old sister and twelve-year-old brother At that time, he also described observing his brother having intercourse with his sister and another juvenile girl in the Jordan area. Finally, he admitted having sexual contact with his stepmother's sister, but denies knowledge of any other adult sexual activity. In a June 1984, statement he claimed that his brother and sister learned this sexual behavior from other children in the neighborhood and denied any knowledge or abuse by adults. He changed that story in July 1984, when he gave a statement implicating his step-mother and seven other adults in sexual abuse of children. In November 1984, however, this individual recanted the portion of his statement implicating other adults claiming he had done so only because Scott County authorities kept pressuring him. He did not recant his admissions about the sexual abuse he perpetrated on his siblings.

Similarly, another older juvenile implicated his own mother and other adults in sex abuse in exchange for criminal immunity. When interviewed by BCA and FBI agents, however, he recanted those allegations, alleging that he made them up out of fear of personal prosecution. At the time of his retraction he took a polygraph test administered by state/federal personnel. He passed that polygraph.

In conclusion, the search or corroborating evidence by the Scott County authorities came far too late to produce anything either useful or reliable. It would appear that this absence of corroboration was an extremely important factor in the dismissal of cases against 21 defendants by the Scott County Attorney.

Investigations Lack of New Evidence

The final factor in the decision to issue no new charges is the lack of new evidence. In spite of the intensive effort of state and federal investigators, no evidence was uncovered which would corroborate the initial allegations of the children. There was, however, one individual who came forward claiming to have "new," incriminating evidence regarding some of the Scott County defendants. The person is a juvenile who claimed to have been at a gathering where two of the defendant couples were sexually abusing children.

State investigators conducted two interviews with this witness. During the second interview they asked this witness to identify the photographs of the individuals alleged to have sexually abused children. Though the witness was able to identify two of the children, the witness could not pick out the photograph of a woman whom he claims has given him oral sex on at least ten occasions. Upon further questioning he indicated that he had not actually witnessed acts of abuse by adults which he earlier claimed to had seen.

Investigators attempted to corroborate other parts of this story. They made use of a hidden body wire in an attempt to obtain incriminating statements from individuals the witness claimed knew about abuse. They spoke to individuals previously not questioned by Scott County authorities whom the witness claimed also were present when child sexual abuse occurred. These other interviews resulted in information directly contrary to the allegations at this new witness. As a result, the investigators concluded that statements from this individual were simply not reliable. As such, they could not be used to support the filing of any new criminal charges.

Conclusion

The Federal Bureau of Investigation and the Minnesota Bureau of Criminal Apprehension concluded that there was no credible evidence of murders in Scott County connected to the activities of any child sex abuse ring. In addition, no reliable evidence of the existence of pornographic materials was discovered. Finally, their recommendation is that there is presently a lack of credible evidence which would provide a basis for pursuing any criminal charges in these cases.

There is no doubt that a number of children in Scott County were victims of sexual abuse. Yet, therapists treating them indicate that many of the children are presently unable to testify in further proceedings. Those able to testify face severe challenges to credibility due to repeated questioning, lack of reports and a cross-germination of information. Moreover, there is a lack of corroborating evidence to support these allegations. Under these circumstances it would not be in the best interest of justice to continue these matters in a criminal forum.

The tragedy of Scott County goes beyond the inability to successfully prosecute individuals who may have committed child sexual abuse. Equally tragic is the possibility that some were unjustly accused and forced to endure long separations from their families.

Although criminal charges will not be forthcoming, this does not mean the children have been forgotten. In each of these cases there has been a thorough review of what actions should be taken to protect the children. The Hennepin, Ramsey and Dakota County Attorneys Offices provided the services of many of their most experienced family court attorneys to handle these cases. We are constrained by data privacy laws from speaking about specific actions in family court cases. Yet, the public should be aware that, where appropriate, the family court can and has required treatment, therapy, protective services, and ongoing monitoring of the family situation, even if criminal charges are never filed. Even if accused adults had not abused their children, the problems caused by long separations must be dealt with by the family as a whole. Family court can facilitate a healthy reunification of a family, regardless of whether sexual abuse has or has not been proven in a criminal courtroom. The role of family court is to promote the well-being of the family, in a safe and supportive environment. That goal is being met in these cases.

In addition, the Scott County cases have caused us to thoroughly review how child sex abuse cases should be handled. During the course of this investigation we conducted a survey of the handling of child abuse throughout the state. Using the Scott County experience in conjunction with the survey, we have developed 21 recommendations for improving the quality of child protection in Minnesota. It is clear that investigators, prosecutors, human service workers and therapists must all examine how they presently handle these cases in light of the Scott County experience. We should all benefit by understanding what went wrong in Scott County.

Both our survey and the Scott county experience should help to spur on efforts to provide more intensive training in the handling of child sexual abuse. What is preferred is a coordinated, multidisciplinary effort in investigating and processing these cases. In our survey of the handling of child abuse throughout the state, it is noted again and again that the system generally works well. In part, this is due to what a number of counties describe as a successful, coordinated effort in dealing with child abuse. In responding to that survey, one county sheriff succinctly addressed this issue:

"My observation is that counties that have a successful and professional child protection effort are those that understand and respect each other's abilities. This is the crux of the multi-disciplinary approach to child protection. It is a team effort that cannot be controlled by one team member....

"In closing, I would like to add that child protection is best dealt with by local authorities. In the wake of a few bad examples of how investigations were conducted, I hope we don't lose sight of the fact that many of us have been doing a good job in this area."

It is hoped that our efforts to combat the horrors of child sexual abuse will not suffer as a result of what happened in Scott County. Yet, at the same time, we have been vividly reminded that in a just and democratic society, those in positions of public power must bring reason and good judgment to their discretion in the exercise of that power.

Recommendations for Action

During the course of the investigation of the Scott County cases, the Attorney General's Office was also in the process of surveys child protection practices in Minnesota. Survey forms were sent to county attorneys, sheriffs, police departments and human services agencies in all 87 Minnesota counties. In addition information was requested from various other states concerning the existence of training standards for individuals involved in child protection.

The survey was intended to provide a general overview of how the legal system in Minnesota is handling child abuse cases. Our focus was on issues such as caseload, training needs, general policies and guidelines, and recommendations for improving the system. It was not intended to achieve a comprehensive analysis of how well the system functions in handling these cases. Moreover, in reviewing the survey responses, it is apparent that additional follow up and review is needed to more fully understand the problems and concerns facing those involved in child protection. We believe that, if a generalization is possible, those involved in child protection are doing a very good job of protecting children, while respecting the rights of the accused. The Scott County cases which we have reviewed must be seen as an aberration.

The survey, together with our Scott County experience, has led to the development of recommendations for providing high quality child sexual abuse protection in Minnesota, several of the more specific recommendations are established practices in many counties. Others are new. Thousands of child sex abuse cases have been successfully and properly handled by local prosecutors in Minnesota. Again we emphasize: the child protection system in Minnesota works well. Nevertheless, we can and should examine ways to improve it.

A final word of caution must precede our recommendations. Any system for child protection, especially involving sex abuse, is extremely complex. There is no single set of rules for how the problem of child sex abuse should be handled. Some counties may do things differently than suggested below and achieve outstanding results. The recommendations in this report are intended to serve as a spring board for a sensitive and well-informed public debate on this subject. Participants in the debate should include: the legislature; county attorneys, who have primary jurisdiction in this area; law enforcement agencies; social welfare agencies; religious organizations; and other groups of interested citizens.

Investigations

The importance of thorough, competent investigations in child sex abuse cases cannot be emphasized. A thorough investigation protects the innocent and provides greater certainty that the guilty will face the consequences of their conduct.

Many counties presently employ a multi-disciplinary team approach involving law enforcement, human services, and prosecution. A team approach may be the most effective means of handling child sex abuse. However, the functions of child protection and criminal investigation are distinct and separate. Law enforcement, human services and prosecution need to recognize their appropriate role distinctions.

Another key to competent investigation is adequate training. In our statewide survey of county attorneys, 100% of those responding cited a need for increased training for law enforcement officials involved in mild sex abuse cases. Law enforcement officers involved in child abuse investigations should have some background in child development and psychology. This would prove helpful in questioning children and evaluating their statements. Similarly, there is a recognized need for increased training for human services workers involved in child protection. Both human services and law enforcement personnel concurred in recognizing the need to improve skills in this area. Adequate resources, both state and local, must be made available for training purposes.

There is no consensus on the specific number of times a child should be interviewed prior to trial. Responses to our survey indicate there is a consensus that contacts be minimized. On occasion, repeated meetings may be necessary to obtain the full story or allay a child's fears about the court process. Nevertheless, the Scott County experience has demonstrated the difficulties that develop from repeated questioning and a lack of reports, especially when the child has been isolated from family and provided inducements to talk about abuse.

In regard to the human services component of investigation, a number of survey respondents cited a need to remove what is known as the "Tennessee warning" in child abuse investigation. The "Tennessee warning" requires that individuals being asked to provide what is defined as private or confidential information to state agents should be informed as to (1) whether he or she may legally refuse to give the data; (2) any known consequences of providing or refusing to provide the data; (3) and the identities of persons or entities authorized to receive the data. Law enforcement is already exempt from giving this warning because of the obvious concern that giving it hinders the investigative process. Because of the investigative process involved in any child abuse inquiry, such an exemption is also warranted for human services workers, this proposal is already being reviewed by the Minnesota County Attorney's Association.

Recommendations

1. Law enforcement officers involved in child abuse investigation may benefit from more extensive training in that area This includes a need for training in child development and psychology and interviewing techniques.

2. Investigation of child sexual abuse should involve a team

approach, including law enforcement, human services, and prosecution personnel. Such an approach should involve extensive communication from initial entry into the case until final disposition. This will also help limit the number of interviews.

3. Where appropriate, search warrants should be used extensively in an attempt to obtain corroborative physical evidence.

4. Basic to any interviewing of child witnesses are three standard and routine procedures,

    a. Interviews with child witnesses and victims must be kept to a minimum. Policies should be established to limit the negative effects of multiple interviews,

    b. Investigators should avoid telling child victims what other victims have alleged.

    c. Interview reports and investigative notes must be maintained in any investigation.

5. Remove the requirement that human services personnel give "Tennessee warnings" when investigating child abuse cases.

Prosecuting Attorneys

Prosecuting attorneys play a central role in the handling of child abuse cases. They have the responsibility of presenting evidence in both criminal and child dependency and neglect cases. It is essential that prosecuting attorneys maintain good working relationships with human services and law enforcement personnel so that investigative problems do not hamper prosecution efforts. Prosecutors must ensure that cases have been adequately investigated before criminal complaints are filed.

It is important that prosecutors work with child victims to ease their anxiety about the court process. However, the Scott

County cases have raised the issue of how close and how much contact the prosecutor should have with child victims.

Prosecutors must also recognize a separation of investigative and prosecution functions. The ABA standards on prosecution functions provide that although prosecutors have an affirmative duty to investigate suspected illegal activity when it is not being adequately dealt with by other agencies, they should ordinarily rely on police and other investigative agencies for investigation.

As prosecutors recognize, the protection of children involves more than just successful prosecution of the offender. From the moment the state intervenes in the family unit until the family problem is resolved, prosecutors must seek to protect children. This requires a recognition and consideration of the impact of the prosecution's effort on the well-being of the child. Prosecutors recognize that, unless termination of parental rights is appropriate, offenders and victims will eventually be reunited. As such, where appropriate, the child's relationship with the family unit should be maintained. This involves attempting removal of the abusing party, rather than victims, from the home. The 1984 Minnesota legislature provided judges with the authority to remove abusers from the house pursuant to Minn. Stat. § 260.191 subd. lb (1984).

There are, of course, circumstances when the protection of children requires their removal from the home. However, the removal of a large number of children from their homes in these Scott County cases is not indicative of how other counties operate. In Hennepin County, for instance, less than two percent of the child protection cases result in removal of children from homes.

In responding to our survey, prosecutors also recognized the need for Minnesota to receive over $900,000 in matching funds to assist in improving the criminal justice system. The Attorney General's Office has worked with the Governor's Interagency Task Force on Criminal Justice in directing that those funds be used to improve the handling of child sexual abuse cases. This includes funding for increased training for prosecutors, law enforcement, human services, treatment and other personnel involved in these cases.

Recommendations

6. Prosecutors should limit the number of interviews and contacts with child victims.

7. Prosecutors should encourage and assist in establishing policies to ensure the speedy processing of child sexual abuse cases.

8. Prosecutors should first seek to protect children by means other than removal from the home. Perpetrators, rather than victims, should be removed from the home.

9. The Minnesota County Attorney's Association should continue its training efforts in working with child victims and prosecuting child sex abuse cases. The legislature should provide the necessary funding for this training.

Therapists

Therapists play an important and necessary role in dealing with child sexual abuse. Working closely with victim, family and perpetrator, they can help the child deal with the effects of abuse and aid in bringing families together. They are necessary experts in family court cases. Even if reported abuse did not occur, therapists can and need to work with the child and the family to help resolve the underlying problems.

In working with sexually abused children questions are raised regarding the role of therapists. Should the therapists perceive themselves as part of the prosecution team or is their role a more neutral one? Is it appropriate, and under what circumstances, should therapists act as investigators?

Recognition of the scope and seriousness of the problems of child abuse has only recently come to the forefront of public awareness. Many issues regarding the treatment and handling of victims are only beginning to be understood. How long should children remain in therapy when they deny being victims? What "incentives" should therapists use in trying to get children to admit they have been abused? To what type of "education" process concerning sexuality should children abused or suspected of being abused be exposed? These and other issues must be more fully explored.

Both the Scott County experience and our survey responses indicate a need for independent psychologists to counsel both victims and families, Regardless of the outcome of criminal or family court actions, victims and families must be aided in dealing with the underlying abuse and problems that may develop as a result of separation and court action.

Recommendations

10. The role of therapists in child sex abuse cases should be more carefully studied. The Minnesota Psychological Association should examine the issue. Among the issues that should be examined are:

    a. When is it proper for therapists to act as investigators while engaged in an ongoing treatment of a child suspected of being sexually abused?

    b. Should therapists limit the number of times they question children about abuse during the course of treatment?

    c. What is the proper relationship between therapist and prosecutor?

Human Services: Foster Care

Our statewide review of child abuse projects that human services agencies experienced almost a twenty-five percent increase in child abuse cases in 1984. The director of Pipestone County Human Services sums up the problem:

Pipestone County has experienced a two hundred percent increase in child abuse, neglect in the period August through September 1984. For a small rural county agency, 25 new cases, involving 27 children, of which 12 of these cases were complaints of sexual abuse, from August 1, 1984 to October 16, 1984, is scary. We need action and especially need training and additional assistance.

The survey also indicates wide disparity in training and background of child protection personnel, as well as case loads. Using the survey results, we compared the projected number of abuse cases in 1984 (based on nine-month statistics) to the number of full-time equivalent staff positions. The result was an estimate of the number of investigations per full-time positions. The range was nine investigations per full-time position in one county to 116 in another. Follow-up review is needed to analyze this data.

There are many concerns which should be reviewed more thoroughly by the Department of Human Services. For example, what is the appropriate role of the state Department of Human Services when local agencies handle child abuse cases? Is there a need for closer monitoring by the state in this area? Is there a need for establishing uniform training or licensing standards for individuals involves in child protection?

Another important issue that needs to be addressed is the delicate balance between protecting the child and keeping the family together. In some Scott County cases, children were removed from the home at a time when there were allegations of abuse against only one parent. The question arises as to when and under what circumstances should children be removed from a home? As set forth in Minn. Stat. § 260.015 (1984), whenever possible, attempts must be made to preserve the family unit.

The use of foster care must also be examined, what type of training is required of foster care providers? What is their proper relationship with the prosecutor? In at least one Scott County case, questioning of a child by the foster parents resulted in that child's testimony being ruled inadmissible in court.

Visitation becomes an issue after a child is in foster care. Everyone involved in child protection has concerns about victims being intimidated by an accused parent, even during supervised visitation. Nevertheless, total isolation from members or even the extended family unit is a serious concern. It presents major barriers to eventual reunification of the family.

We need to understand that very few child sexual abuse cases result in termination of parental rights. Even if an offender serves time in jail, eventually he or she will return to the family. Again, the stated objective of family court is to preserve and strengthen family ties.

Recommendations

The Department of Human Services should examine its role with respect to local agencies. Licensing and continuing education programs for child protection workers should be considered.

11. The Department of Human Services should examine its role with respect to local agencies. Licensing and contin-

uing education programs for child protection workers should be considered.

12. Child protection service workers should be provided with updated training and practice standards for assessment and intervention.

13. Foster care providers should receive training in understanding physical and sexual abuse. However, foster care should be a neutral setting. Foster parents should not initiate questioning of children about sexual abuse.

14. Total isolation of children from their families (or clergy who have worked with the family) during the pendency of sex abuse cases should be avoided, by means such as supervised visitation.

Court Systems

The report on the FBI/BCA investigation did not focus on the role on the courts, a major component in handling child abuse cases. After the conclusion of the one case that went to trial there was concern about the trauma child witnesses possibly had to endure. A number of survey respondents felt a need to reexamine trial procedures and rules of evidence to provide more protection for child victim/witnesses. The question of how to achieve the protection in a manner consistent with the constitutional rights of the accused is a difficult issue to resolve. Much at this is dependent on the sensitivity and training of trial judges.

Proposals have been made which would allow judges to protect children by rules of cross-examination. We recognize that in seeking to protect child witnesses, any proposal that limits the rights to cross-examination may raise constitutional issues. Those concerns carry greater weight in a criminal action where loss of liberty is a potential penalty. In family court the trial judge may have greater discretion in protecting child witnesses.

In addition, in dependency and neglect cases a family court judge presently does not have jurisdiction over the parents. In certain instances the court's ability to achieve its goal of family unification can be more effectively achieved if it were to have authority over parents at the disposition stage of a case.

Delays in disposition of cases are also a major concern. Delays or continuances in these cases have both a negative impact on children and some families. For example, an important consideration is the effect that time has on the memories of young witnesses. In addition, families should not suffer the pain of separation for an unduly long period of time. By requiring speedy action one sets in motion the possibility of early treatment or other corrective actions needed to reunite the family.

Another area of concern is the need to provide greater anonymity for both victims and the accused. Minnesota statutes, sections 3641 to 3644 are outlined as various degrees of intra-familial sexual abuse. The mere filing of a criminal complaint under these provisions almost invariably results in the victim being identified as a family member. In our survey, one county attorney noted that the mere filing of charges is more devastating to the victim than to the accused.

Finally, it must be recognized that the Scott County experience has and will continue to have an impact on the prosecution of child sexual abuse. It has provided an opportunity to challenge the credibility of children by claims of manipulation. This is an unfortunate occurrence because the Scott County experience is simply not representative of how these cases are handled elsewhere in Minnesota.

Recommendations

15. Child sex abuse cases should have priority in scheduling. Judges should establish guidelines to ensure expeditious handling of child sex abuse cases.

16. Re-examine rules of evidence to provide greater protection for child witnesses. These might include:

    a. Utilizing informal (e.g., in chambers) settings when questioning children;

    b. In family court, upon motion of counsel, have questions submitted to, and asked by, the judge;

    c. Further study of an option which would provide that questions on direct and cross-examination be submitted to a guardian ad litem who would question the child on video tape. That videotape could, at the motion of either party, be moved as substantive evidence in a family court proceeding.

17. Family court judges should have jurisdiction over parents in neglect and dependency matters. This includes use of contempt sanctions.

18. Family court judges should have discretion to order counsel to submit questions on cross-examination to the court for questioning by the court when necessary for protection of the child.

19. Efforts should be made to provide greater confidentiality for victims and defendants. "lntra-familial sexual abuse" should be rephrased. This proposal is presently being pursued by the Minnesota County Attorney's Association.

20. Because of the valuable role of family court in protection of children, it should continue to play an integral role in resolving child sex abuse cases.

Community Concerns

Finally, a brief note regarding the City of Jordan. It is accurate to state that the City of Jordan should also be listed among the victims of the so-called sex-ring cases. Over sixty of its citizens were either charged with or suspected of abusing over one hundred children. State/federal investigators simply do not believe that accusations of such wide-spread abuse were accurate. The citizens of Jordan, most importantly the children, both those who were abused and those who were not, have suffered as a result of these public accusations. The impact those accusations have had on the community may well be extensive and far-reaching. At the same time, the precise nature of the impact will likely be difficult to discern.

Recommendations

21. State officials, the universities and colleges, the churches, leaders in Jordan and Scott County, the therapeutic community, law enforcement, the medical community, and private foundations should undertake a combined effort.

   a. To identify and analyze the impact on the Jordan community,

   b. To develop and implement ways to meet the needs of the community, and

   c. To ensure that there is greater public understanding of the short-term and long-term effects of "community trauma."

We have an obligation to the citizens of Jordan to help address, treat and learn from these unfortunate events. This is an opportunity to develop a positive conclusion to this story for the citizens of Jordan and for the citizens of Minnesota.

39

▼

Attorney General's Task Force on Child Abuse Within the Family

Following the Humphrey Report on the Scott County Minnesota child sexual abuse cases that was issued in February 1985, Attorney General Hubert H. Humphrey III appointed a task force on Child Abuse Within the Family. The report was published October 2, 1986.

Some have criticized Humphrey for appointing his political supporters, Marvin Borman and Geri Joseph to co-chair the Task Force. Other members of the Task Force came from many disciplines: Religion, business, judicial/legal, education, charity, human services, League of Women Voters and Urban League.

Attorney General's Task Force On Child Abuse Within the Family

Co-chair:
Marvin Borman, Esq.
Geri Joseph
Staff:
  Norman Coleman, Solicitor General
  Maureen Kucera, Attorney General's Office
  RaDene Hatfield, Humphrey Institute

A Report to
Hubert H. Humphrey III
Attorney General

October 2, 1986

Hubert H. Humphrey III
Attorney General
102 State Capitol
St. Paul, Minnesota 55155

Dear Attorney General Humphrey:

The Task Force on Child Abuse Within the Family, which you appointed on January 16, 1986, has completed its work and formulated its recommendations, which are contained in the attached report.

The task force held eleven public hearings, heard from over seventy-five witnesses and solicited written comments from over two hundred child abuse professionals. Testimony was given by representatives from all segments of the criminal justice and human service systems. In addition, it heard the anger and frustration from survivors of abuse, current victims and those who felt unjustly accused.

Our response to that testimony is the attached 85 recommendations. They range from expressions of support for present policy to suggestions for new programs aimed at increasing intervention. They reflect the following broad principles:

1. The need for greater focus on prevention of child abuse.
2. The importance of increased training for all involved in the processing and treatment of child abuse cases.
3. Establishing effective interdisciplinary child abuse teams to ensure the most appropriate handling of the cases.
4. The tremendous need for statewide leadership in the human services area.
5. The acceptance of the fact that the system is not perfect, but that we can solve today's problems, anticipate there will be new ones tomorrow, and that we need the courage to experiment with a variety of ways of resolving family abuse and lessening trauma.

When this task force accepted your charge to examine our system of child protection and develop ways to lessen the trauma to victims and families, it was with the understanding that a concerted effort would be made to translate our efforts into action. We agreed and understood that what was desired was more than mere study and reflection. We believe we have met our charge.

The task force is committed to seeing that these recommendations are implemented. We urge your support and assistance in this effort. The result will be an improved system of child protection in Minnesota, sensitive to the needs of both families and victims.

Very truly yours,

Attorney General's Task Force on Child Abuse Within the Family

Task Force Members
Marvin Borman, Esq. Senior Partner
Maslon, Edelman, Borman & Brand
Minneapolis (Co-chair)

Geri Joseph, Senior Fellow
Hubert H. Humphrey Institute of Public Affairs
Minneapolis (Co-chair)

Eugene L. Baker
Senior Vice President
Control Data Corporation Minneapolis

Beverly Barker, Director
McLeod County Human Services
Glencoe

Bishop Robert Carlson
Archdiocese of St. Paul and Minneapolis
St. Paul

Rabbi Barry Cytron
Adath Jeshurun Synagogue
Minneapolis

W. D. Conley, Vice President Public Affairs
Honeywell, Inc.
Minneapolis

Bishop Lowell Erdahl
American Lutheran Church
St. Paul

Margaret Matalmaki
Vice-Chair of Board of Trustees
Blandin Foundation
Grand Rapids

The Honorable Lynn Olson
Judge of District Court
Anoka

Roy Garza, Director Community/Governmental Relations
United Way
St. Paul

Nora Hakala, Supervisor
Indian Education Field Office Department of Education,
Duluth

Joan Higinbotham, President
League of Women Voters of Minnesota
St. Paul

Ron Jandura, Superintendent
District 742 Community Schools
St. Cloud

Thomas Johnson
Hennepin County Attorney
Minneapolis

C. Paul Jones
State Public Defender
Minneapolis

John Taylor
Senior Vice President
First Bank St. Paul
St. Paul

Judy Traub, President
National Council of Jewish Women,
Greater Minneapolis Section, Minneapolis

Mark Shields, Executive Director POST Board
St. Paul

Emily Ann Staples Director of Community Relations
Spring Hill Conference Center
Wayzata

Willie Mae Wilson, Chief Executive Officer
St. Paul Urban League
St. Paul

STAFF
Norman B. Coleman, Jr.
Solicitor General
Attorney General's Office
St. Paul

Maureen A. Kucera, Legal Assistant
Attorney General's Office
St. Paul

RaDene Hatfield
Research Assistant
Hubert H. Humphrey Institute of Public Affairs
Minneapolis

The very impressive list of the many witnesses who testified
before the task force:
1. Dr. Robert ten Bensel, Director of Maternal and Child Health,
   the University of Minnesota, Minneapolis
2. Fern Sepler-King, Executive Director, Minnesota Crime
   Victims and Witnesses Advisory Council, St. Paul
3. Dr. Ralph Underwager, consulting psychologist, Institute for
   Psychological Therapies, Minneapolis

4. Hollida Wakefield, a licensed psychologist, Institute for Psychological Therapies, Minneapolis
5. Dr. Sandra Hewitt, licensed consulting psychologist, St. Paul Children's Hospital, St. Paul
6. Dr. Sharon Satterfield, child and adolescent psychiatrist, University of Minnesota, Minneapolis
7. Susanne Smith, Hennepin County Guardian Ad Litem Program, Minneapolis
8. Elaine Dietrich, Family and Children's Services, Parents Anonymous, Minneapolis
9. Michael Clancy, intake supervisor, Washington County Social Services, Stillwater
10. Robert Carolan, Dakota County Attorney, Hastings
11. Robert King, Assistant Dakota County Attorney, Hastings
12. Mark Ponsolle, Assistant Dakota County Attorney, Hastings
13. Judge Lindsay Arthur, Hennepin County District Court, Minneapolis
14. Paul Gerber, Bureau of Criminal Apprehension, St. Paul
15. Peg Doe, VOCAL, Minneapolis
16. Michael O'Brien, PHASE Program, Stillwater
17. Stephen Peterson, Assistant Hennepin County Public Defender, Minneapolis
18. Dwaine Lindberg, Child Protection Supervisor, Minnesota Department of Human Services, St. Paul
19. Stephen Rathke, Crow Wing County Attorney, Brainerd
20. Robert Johnson, Anoka County Attorney, Anoka
21. William Seals, Director, Seals and Associates, Inc., Minneapolis
22. Mary Lou Bauer, VOCAL, Minneapolis
23. Jane McNaught, Ph.D., licensed consulting psychologist, Minneapolis
24. Lucy Berliner, M.S.W., Director, Sexual Assault Center, Harbor View Medical Center, Seattle, Washington
25. Robert "Bud" Cramer, Jr., District Attorney, Huntsville, Alabama
26. Gary Melton, Ph.D., Professor of Psychology and Law, University of Nebraska, Lincoln, Nebraska
27. Dr. Carolyn Levitt, St. Paul Children's Hospital, St. Paul

28. Lt. Beverly Ecklund, Duluth Police Department, Duluth
29. Don Bacigalupo, Canton County Human Services, Cloquet
30. Julie Spare, Canton County Human Services, Cloquet
31. Tom Papin, Itasca County Social Services, Grand Rapids
32. Rev. Dale Sewall, First Presbyterian Church, Brainerd
33. Nancy V. Cairns, Ph.D., licensed consulting psychologist, Northland Mental Health Center, Grand Rapids
34. Adrienne (Jay) Bendix, Minnesota Chippewa Tribe, Cass Lake
35. Jo Richmond, Coordinator, Sexual Assault Services, Women's Center of Mid-Minnesota, Brainerd
36. Kathy Bieler, Range Mental Health Center, Virginia
37. Loree Miltich, Director, Marriage and Family Development Center, Grand Rapids
38. Ricky Fred-Boham, Sexual Assault Program, Bemidji
39. Jodi Metcalf, Assistant Cass County Attorney, Walker
40. Nancy Steele, Transitional Sex Offenders Program, Lino Lakes Correctional Facility, Lino Lakes
41. Raymond Schmitz, Olmsted County Attorney, Rochester
42. Donna McNamara, Illusion Theatre, Minneapolis
43. Randy Bachman, Olmsted County Human Services, Rochester
44. Barbara Andrist, Olmsted County Health Department, Rochester
45. Debbie Anderson, The Rapeline Program, Rochester
46. Cathy Zupan, The Rapeline Program, Rochester
47. Deb Wellnitz, Brown County Family Services, New Ulm
48. Virginia Dixon, Director of Special Services, Rochester Area Pubic Schools, Rochester
49. Caren Markley, Rice County Social Services, Faribault
50. Judge Ancy Morse, District Court Judge, Olmsted County, Rochester
51. Bill Price, Survival Skills Institute, Minneapolis
52. Kambon Camara, Survival Skills Institute, Minneapolis
53. Ira Schwartz, Senior Fellow, Center for the Study of Youth Policy, The Hubert H. Humphrey Institute of Public Affairs, Minneapolis
54. Deborah Anderson, RESPONSES, INC., Minneapolis

55. Sister Giovanni, Guadalupe Area Project, St. Paul
56. David Robinson, Director, EAR, Control Data Corp., Bloomington
57. Bernard Bauer, VOCAL, Minneapolis
58. Karen Ray, Project Director, Project IMPACT, St. Paul
59. Karen Mueller, Southwestern Mental Health, Windom
60. Irma Cattoor, Public School Nurse, Marshall
61. Autumn Cole, M.A., Coordinator, FSATP, Community Services Center, Inc., Willmar
62. Gwenn Johnson, Southwest Minnesota Sexual Assault Program, Marshall
63. Dr. Barbara P. Yawn, Worthington Sexual Assault Program, Worthington
64. Charlotte Dokken, Chippewa County Family Services, Montevideo
65. Pam Otterman, Chippewa County Family Services, Montevideo
66. Ron Ottersted, Beltrami County sheriff's Office, Bemidji
67. Noel (Chuck) Koenigs, Swift county social Services, Benson
68. James L. Morrison, Northern Pines Mental Health Center, Brainerd

The task force also heard from 11 people who gave personal testimony concerning their own experiences with child abuse.

Some members of the Attorney General's staff and members of the Minnesota task force worked on the Humphrey Report on the Scott County investigations that was issued in February 1985. Also, many of the witnesses who appeared before this task force were also provided information for Nightmares and Secrets.

Dr. Sharon Satterfield, child and adolescent psychiatrist at the University of Minnesota was asked, "What happens to the children who have been falsely identified as being sexually abused?"

She replied, "The most horrendous thing that can happen to a family is to be falsely accused. There are many well-documented cases of reported abuse where abuse did not occur. It is a nightmare for both the accused and the children." She continued, "the acute symptoms of families who have been falsely accused are similar to those symptoms of families where abuse has occurred. It is a post-traumatic stress disorder that these families go through."

In October 1986, the final report on the Minnesota Task Force included the statement, "Not every allegation of abuse is true. The impact of false allegations on families can be devastating–the stigma within the community, the potential loss of employment, and the trauma to all within the family."

The complete 73-page report can be requested from Attorney General Library, 445 Minnesota Street, St. Paul, Minnesota 55101-2108.

"Pain forces even the innocent to lie."
– Publilius Syrus

40
▼

As I've Been Told...

"To create an unfavorable impression,
it is not necessary that certain things should be true,
but that they have been said."
– William Hazlet

With talking with the alleged victims of the Jordan scandal, different ones have repeatedly told me psychologist tried many times to get them to make false statements about their parents and others.

The *Minneapolis Star Tribune* reported on February 13, 1985: "State Attorney General Skip Humphrey asked the Minnesota Psychological Association to examine the issue of when it is proper for a therapist to act as investigators while engaged in an ongoing treatment of a child suspected of being sexually abused. He also suggested the association determine the proper relationship between therapist and prosecutors."

The *Minneapolis Star Tribune* November 15, 1987 reported on an 11-year-old boy who denied being abused for three months, and then changed his testimony for therapists after being questioned repeatedly. He said 19 different adults had abused him.

Even today, a psychiatrist told the (boy's) parents that he suffers the lingering effects of traumatic stress caused by the intense interrogation by police, psychologists, social workers and County Attorney Kathleen Morris.

Two child psychiatrists from the University of Minnesota treated children from a few of the Jordan's accused families. They wrote a report suggesting that repeated questioning of child witnesses could cause damaging anxiety for children.

The therapists, cops, social workers were not really interested in the health and welfare of this child. They were helping prosecutor Morris build a case against someone she had accused of child sexual abuse. Their motivation, their mission, and their job became to gather evidence and confessions that would help Morris. This process may have inflicted more confusion and frustration on the children than the therapists' true duty, which is to care for the health of the child.

Dr. Jonathan Jensen, Director of the University of Minnesota child psychiatry clinic and Dr. Barry Garfinkel said, "In the Scott County system, the procedure of removing the child from the home for a long period of time, changing a child's identity with a new name, the separation from siblings, the change of religion and the instructional prompt not to reveal any identifying information about themselves, produced a strong undermining of the children's personality structure."

Dr. Margaret Hagen, who has a PhD in developmental psychology from the University of Minnesota wrote a book, *Whores of the Court: The Fraud of Psychiatric Testimony and the Rape of American Justice.*

Some psychologists paid by Scott County to help Kathleen Morris build her cases against those she accused of child sexual abuse were and are whores of the court.

41
▼

Minnesota Attorney General Makes a Statement on Scott County Court Case

The following is the text of Tuesday's remarks by Minnesota Attorney General Hubert Humphrey III as it appeared in Wednesday, February 13, 1985, *Minneapolis Star Tribune*:

I am announcing today that the investigation by the Federal Bureau of Investigation and Minnesota Bureau of Criminal Apprehension into allegations of homicide, pornography, and sexual abuse in Scott County has been completed. That investigation concluded, first, there is no credible evidence to support allegations of murder or pornography, which arose during the sexual abuse investigation, and second, there is insufficient evidence to justify the filing of any new sex abuse charges. I will not file any new criminal charges in these cases.

I have concluded there is no probable cause to proceed with the filing of criminal charges. Based on the investigation by state and federal authorities over the past four months, we have determined that there is an absence of credible testimony and a lack of significant corroboration of the allegations.

The credibility problem resulted from the initial handling of these cases by Scott County authorities, including, repeated questioning, a lack of investigative reports, and cross-germination of allegations. In addition, the opportunity to obtain corroborating evidence was lost by the filing of the original criminal charges in Scott County before the completion of thorough investigations. The manner in which the Scott County cases were handled has resulted in it being impossible to determine, in some instances, whether sexual abuse actually occurred, and if it did, who may have done these acts. These factors lead to the inevitable conclusion that no new criminal charges are warranted.

We know that some of the children in Scott County were abused because James Rud and some juveniles have admitted sexually abusing a large number of children. Rud has been convicted and the juveniles have received immunity and undergone treatment.

In other instances children strongly maintain that they have been abused by other adults. Some therapists and others involved in these cases believe and support those allegations. But, in the circumstances of these cases, the belief that a child is telling the truth, by itself, cannot support a criminal conviction or establish proof beyond a reasonable doubt. The presumption of innocence and proof beyond a reasonable doubt are fundamental standards upon which our American system of justice is based.

My conclusions today are based on the thorough investigation by the state and federal team over the past four months. The state-federal investigation began last October at the time the Scott County attorney dismissed criminal charges against 21 citizens accused of child sexual abuse.

Our investigative effort was comprehensive. It involved over a dozen experienced state and federal agents. It included contacts with law enforcement authorities in several states; experts were consulted from the FBI Behavioral Sciences at Quantico, Virginia, who were familiar with similar investigations concerning, sexual abuse in other parts of the country.

The basics for my conclusions and a fuller discussion of the investigative efforts are set forth in the report I am releasing today. Prior to completing the report, I conferred with legislative leaders and representatives of the law-enforcement community, county attorneys, and public defenders.

Now–let me comment on the nature of the charges in these cases. Child abuse is horrible and shocking behavior, which has, until recent years, often been hidden or ignored. The Scott County Attorney has been in the forefront of raising public awareness about this issue.

Protecting children is a concern shared by all of us involved in the criminal justice system. Hundreds of child abuse cases are successfully pursued every year by Minnesota prosecutors. They have done so in a manner, which recognizes the delicate balance between the interests of children and the rights of the accused. One of the positive experiences for me in this matter has been working and communicating with numerous county attorneys in this state who, in the way they handle their cases, demonstrate their sensitivity to that delicate balance.

The child protection system in Minnesota works. But in Scott County something went wrong. This is not to suggest that the motives of Scott County authorities were improper. There is no reason to believe that their concern was for anything, other than protecting children.

The concern for protecting children can best be addressed when cases are investigated and handled in a manner, which results in the development of credible evidence. The best way to protect children is to develop evidence, which will lead to the discovery of what really happened and will lead to convictions, if justified by the evidence. This did not occur in Scott County.

The issue in these cases is not whether we believe the children. There is no question that children can be credible witnesses. But it is unfair to the children in these cases to rest upon their shoulders, the issues of guilt and innocence when the responsible authorities have not done a thorough job of developing other physical evidence or testimony. It is unfair to place such a burden on children when they have been through a process that has severely undermined their credibility as witnesses.

The report I am releasing today discusses these problems in detail. In regard to the homicides, the lack of credible evidence is clear. Three individuals recanted their earlier allegations of homicide. Four other children who had been identified as having talked of homicide stated they never witnessed any killings. The only child to continue to talk about homicides gave three entirely different versions of what allegedly happened, all within the span of one interview.

In regard to allegations of pornography and sexual abuse, these cases rested almost exclusively on the testimony of the children. Stories such as the homicides, plus a combination of other factors, have served to undermine the credibility of children in these cases. Those other factors, as I noted earlier, include repeated questioning, lack of reports, and cross-germination of information.

In addition, there is a lack of corroborating evidence, which, if it existed, might have served to support the testimony of children. This lack of support stems primarily from the haste in which criminal complaints were filed.

I understand the need to move quickly when the safety of children is at stake. But under Minnesota law there are ways to protect children without filing criminal complaints before a thorough investigation.

The fact that criminal charges are not being filed today does not mean that the children are being abandoned. When the criminal cases were first dismissed by the Scott County Attorney, the family court proceedings related to these cases continued on. To handle those family court cases, I called upon assistance of metropolitan area county attorneys, Tom Foley, Thomas Johnson, and Robert Carolan. Recognizing the need for responsible and immediate action, they volunteered the services of many of their most able and experienced family court   practitioners. With their assistance in family court, we addressed and resolved many of the problems of the children and the families. I am constrained by data privacy laws from speaking about specific actions and family court cases. Yet, the public should be aware that, where appropriate, the family court can and has required treatment, therapy, protective services, and on-going monitoring of the family situation, even if criminal charges are never filed. Even if accused adults had not abused their children, the problems caused by long separations must be dealt with by the family as a whole.

It is important to recognize that the Scott County cases are unique. They do not represent how cases are usually handled elsewhere in our state. County attorneys, local law enforcement and county protection services are doing their job throughout Minnesota.

The Scott County experience has been a tragedy from many perspectives.

The children have clearly suffered. They have been subject to a process, which undermined their credibility, and, as a result, individuals who may have committed sexual abuse will not be prosecuted.

We must also recognize the possibility that some citizens of Scott County may have been unjustly accused–not because of any improper motives of the part of authorities or accusers–but because of a process which encouraged accusations.

I am hopeful that the Scott County experience will not undermine the responsible actions taken daily by those involved with child protection services in Minnesota.

Hopefully these cases will help us reflect on what we are doing and how we can do better.

Towards this goal, I have included in my report a series of recommendations for action. They are the results of our   experience with Scott County and some suggestions for change developed from our statewide survey of child protection.

In some instances they reflect what is already standard procedure in several counties. In other instances they are a call for study, review, and action.

We should not fear self-examination–we should strive to make the system better.

Let the lesson of Scott County focus on improving a system, which is so important to all of us. At stake are both the protection of our children and the preservation of our families.

42

*"It is a sad moment, really, when parents first
become frightened of their children."*
– Ama Ata Aidoo

Abuse Abuse:
The Therapeutic State
Terrorizes Parents in
Jordan, Minnesota

The following article is written by the E. Michael Jones,
Ph.D., editor of Fidelity Magazine, described as "a magazine
on the family that is as Catholic as the Pope." Subscriptions
can be ordered from Fidelity Magazine, 206 Marquette
Avenue, South Bend, IN 46617

Dr. Jones gave me permission to print verbatim this article
on the Jordan sex abuse cases that appeared in Vol. 4, No. 3 of
Fidelity Magazine dated February 1985.

*"The therapeutic individual gradually becomes
morally stupid and is able to respond only to gross
evils which have become 'causes.'*
– James Hitchcock, Catholicism and Modernity

"You don't need a penis to hurt kids."
– Kathleen Morris, Scott County Prosecutor quoted in
Newsweek, May 14, 1984

When Robert Bentz got home from work at 6:00 p.m. on January 20, 1984, he found his house uncharacteristically dark. Usually his three sons – ages 13, 10, and 7 – were there to meet him. This time no one was there. When his wife worked the afternoon shift, his oldest son babysat until their father got home. This Friday evening in Jordan, Minnesota Bentz went to his neighbors' house to find out what was going on and if his children were there. The neighbors told him that ten minutes before he arrived seven policemen and four social workers had arrived in four squad cars and had taken his children into custody. Protective custody, he was to find out shortly. After returning home Bentz got a call from his wife. The police had called her at work; the Bentzes were wanted for child abuse; the

county had their children in custody; they were to turn themselves in at the police station. The Bentzes had no other alternative but to comply. Since it was a Friday, they had no opportunity to post bail. Spending the weekend in jail, however, was just the beginning of an ordeal that hasn't ended for them yet.

THE SEX RING CASE

What has come to be known in the media as the sex ring case in Jordan, Minnesota began in the fall of 1983 when two children went to their mother and said that James Rud, a 27-year-old trash collector who also did babysitting, molested them sexually. The parents of the children then filed charges against Rud, who had already been convicted of child molesting twice before. Once Rud was in custody, the police, the prosecutor, and the social service professionals began interrogating the two children and then expanded their investigation to include other children who had known Rud. Under the pressure of the investigators, the circle of those involved in sexual abuse gradually grew until it included the parents of the children themselves. Testimony against parents increased dramatically once the children were removed from their homes and put under the custody of the state.

Before long a routine case was on its way to becoming a national media event and as the publicity grew the investigation got more and more out of control. Greg Myers, a patrolman on the Jordan, Minnesota police force who was also accused of sexual abuse, gives some indication of how things developed. Myers had not been involved at the beginning of the case because he was about to go on vacation when it began. As the case grew though, it became impossible to ignore, and the more Myers saw, the less he liked.

"DID YOUR MOMMY AND DADDY HURT YOU?

"The only time (the police) got allegations," he said, "was after they took the kids out of the home.... It initially started out where the parents brought the kids in when Rud was arrested. The parents brought the kids in because they had told them that they had been abused by Rud. After that (the investigators) just started using the kids. The kids gave them other names of parents or friends of theirs or kids in another family, and then they'd proceed to continually question the kids until they said, well yeah, they might have been abused. So they come and pull the kids out of the home and question them and say to a five-year-old, `Did your mommy and daddy hurt you?' Well, hurt to them was a spanking or something on that order, and that's how they proceeded after that."

In addition to Rud, 23 people were indicted over a six-month period on the average of one a week, one Jordan resident said later. All were charged with criminal sex abuse by the state. There was no other corroborating evidence in these cases. Medical examinations showed no tears or scars. The hymens of the girls were all intact.

Fidelity (February, 1985).

The Bentzes were arrested only

three hours after their names came up in the interrogation of children who had been taken from their parents some time before. In three hours, Bentz mentioned later, the police have barely enough time to do the paperwork necessary for the arrest, much less the investigative work required by state law.

Myers said he was under court order not to discuss his children. He hasn't seen them since February of 1984 in spite of the fact that all criminal charges have been dropped. Bentz, who was arrested on January 20, also has not seen his children as of this writing (December 1984) even though he was acquitted of criminal charges in September. He has spoken with his 13-year-old over the phone about a number of things but also about the interrogation tactics of the county prosecutor.

"YOU BETTER SAY YOUR PARENTS DID SOMETHING"

"Kathleen Morris," Bentz said, "told him you better say your parents did something. She said, `If they go to trial, they're going to lose for sure. First she's telling my kid we're going to lose my trial. She said that the judge thinks they're guilty. She said, `If they

go to trial, they'll get five to 30 years in prison. Now if you say something, that they did this stuff to you they'll only get treatment like 28 months in treatment, and then you'll be able to go home.' They put the fear of God into these kids, and they think they're helping their parents by saying, 'Yeah, they did something,' and they'll get help and we'll be home... They used some rotten tactics, boy."

MEDIA BARRAGE

Between the time of the Bentzes' arrest on January 20, 1984 and their acquittal on September 19 of the same year, after star witness Rud was unable to identify Bentz in court, the nation was subject to what can only be described as a media barrage on the subject of child abuse. Articles appeared in Time, Newsweek, Ladies Home Journal, People, Rolling Stone, Working Woman and a whole raft of other periodicals, describing what Newsweek was to call a "hidden epidemic." Instead of focusing on the issue at hand, which, as in the case of the day care center in Manhattan Beach, California, had to do with non-relatives and sexual abuse, the major media pose to see the few documented instances as evidence of something bigger and darker, truths having to do with the nature of the family itself. In May of 1984, in the middle the proceedings in Jordan, Newsweek was talking as it had discovered the tip of the proverbial iceberg. "All at once," we read, "the sexual abuse of children seems as ambiguous as it was unmentionable."

"It is fair to speculate," intones David Finkelhor of the Family Violence Research Program, "that between 2 and 5 million American women have had incestuous relationships." Fair or not, Newsweek was only too willing to treat the self-serving conjectures of the therapeutic lobby as if it were clearly documented fact. "If molestation has suddenly become another hot-selling topic for the news media, perhaps that's all to the good–the first sign that attention is finally being paid to a guilty secret that generations have dreaded to face.

"HIDDEN EPIDEMIC"

Right in the middle of all of the concerned professionals talking about the "hidden epidemic" of child abuse, the reader comes across the prosecutor from Scott County, who felt that women could be abusers too.

"You don't need a penis to hurt kids," says Kathleen Morris, a county prosecutor in Minnesota. One of her current cases involves the small town of Jordan, where 16 adults have been accused of belonging to a sex ring that abused more than two dozen children. Eight of the alleged offenders are women.... Members of the sex ring in Jordan, Minn., are accused of inserting curlers and candles into their little victims.

In marked contrast to her cooperation in the Newsweek story, Morris isn't talking at all now. Fidelity's calls to her office were not returned. Sources in Jordan said that she is unavailable to the press in general and had recently turned down an interview request from Nightline. Since Morris is the key figure in the Jordan case, understanding her role is crucial, but even more important at this point is setting her role in its proper context.

By the spring of 1984, when the Jordan case was at its height, a number of things had happened across the country and in Scott County that made this type of thing, if not inevitable, then at least comprehensible. Morris had already made a name for herself in Minnesota by successfully prosecuting James Cermak for child abuse a few years earlier. This early sex abuse conviction helped Morris get reelected in 1982. Newsweek mentions Morris' role in the Cermak case in their May 14, 1984 issue as well as the stiff 40-year sentence he got. At the same time that Morris was making a national reputation for herself as a crusader against child abuse, the nation at large was all but officially certifying child abuse as a national disaster. The Secretary of the Health and Human Services Department, Margaret Heckler, had declared April National Child Abuse Month, and as if to dramatize that announcement, Senator Paula Hawkins announced less than a month later at the Third National Conference on Sexual Victimization of Children that she too had been the victim of child abuse, a story which brought nation-wide attention to what was already a sensational and all but ubiquitous topic.

LAWS LIBERALIZED

As a result of public pressure orchestrated by legal and counseling professionals, laws governing the prosecution of child molesters had been increasingly liberalized over the years. It was becoming increasingly easy for prosecutors to get convictions against alleged sex offenders.

In the issue that it devoted to the subject in September 1983, Time magazine reported that, some liberals sound illiberally willing to cut corners when it comes to prosecuting private-violence offenders... States are changing their laws so that simply a victim's say-so may be evidence enough. The Washington State legislature, angry over the difficulty of prosecuting a child molester, passed a law last year allowing hearsay testimony in certain criminal trials to corroborate other evidence.

In Newsweek we find the Scott County Prosecutor saying much the same thing:

"We have to quit pretending that kids have to testify like adults," says Kathleen Morris, a prosecutor in Minnesota. "If all they can do is show, that should be enough."

"Legal procedures," Time opines, "appear to have made prosecution easier." According to an article appearing in the June 25, 1984 issue of The National Law Journal, "Dramatic reforms are being adopted nationwide to change courtroom procedures, sentencing laws and rules of evidence to facilitate prosecution of accused child molesters. But some question whether the trend is an over reaction at the expense of constitutional rights."

These reforms include:

• Abolishing statutorily set ages below which children are presumed to be incompetent as witnesses.

• Abandoning corroboration requirements. Only two jurisdictions Nebraska and the District of Columbia still retain blanket prohibitions against finding someone guilty of sexual abuse solely on the word of a child.

• Changing hearsay rules to allow into evidence both out-of-court statements from children and videotaped interviews.

The powerful emotions stirred up in child abuse cases have many observers concerned that defendants may not be adequately protected. "The more afield we get," said one prosecutor, "the more nervous I am that some poor innocent guy will go down the tubes." One defense lawyer described the current climate of opinion as bordering on hysteria. "It's gotten so that I'm afraid to get into an elevator with a little girl," he said. In addition to these developments,

one would have to add the feminist orchestrated attack on the family as an authoritarian institution that conditioned people to accept male domination and violence. "There is no place so violent as home," Time tells us solemnly. "Every parent has the capacity to abuse." The psycho-socio professionals had been alleging parental incompetence for years; the feminists had accused parents, particularly fathers, of things even worse, and the courts had proven willing to assist these groups in undermining parental authority, most notably in the parental notification, parental consent battles over abortion.

By late 1983 the whole therapeutic, antiparental, legal-activist Zeitgeist came together an one person: Kathleen Morris, a feminist prosecutor with political ambitions who had a knack for using the media to her advantage, a budding national reputation as a crusader against child abuse, an ability to intimidate those who opposed her, and an even greater ability to mobilize the professions that had a vested interest in showing the family incompetent or abusive.

ONLY ONE PROBLEM

There was only one problem. As

time went on it became clear that the prosecutor had no hard evidence in the case. She had built her indictments around testimony which would not stand up in court, the testimony of children. The only adult witness in the case was a twice-convicted child molester who agreed to testify as the result of a plea-bargaining arrangement.

When at became evident that the Bentzes fully intended to go to trial, Morris tried two tactics. She added extra counts to their indictments, something which postponed the trial date, and at the same time she offered them increasingly attractive plea bargaining arrangements. When Rud agreed to testify against the Bentzes and other parents, he had the charges against him reduced from 108 to 10 counts. Morris tried the same tactics with the Bentzes, the Browns, and the Myers.

"We all got real good deals in plea bargains," said Robert Bentz.

"What kind of deals?" I asked.

"Well, with my wife and I it started out we'd get ten years instead of 40. And then we'd say, 'No, we're going to trial because we didn't do it.' And then it got to be treatment, no jail time just treatment, and then it got to be we

could just get off completely with nothing (if) we went up to everyone else's trial and testified."

"Testified against them?"

"Against them, right. That's why she needed adults, and the only adult she did get two weeks before the trial was this Rud.... He took the stand at our trial in August. He couldn't identify me at the trial even."

GREAT PLEA BARGAINS

Officer Myers makes much the same point. Once it was clear that there was no hard evidence in the case, plea bargaining became the prosecutor's only hope. "Once they got in and started getting in so deep," Myers said, "they didn't know how to get out. They were just hoping that by offering great plea bargains ... that somebody out of the group would break down and say everybody did it."

"Were you offered plea bargaining?" I asked.

"Oh yeah."

"What were the terms?"

"I was offered a change of identity, relocation, no jail time, money to get reset up."

"In exchange for what?"

"Testimony."

"Testimony against the other people?"

"Right."

"And when was that offer made?"

"The first part of July."

The Bentzes went to trial on August 20. They were acquitted on September 19 after Rud was unable to identify Bentz. According to an Associated Press story, Rud pleaded guilty in August to 10 first-degree counts in a plea bargain with Scott County Attorney Kathleen Morris, which provided for him to testify against others in the case."

In November of 1984, Rud admitted in a telephone interview from the Scott County Jail with station WTCN that he was lying when he implicated the other 23 defendants.

"...THE CHILDREN LATER RECANTED."

"I'm relieved the truth has finally come out," he said. "It's finally off my conscience." "Just before the second trial was to begin," runs a November AP account, Morris dropped all charges against the remaining 21 defendants, saying she was doing so to protect the children in the case and to avoid jeopardizing a larger investigation. "Of the alleged murder charges which surfaced during the interrogation of the children, the FBI said "they were dropping the murder investigation because they had not found evidence to support the allegations, and the children later recanted."

And so the so-called sex ring case of Jordan, Minnesota collapsed in a cloud of denials, perjury, and recantations in November of 1984. However, even if the criminal charges have been dismissed, the trauma created by the investigation continues. After the Bentzes' acquittal, Morris said that she was sick of hearing people talk about the presumption of innocence and swore, according to the Bentzes, that they would not get their children back. As of this writing, they still haven't, although their 13-year-old is scheduled to return home by mid-December. The Bentzes have not seen or talked with their seven-year-old since he was taken away from them in January of 1984.

THERAPISTS FOR CHRISTMAS

The Browns' children are still in protective custody with no end in sight.

"What has happened since Rud said he made it all up?" I asked Mrs. Helen Brown.

"Nothing," she answered. "It

didn't change a damn thing. You get so frustrated with the kids admitting they have lied and Rud admitting he has lied, we should have our kids back. And chances are we won't even get visitation for Christmas. When my kids found out that they couldn't spend Christmas day with us here at home, they proceeded to cry.... The therapist said we could spend 2 hours in his office on Christmas Day, and I said, "How can I make a Christmas meal here?' But we did have two therapists, one is ours, who volunteered to supervise a home visit on Christmas Day, which is pretty damn nice, you know, but we don't know if that can be granted yet."

Even when the parents are able to visit their children it is only in the presence of a number of therapists, who often censor the family's conversation. "I asked my son," said Mrs. Brown, "if he had been abused, and both my son's therapist and my daughter's therapist jumped up and said, 'You can't be talking about that,' and my son slammed his fist down on the couch and said, 'We are a family. We are supposed to be able to talk about anything. I thought this was America.' And they just told us, "No, we can't talk about that."

When asked why his children hadn't been returned to him yet, Bentz replied that he didn't know. His lawyer said the same thing. Myers said that a court gag order prevented him from talking. Mrs. Brown also didn't know why her children hadn't been returned but offered a theory. "I think they're in the process of trying to deprogram the children," she said. "It's just frustrating to know that innocent people and innocent children can be victimized by the state."

THE MOTIVE

In trying to put all the pieces together in a case like this, one invariably looks around for motive, and in looking for one, we come across an as yet unacknowledged constituency in this country whose interests are served by attacks on the family. Encouraged by liberalized rules of evidence in recently modified child abuse laws, the prosecutor sees an easy way to get convictions and make a name for himself. Rules regulating the admission of evidence are lenient; opposition is easy to intimidate; no one wants to seem pro child abuse. As the case progressed those who spoke out in defense of other parents got arrested for speaking out. It's easy for the police to become implicated in the prosecutor's power play and then try to extricate themselves first by intimidating the children into denouncing their parents and then by arresting those who disagreed with them. The media, which according to one of the parents seemed to know about the arrests before those who got arrested did, were willing to cooperate in order to have first crack at what was becoming a national news story.

The motivation behind the actions of the therapists and social workers is more difficult to fathom. Bentz said that each of the children was interrogated between 25 and 40 times. The therapists who questioned them were being paid $95 to $105 an hour. "The kids," Bentz said, "were a goldmine for these therapists."

In a Nightline segment broadcast on October 25, 1984, Dr. Carolyn Levitt, a pediatrician employed by Scott County to examine some of the children involved in the case, denied the allegation that the psychologists and other professionals were financially motivated. More disturbing though than any amount of money they may have earned was Dr. Levitt's description of her method of interrogation. "One thing a physician can do which no one else can do," she told Nightline correspondent James Walker, "is we can actually use the child's body, and I do that because I'm a female physician and I feel comfortable doing that. I actually put my finger in a little girl's vagina and asked her is this what they did to you, and do you think it went in that far, and did it bleed?"

Levitt concludes: "I have no doubt that these children were abused," and after hearing about her methods, it's hard to disagree. The real question, though, is who is doing the abusing.

CHILDREN BETTER RAISED BY THE STATE

When asked about the motivation of therapists in a case like this, psychologist W.R. Coulson took a longer view: "I think that they generally believe that parents are incompetent and destructive and that children would be far better raised by the state than by parents because parents don't have training. I think that any kind of evidence they can get on parents, they're eager to jump on it, and it causes them to lose perspective…. It comes in my judgment from sitting in therapy and counseling and hearing hour after hour stories from patients about their upbringing. It's very hard to be a practicing psychologist and not develop an antiparental attitude because you hear all these horror stories, which by and large are in the realm of fantasy or certainly are embellished by the nature of the engagement between the therapist and the patient.

"Therapists also become competitive with parents. They see parents as having inordinate influence not only over a person's pathology but on their personalities, and they say in effect, 'I want to be your father,' and so they'll take whatever chance they have to symbolically kill the blood father in favor of their own paternity."

The social workers in the Jordan case seemed to exhibit a type of possessiveness when it came to the children. Helen Brown brought it up in describing her attempt to get custody of her sister's children after her sister was arrested.

"The Scott County Human Services," she said, "were given a court order to do a complete home study on myself, my husband, and our family. One of the social workers told me to my face in front of witnesses that he was not going to do it, and I asked him why, and he said because nobody's getting the kids out of our custody. So I told him you better do it because you have a court order. Well, the court order stated that the study had to be done by January 15, 1984. January 11 at 4:20 p.m., a Wednesday, I was arrested, my husband was arrested, and my children were taken."

THE STATISTICS

When asked about the self-interest of the psychological profession as a whole, Coulson said, "Therapists love child abuse because it makes more work for them. There hasn't been a lot done on the fact that the growth in statistics on child abuse comes from people in whose advantage it is to discover it."

Coulson also saw a similar attitude extending beyond the social worker/therapist professions. "Our society is in love with child abuse now – I hate to say it, but I believe it's true and another reason for it is that all those people who are divorced and child-abandoning really are able to steer the attention away from their own sin by pointing at this awful thing which others do. They're able to say, 'Well, at least I'm not a child abuser. I'm only a child abandoner. I'm a wife leaver, but I'm not a wife beater.' And so I think you'll find that the more disrupted the family is, the more popular are going to become these causes like wife beating…and child abuse because it's a way for people who commit seemingly lesser sins to say, 'I'm not so bad.'"

Coulson does feel though that there is an economic dimension to the child abuse "epidemic," and that the family will come under increasing attack as more and more professions get involved in therapy and begin competing among themselves

NON-THERAPEUTIC PEOPLE

"Things are going to get worse in this kind of pointing the finger at non-therapeutic people as being the cause of our children's ills because so many professions have come into the business of therapy and are competing with one another trying to establish their credentials. They will find even more horrible crimes which demand their services.... This means you have all of these dozens of different professionals racing to see who can uncover the worst forms of abuse on the part of families or parents."

When asked if child abuse were actually on the increase, Coulson spoke of his own experience as a therapist.

"Here's the thing I see in patients myself.... Whatever the media are popularizing, my patients tend to bring it to me as their own personal problem, and so one tends to hear reports of abuse in therapy more frequently than you used to because one reads about it in People magazine, and, 'by golly, that happened to me too. I better get help with this.' It's hard to know if there's any objective data on child abuse."

"As a parent I couldn't be more delighted to see genuine child abusers pursued and brought to justice," Coulson said. However, knowing the attitudes prevalent in his profession, he added that the child abuse epidemic "is a way of putting down parents, and psychologists are always putting down parents, so it doesn't surprise me that child abuse is a favorite interest of psychologists."

SELF-SERVING NATURE OF ABUSE CRUSADES

On county prosecutors, one

might add. It's time we started to recognize the self-serving nature of the various abuse crusades that get launched with ever-increasing regularity by that coalition of groups in our society–social workers, therapists, the media, the courts, the shelters, etc. which make their living by exploiting, and oftentimes creating, family pathology. It's time that we also realized that giving money to these professionals can have the exact opposite effect than the one intended. Too often the professionals create false dichotomies which pit the child against the institution, the family, which is there to support him. "Who are we trying to protect," wonders a police officer in an article on abuse in Ladies' Home Journal, "the child or the entity known as the family?"

It's time to stop the funding of parasites who make their living by creating problems for themselves to solve.

The health of society is directly dependent on the well-being of the family. Those professionals who would become surrogate parents in the name of concern for children do nothing more that guarantee future business for the therapeutic state. By attacking the family they create, willingly or not, a nation of patients ready to seek them out for treatment.

Author's Note: I believe Dr. Michael Jones accurately defines and describes Kathleen Morris and her sycophants as "self-serving abuse crusaders."

43

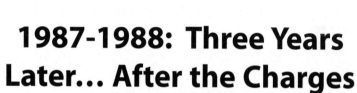

1987-1988: Three Years Later... After the Charges Were Dropped

"The truth is one thing, but in a way it's the other thing, the gossip, that counts. It shows where people's hearts lie."
– Paul Scott

Sunday, November 15, 1987, three years after Scott County Attorney Kathleen Morris dismissed charges against 21 adults charged with child sexual abuse in Scott County, the *Minneapolis Star Tribune* reported on what happened to those who were arrested and charged.

Robert and Lois Bentz were the only people to go to trial. Acquitted of all charges, the family moved from Scott County. The couple divorced and after the divorce, Lois Bentz and two of her three children returned to Jordan. The children indicated they wanted to be near their friends in Jordan. Lois Bentz claims stress from the investigation, accusations, arrest and the trial led to her divorce. The Bentzes owe relatives at least $20,000 borrowed to pay lawyers to defend them.

Christine Brown lost parental rights to her five children, four of whom are in foster care. She was charged with 10 counts of criminal sexual abuse. All charges were dismissed. She divorced her husband, Jim Brown, but later remarried him. Jim and Christine live in Anoka County with their third youngest daughter, of whom Jim Brown obtained custody in 1985. Jim Brown is studying to become a United Pentecostal Church minister. He was charged with five counts of criminal sexual conduct. All charges were dismissed. Currently, he is a self-employed painter. Jim said he paid more that $10,000 in legal fees by refinancing his home.

Tom and Helen Brown's two children were removed from their home for about 13 months. The Browns were each charged with 14 counts of criminal sexual conduct. All charges were dismissed. Helen Brown, 37, lost her job as a cook at a truck stop after she was arrested. Tom Brown, 39, lost his mechanic's job. His boss said he didn't want his company to be associated with people arrested for child sexual abuse. Out of work, the couple couldn't make mortgage payments on their home and were forced to sell it. They have moved to Dakota County and have found new employment.

Donald and Cindy Buchan's three older children, who were taken away after their arrest, have been returned. Another child, their youngest daughter was born after the criminal charges were dismissed. The Buchans are contemplating filing bankruptcy because of legal fees that arose from their case. Donald Buchan was charged with 55 counts of criminal sexual conduct. Cindy Buchan was charged with 22 count All charges were dismissed. The Buchans moved from Scott County to LeSueur County.

Scott and Marlene Germundson moved away from Jordan. After her arrest, Marlene Germundson lost two jobs.

Scott Germundson was charged with eight counts of criminal sexual conduct. Marlene Germundson was charged with 17 counts. All charges were dismissed.

Judith Kath was charged with five counts of promoting a minor to engage in obscene works and 18 counts of criminal sexual conduct. All charges were dismissed. Kath, 43, lost her factory job while she was jailed. She lost parental rights to her 14-year-old daughter.

Charles and Carol Lallak moved their family to southern Minnesota. At the time of their arrest, their children were living with relatives and were not taken by Scott County and placed in foster homes. The Lallaks were each charged with six counts of criminal sexual conduct. All charges were dismissed. Charles Lallak had $40,000 in legal fees. He is now employed as a welder.

Irene Meisinger, 36, and her children moved to Arlington, Minnesota. She was charged with 11 counts of criminal sexual conduct. All charges were dismissed. Two of her three children were removed from her home for more than a year. Meisinger and her children have been seeing a psychiatrist. The bank repossessed Meisinger's home. Her parents paid legal fees in excess of $25,000.

Terry Morgenson was charged with two counts of criminal sexual conduct. The charges were dismissed. He said he had been financially ruined and took a disability retirement from the Scott County assessor's office. Morgenson's wife Paulette was not charged and their children were not removed from their home.

Greg and Jane Myers moved to LeSueur County. Greg Myers was charged with 16 counts of criminal sexual conduct His wife, Jane Myers was charged with eight counts. All charges were dismissed. Greg Myers gave up his job as a

Jordan police officer, a position he held for 10 years. He has been working construction. He says he suffers from stress-related physical pains.

Duane and Delia Rank were each charged with six counts of criminal sexual conduct. All charges were dismissed. Now both in their 60s, they have moved from Jordan to another Scott County community. They paid more than $50,000 in legal fees. After exhausting their savings, their five grown children helped pay bail and legal fees. The Ranks' 12 grandchildren have suffered because of the publicity surrounding their grandparents' arrest.

Coralene Rawson divorced Robert Lee Rawson, 56, after Scott County authorities removed their daughter. He was charged with 18 counts of sexually abusing children. All charges were dismissed. Rawson's daughter is still in foster care. He is allowed to visit twice a month with a social worker present. Coralene Rawson was charged with 10 counts of criminal sexual conduct. All charges were dismissed. Coralene Rawson, 53, still lives in Scott County and continues to fight to get custody of the child. Robert Lee Rawson has paid more that $10,000 in legal fees.

Alvin and Rosemary Ann Rud were last known to be living in Rosemount, Minnesota. They were each charged with eight counts of criminal sexual abuse. All charges were dismissed against James Rud's parents.

James Rud, 30, is serving a 40-year sentence at the state prison in St. Cloud, Minnesota. Rud was the only defendant to admit guilt in the cases. He was charged with 110 counts of sexually abusing children and pleaded guilty to 10 counts of criminal sexual conduct. The remaining 100 counts were dropped.

44
▼

Help for the
Falsely Accused

"Life can only be understood backwards,
but it must be lived forwards."
– Soren Kierkegaard

Who should one call if you are falsely accused of child sexual abuse? Help is available.

- A first step is to use the Internet. Specific references are listed for people who can help you defend yourself against false accusation and false arrest.

- Many sites are listed for specifically helping one defend against false allegations of child sexual abuse.

- Also, check with lawyers who have successfully defended clients charged with child sexual abuse. Twin City attorneys Earl Gray and Barry Voss successfully defended Robert and Lois Bentz, the only case to go to trial. A jury found the Bentzes not guilty and soon after charges were dismissed against 21 other adults accused of criminal child sexual abuse by County Attorney Kathleen Morris.

Lawyers who defended those falsely accused in the Scott County Child Sexual abuse cases such as Carol Grant, Marc Kurzman, Robert Niklaus, Tom Hunziker, Dale Albright, Robert Grubbe, Paul Rogosheske, and other lawyers with this expertise should be contacted as soon as you are charged with a crime.

The defense attorneys who represented the falsely accused in Scott County adamantly told me they believed their clients were innocent. They said they would not represent someone guilty of child sexual abuse. Before agreeing to represent those accused in the Scott County cases, lawyers thoroughly interrogated prospective clients.

- A Web site I recommend is www.beanswers.com hosted by Bob and Elaine Lehman of Taneytown, Maryland. Elaine Lehman says our justice system is supposed to follow two basic premises:

  1. An accused person is innocent until proven guilty.
  2. It is better to let 10 guilty people go, than to incarcerate one innocent one.

  Bob and Elaine Lehman assert the Mondale Act (referenced several times earlier) is responsible for much of the unfounded reported cases of child abuse. Elaine Lehman is available as an expert witness for the defense in cases of false allegations of child abuse.

- Another important resource to contact if you are accused of criminal child sexual abuse is www.a-team.org. Trial consultant Kenneth R. Pangborn, M.S. met with some of the accused in the Scott County sex abuse cases. He said people were falsely accused.

  The A-Team is comprised of professional people who believe innocent people are falsely accused, arrested and convicted. The A-Team will only take clients they believe are innocent. They have an excellent track record for getting innocent people exonerated. Pangborn is a true believer in protecting and defending the innocent from false accusations of child sexual abuse.

- Another resource is Allen Cowling of Cowling Investigations Inc. at www.allencowling.com. Cowling will provide links to experts in false allegation cases. He knows the experts and this False Allegation Defense Web site will educate you about what to do to defend yourself should you be falsely accused of child sexual abuse.

- The Institute for Psychological Therapies (IPT), 13200 Cannon City Boulevard, Northfield, MN 55057-4405. IPT's primary work is related to allegations of child sexual abuse, but also deals with cases of sexual harassment, claims of recovered memories of childhood abuse, accusations of rape, allegations of improper sexual contact by professionals, forced and coerced confessions, false confessions, personal injury claims, insanity and diminished capacity, murder, mitigating factors in sentencing, custody, and medical and psychological malpractice.

If you are falsely accused of child abuse, take immediate action: Don't trust the arresting officer, the prosecuting attorney, child protection workers, psychologist and therapist being paid by the state or county. Contact a defense lawyer; preferably one who has had some success defending falsely accused clients. Visit a Web site dealing with false accusations of child abuse.

45

▼

The Problem of Knowing Where to Go For Help

"What hurts the most is not the punishment,
but the injustice of it, the unreasonableness."
– Victor Frankl, Man's Search for Meaning

If you are a victim of sexual abuse or if you suspect someone of being an abuser, what can you do? Who do you call? Where can you go? Who can you tell? Who can you trust?

Finding someone trustworthy may be easier said than done. Who can you confide in?

- **Teachers**. But not all teachers are trustworthy. James M. Simon was teaching at Jordan in 1984. In January 2003, Simon acknowledged that he molested numerous minors during his more than 20-year career as a teacher. Judge Thomas Howe sentenced Simon to 86 months in prison for Criminal Sexual Conduct.

- **Police**. Not all police are trustworthy. Eight-year veteran Jordan policeman, Greg Myers was arrested for child sexual. Scott County Deputy Sheriff Donald Buchan was charged with criminal child sexual abuse.

County Attorney Kathleen Morris dismissed charges against Myers and Buchan, hence they never went to trial. Shakopee Valley News June 24, 2004 reported that former Jordan police officer, Tim Weirke, pleaded guilty to fifth-degree criminal sexual conduct.

The Jordan School District hired the Illusion Theater to put on a production to help children and parents identify and report child sexual abuse. The presentation recommended going to the police. The Jordan cases proved this might not always be good advice.

- **Medical doctors.** We observed conflicting medical testimony from medical doctors who examined victims in the Jordan sex cases. Some doctors saw no evidence of sexual abuse. Some said they saw physical evidence of sexual abuse. Some said that they couldn't find physical evidence, but that abuse probably happened anyway. Medical doctors are often hired guns for the prosecution or the defense. Their evaluations and conclusions are paid for and may not be entirely honest and objective. So, perhaps, a Ph.D. or M.D. is not always synonymous with trustworthy.

- **Clergy**: In Jordan both the accusers and the accused found the clergy untrustworthy. With all the pedophile priest stories, along with the expositions of sexual misconduct by ministers and television evangelists, one must have reservations about talking to the clergy about sexual issues. They may not be as virtuous and trustworthy as their stature would imply.

- **Therapist and psychologists**. The Jordan sex cases demonstrated that many of these experts are dishonest masters of manipulation. They are hired to testify for the prosecution or the defense. They are hired guns lacking any genuine personal integrity. Because of their learned skills, mental health professional are often powerful, deceptive, and deceitful. They are likely to be untrustworthy due to their biased support of the courts. Margaret A. Hagen, Ph.D. describes the profession in the title of her book, Whores of the Court.

• **Child Protection Services (CPS)**. The Jordan cases illustrated that some people paid to help investigate child abuse are themselves very abusive people. Some form strong alliances with the prosecution.

• **Lawyers**. Lawyers in the Jordan cases lied. County Attorney Kathleen Morris was found guilty of lying to a judge.

• **Reporters**. The Jordan cases demonstrated how reporters sensationalize an event. They are looking for a big, bad news story. They may be less than honest and trustworthy.

• **A friendly judge**. The Jordan cases point out that judges may have an agenda or personal preference and may not be impartial or trustworthy. Suspicions of a judge being in cahoots with the county attorney in the Jordan cases are credible.

• **An elected official**. County Commissioner, County Attorney, State Attorney General, Governor, State Representative or State Senator, or Federal Congressman. The Jordan cases proved this was a futile exercise. Elected officials often played politics and were evasive or hid out under the protection of gag orders.

• **A neighbor**. The Jordan cases proved that discussing possible child sexual abuse could be dangerous and unwise. Any such conversation could lead to assumed guilt by association. A confidential conversation with a friend or neighbor could result in getting your name on a list of possible suspects published by the county attorney.

"Stop It Now" Hotline

A place to begin is to call 1-888-773-8368, the Stop It Now Help Line. The Stop It Now literature states this is a place to ask confidential questions of a trained staff about child sexual abuse.

Stop It Now is a nonprofit organization. They recommend you call:

- When you are concerned about a child's or an adult's sexual behavior.

- When you are unsure if what you see is inappropriate sexual behavior or sexual abuse.

- When you have a gut feeling, but just don't know what to do.

- When you want to talk about it, but can't find the words.

The kind of help you will get from Stop It Now:
- If you know about a situation of sexual abuse, they will talk with you about reporting that abuse, ensuring that everyone is in a safe situation, and seeking help for everyone involved.

- If you suspect child sexual abuse, but are unsure or do not have any evidence, they will talk with you about your options, how to ask questions of everyone involved, and identify local resources that may be of help to you.

- If you are concerned, about sexualized behavior in an adult or child, they can provide information about healthy sexual development concerning behaviors and child sexual abuse.

Minnesota has its own affiliate chapter called Stop It Now Minnesota. Their web site: **www.stopitnow.org/mn** is loaded with helpful information about what to do about suspected child sexual abuse.

Immediately upon suspicion or evidence of child sexual abuse, contact Stop It Now Minnesota and CornerHouse on their web sites to gather information and assess your personal situation.

www.stopitnow.org

www.cornerhousemn.org

Not all teachers, lawyers, psychologist, judges, policemen, doctors, child protection workers, politicians, clergymen, reporters, and neighbors are untrustworthy. There are many honest, trustworthy professionals in our communities. We must learn how to differentiate professionals with their own motives and agendas. Because of the Jordan sex cases, that is not easy.

CornerHouse

CornerHouse is a local nonprofit organization that assesses suspected child sexual abuse, coordinates forensic interview services and provides training. Considering the needs of the children first, services aim to reduce trauma to children and their families and to ensure the rights of those accused of abuse.

An updated mission statement that appears on the web site reads: "The mission of CornerHouse is to assess suspected child sexual abuse, to coordinate forensic interview services and to provide training for other professionals."

Amy Russell, Executive Director of Corner House, informed me that CornerHouse was formed in 1989 as a response to a task force that resulted from the Jordan Child Sexual Abuse Scandal. She said the then Hennepin County Attorney, Tom Johnson said he didn't want something to happen in Hennepin County that happened in Scott County.

Ms. Russell showed me an interview room where children are questioned about possible sexual abuse. The room is about 10x12 foot with two small sofa-like couches to sit on. On one wall, there is a large sketchpad. She said children use this to draw their interpretation of what happened. There are two cameras overhead to videotape the entire interview. Also, there is a large wooden box containing anatomically correct dolls. The dolls are male and female and black and white to help the children identify.

I asked Ms. Russell if the tapes would eliminate the necessity of children testifying in court. She said children could still be made to testify, but usually after the video is played to the accused and their lawyer, they want to plead down to a lesser charge.

I asked if CornerHouse ever found anyone innocent. She said not very often, but did cite a recent example. A young girl had bloodstains on her underwear and the mother who was in the process of divorcing the girl's father suspected the soon-to-be-ex of child sexual abuse. CornerHouse professionals interviewed the young girl and determined the bloodstains resulted from normal menstrual bleeding and no sexual abuse happened.

Since CornerHouse was founded in 1989, more than 7,000 children have been interviewed about abuse. Since 1991, CornerHouse has provided training services to more than 8,000 professionals from across Minnesota, 26 other states, and from Canada, Russia, South Africa, and Uruguay, and elsewhere. CornerHouse, in collaboration with the American Prosecutors Research Institute's (ARPI) National Center for Prosecution of Child Abuse, has recently founded "Half a Nation by 2010." This is an initiative to establish in 25 states by the year 2010 a high-quality, five-day forensic interviewing course based upon the CornerHouse forensic interview protocol.

Ms. Russell is a member of the American Professional Society on the Abuse of Children (APSAC), the International Society for Prevention of Child Abuse and Neglect (ISPCAN), the National Association of Forensic Counselors (NAFC) and the Association for Traumatic Stress Specialist (ATSS).

Esme Murphy, on WCCO-TV, interviewed Amy Russell July 11, 2005. Murphy mentioned that there is a lot of controversy about false reporting and how can you tell when a child is really telling the truth. Ms. Russell responded, "Kids generally don't give false reports about sexual abuse. It's not something they want to come forward and say 'This is what's happening to me' because it's very embarrassing, so we need to make sure that if there's a child who's come forward to us at all and give us any indication, that we make those calls. We call the police and let the professionals follow up."

Director Russell said that the worst thing that might have happened in the Jordan sex case is that an abused child was returned to the abusers. If the system failed to rescue and protect the children, the system must be changed.

CornerHouse offers a course that could correct a major problem in the Jordan investigation and prosecution. According to the Humphrey Report, mandatory reporters did not report suspicions or incidents of child sexual abuse. CornerHouse offers a course: "Making the Call: CornerHouse Child Sexual Abuse Training for Mandated Reporters." In order to get federal monies for child protection services and foster care, states have to have mandatory reporting laws in effect. Minnesota has such laws, but apparently in the Jordan sex cases, these laws were not enforced. No mandatory reporter was charged with the legal offense of failure to report.

The training for mandatory reporters offered by

CornerHouse would make such reporters more knowledgeable and willing to report child sexual abuse.

Lawyers, judges, police, investigative reporters, politicians, and others concerned with protecting children have told me that the Jordan debacle would not have happened if CornerHouse had been around in 1984. Investigator Deputy Michael Busch, who extensively interrogated convicted sex offender James Rud, said an operation such as CornerHouse would have changed the outcome of the Jordan cases.

CornerHouse is a private non-profit organization. It is funded by private contributions. Perhaps the most famous contributor is Josh Hartnett, local actor who went on to Hollywood to star with Harrison Ford in the movie "Hollywood Homicide." On June 4, 2003, Hartnett hosted a special charity showing of the film at the Megastar Cinemas in Edina and according to Amy Russell, the evening netted $75,000 for CornerHouse. On September 2, 2004, Hartnett hosted the premiere of his new movie "Wicker Park" and all the ticket money went to the CornerHouse child abuse evaluation center.

CornerHouse has an extensive library containing books, academic journals, and research related to child abuse and child interviewing. It is open to all interested professionals and members of the community.

Although CornerHouse is more aligned with prosecutors than with defense lawyers, they are careful not to make any false accusations or interfere with police investigators. Protecting children from abuse, especially sexual abuse is the primary purpose of Corner House.

46

▼

School Days, School Days... Good Old Golden Rule Days

"I can't forget, but I will forgive."
–Nelson Mandela

Jordan School Board Chairman Ken Hicks was quoted "We've all come to feel like victims, feeling the guilt, the shame, the denial–feeling embarrassed to tell people where we even live."

Theresa Monsour's heroine in *Cold Blood* asks, "When do you suppose we stop keeping tabs on the kids we went to high school with? What's the big deal about high school?"

Her boyfriend Eric replies, "High school's important because the person you become then, is the person you stay the rest of your life."

These quotes were previously published in newspapers twenty years ago:

Teenagers from Valley Green Park received degrading innuendos and verbal abuse. Nancy Henriksen said, "Everyone was down on anyone who lived in Valley Green. Just because you lived there you were guilty."

Several other teenagers from Valley Green told about a lot of hurtful teasing in school. Fellow students told them they were "Rud-lovers," and "they lived in Rudville," or in "perverts paradise."

Scott Henze, 17, described an incident when he was milling around at a bowling alley parking lot in nearby Montgomery, Minnesota. "A guy says there's some people from Rudville!–So Bam! I smacked him in the face. Then the cops come and we all split."

Laura Henriksen, 16, described an incident at a football game in 1984 in LeCenter, Minnesota. "One of the LeCenter kids asked me what I charged per hour. A substitute teacher came over and told the kid to get away."

Tracy Dominik, 13, said, "Girls who lived there were labeled sluts."

Lorie Elliot, 15, commented: "Some of our friends dropped us like hot potatoes. They wouldn't even look as us anymore."

Some nasty jokes circulated in the high school and at community events. Pastor Voss said, "I think the jokes disguise their discomfort. I challenge people to tell me what's funny about children being abused."

Just as the arrests began, Judy Pilz joined the Jordan school system on October 1, 1983 as a social worker. She talked with teachers who noticed some anti-social, obnoxious behavior of some children.

It was awkward for people in school. Police officers and social workers just coming in and taking kids out of classes and escorting them to hour-long interviews in Pilz's office. The children were interviewed in school to avoid alerting parents who were suspects.

Pilz told the Minneapolis Star Tribune: "Whether to take them to emergency foster care was a real weighty decision for the child protection workers to make in two hours. It was an emergency, a crisis. But if the kids were to go home and talk to their parents, the parents would obviously tell them not to talk. They'd tell kids that foster parents are evil people who won't feed you, that they themselves would go to jail and never be able to see them again. The kids wouldn't talk to the people they needed to talk to."

Superintendent Ken Hanson said it was difficult for teachers from classes where kids had been removed. Children were asking questions, like: "Where's Jerry? What happened to him?" They wanted to understand the atmosphere that filled their environment.

You have to clarify with children: "No he's okay, there is a problem in his family right now and they're trying to work it out."

High school kids developed a strong fear of police. They knew what was really happening because the parents of the kids taken away might be on the TV news that night, escorted by uniformed officers.

At a cost of nearly $2000, Superintendent Hanson brought in the Illusion Theatre from Minneapolis to do shows about sex abuse in December 1983 and January 1984. The program was mandatory for all school children, including kids from the Catholic Elementary School, though no Catholic children had been identified as victims of child sexual abuse.

Superintendent Hanson and the local clergy were given much credit for initiating educational programs to help people identify and prevent child sexual abuse.

Hanson initiated a policy on how to handle child sex abuse cases in school. State law mandates that teachers suspecting abuse must report it immediately to proper authorities. This is known as the Mandatory Reporting Law and failure to report or falsely reporting are punishable offenses.

Hanson instructed teachers to report their suspicions to the school counselor or social worker who would screen cases. Hanson was asked about his policy: "Aren't you in conflict with the law?"

"Yes," he replied, "The problem we can't get around is that with 110 staff members, we have kooks out there teaching for us, too, who overreact to everything. You don't want some of your teachers, who don't make very good decisions, dialing up the courthouse three times a day."

Social worker Judy Pilz defended Hanson's policy. She said, "Teachers who might otherwise ignore mild suspicion would be more likely to pass the word along to a person they know than to contact a stranger." She added that teachers aren't well-trained evaluators.

When Kathleen Morris was told of Hanson's policy, she said, "That's not what the law says."

Superintendent Hanson said the Jordan schools incorporated material on sex abuse in their curriculum and are selling this curriculum to other school systems.

High school counselor, Jerry Langsweirdt spoke about the production of the Illusion Theatre: "The message of the Illusion Theatre was, if you can't tell anyone else–if you can't tell your parents, your teacher, your clergyman or anyone else–then go to the police. A couple weeks later, a police officer was arrested, so the timing wasn't great."

Superintendent Hanson mentioned in 1984 that unlike many other school districts, including nearby Shakopee, Minnesota, no employee of the Jordan school system had been arrested for sex abuse. The truth was he just hadn't been caught yet. Because twenty years later a Jordan schoolteacher confessed to sexually abusing several Jordan students as far back as 1983.

The pedophile teacher, a member of Superintendent Hanson's faculty, was convicted of child sexual abuse and is now serving a long prison sentence. Superintendent Hanson, social worker Judy Pilz, school counselor Jerry Langsweirdt and other teachers worked on a daily basis with this child abuser–and never recognized a problem.

As mandatory reporters, if they knew or suspected, they failed to report child abuse as required by law. *Should they be held accountable?* The presumption of innocence was afforded to the faculty, but the accused outside of the system were presumed guilty. School administrators, social workers, counselors and teachers supported County Attorney Kathleen Morris and she solicited their help to find child sexual abusers.

After twenty years of research, and hundreds of interviews, I have not found one teacher, social worker, counselor, or administrator who questioned the investigations or Kathleen Morris. They were complicit with Morris and the Child Protection Service in having children removed from their parents and placed into the foster care system.

Although I believe the Jordan faculty sincerely wanted to help stop child sexual abuse and put the abusers in jail, some of them behaved cowardly. Jordan educators aided and abetted Morris in carrying on with her "presumed guilty" tactics.

Some of those teachers today still praise Morris and contend she looked out for us and protected us. Some of those teachers were and are gutless wonders.

I talked to many students from the class of 1984 and others wrote me comments about their high school experience. Many feel they were robbed of what should have been the best time of their lives. Some just want to get on with the rest of their lives. But others harbor some strong feelings and resentments.

Jordan High School is not famous for winning many athletic championships. The class of 1984, however, does boast of winning the Minnesota State Football Championship.

Here is what is printed in the 1984 class yearbook:

Hubmen win State Football Championship
Crush Breckenridge 27-0 at Metrodome
We're Number One!
November 19, 1983

Jordan vs. Breckenridge for the Class B Title! All week long people in Jordan talked football, businesses hung signs, pep rallies were held, while players and coaches enjoyed the media spotlight.

The game was scheduled for 10 a.m. at the Hubert H. Humphrey Metrodome, the first of five games in Prep Bowl II.

A large crowd of Jordanians was on hand, leaving the community a ghost town. After all the pomp and preparation it was time to play football.

And Jordan gained a quick upper edge as Gary Fahrenkamp raced past a couple of Breckenridge defenders to catch a Prep Bowl record 73-yard TD pass.

The Hubmen tallied two touchdowns in the second quarter, a great catch by Affolter and a run by Allar.

McFarland closed out the scoring for Jordan in the final quarter as the Hubmen cruised to a 27-0 victory to take the state title.

Jordan dominated the contest gaining 321 yards to only 99 by the Cowboys.

After the game the Jordan players raised the championship trophy high and saluted the Jordan fans that drove over 800 miles this season to show support for the Hubmen.

It was a fitting climax to a dream season and the players and coaches will have this memory forever.

A young man from the Jordan High class of 1984 wrote me this:

"During our practice sessions at the Metrodome, the captains of the football team were interviewed by one of the Twin Cities news stations. The first question we were asked was not about the game at hand, but about the sexual abuse scandal that had just broke. Thank goodness the coaching staff and athletic director did not let that interview air.

"As a teenage kid, I didn't think much of the questions being asked. Looking back now as an adult, I appreciate the energy that was expended by the coaches and athletic director to not let the interview overshadow the game."

Several newspapers mentioned the inappropriateness of the team being questioned about the sex scandal rather than the championship game.

47

▼

Going Back to Those Affected: Jordan's Graduating Class of 1984

"The evil that men do lives after them.
The good is often interred with their bones."
– Shakespeare's Julius Caesar

I solicited comments from the Jordan High School class of 1984 about their high school experiences and their current reflections and opinions. I received many responses and was given permission to include some in this book. Most did not want their name listed for various reasons: Some comments from the JHS class of 1984:

• A woman wrote, "The story had a snowball effect on the media. It just kept rolling and getting bigger. The news stories were all about child abuse, not about Jordan and Jordan high school, it was about smearing our name."

- A young man in 2003, "Even today when people hear you're from Jordan, they ask about it…"

- A woman wrote, "I still have relatives around Jordan and return to visit–but we do not talk about what happened a long time ago. Maybe you shouldn't either."

- A successful Jordan resident, "I graduated in 1984. I'm proud to be from Jordan. I wouldn't want to live any other place on earth."

- A woman who insisted that she not be identified but wanted her comment included: "I'm ashamed to say I lived in Jordan and graduated from Jordan High School. A lot of people should be ashamed of what happened in Jordan."

- A Jordan man, "I'm a Jordan boy through and through. Several generations of us made Jordan our home. Jordan High School is a top-notch school. Our class of 1984 was full of a lot of good people. Many of us still live in or near Jordan and we won the football championship."

- A young woman, Jordan will always have a bad reputation. Many people have forgotten about the sex stuff, but not completely. It never got settled."

- A young woman, "Because of my 1984 experience at Jordan High, I became a worrier, and I still worry too much today."

- In interview with a young lady. she said, "I just wanted to get the hell out of Jordan. There were some neat kids n our class, but some think there was a lot abuse and others think Kathleen Morris was on a witch hunt. My senior year was not a lot of fun."

- A young man told me, "I joined the Army after high school. I doped and drank too much and wound up in treatment a few times. I'm just now not blaming Jordan and Jordan High School for my problems."

- A JHS 1984 graduate now living out of state, "Jordan High School is not one of my fond memories."

- A woman said, "Teachers should have been our confidants–but I didn't trust any of them. Ya, that's what my class of 1984 was about–not trusting anybody."

- A young man: "I was fearful my whole senior year. I always wondered who would get arrested next. Would it be my friend's parents. I know they didn't abuse anyone, but high school was 'camp fear.'"

- A young lady who left Jordan shortly after graduation in 1984 said she has no desire to return, not even for a class reunion. She said when people asked where she attended high school, she tells them in a Minneapolis suburb.

- Young man wrote, "My first year at college, I received several phone calls that refreshed the scandal; needless to say they weren't phone calls made to comfort me. They just made me shake my head at how people try to make themselves feel better by making others feel bad."

- A young man wrote, The faculty, especially the tenured faculty, ironically, were disrespectful to the same students they were supposed to be teaching respect. I believe there was an underlying complacency and disrespectfulness in the high school that was part of the community. A community that was quick to blame and slow to understand. The community climate along with very overzealous county attorney with a separate agenda allowed a nearly fictional case to get out of hand. High school sucked."

- A young lady, "My high school days should have been filled with pleasant memories and I do have some. But what I have been trying to forget and put out of my mind is the sex scandal. Being a girl from Jordan in 1984 wasn't easy. Our reputations were tarnished–simply because we went to Jordan High School."

48

Violated People
Are Violated Again!

*"Nothing on earth consumes
a man more completely than
a passion of resentment."*
– Friedrich Nietzsche

Attorneys for the falsely accused defendants sued Kathleen Morris and other officials for more than $500 million dollars. The lawsuits alleged that Morris conspired with sheriff's deputies, guardians, therapists and court-appointed attorneys to elicit false statements from children, on whose statements the charges were based.

District Judge Harry McLaughlin dismissed the lawsuits. The three-member U.S. Eighth Circuit Court of Appeals upheld McLaughlin's decision and ruled that Morris and other officials were acting within the scope of their jobs while investigating, arresting and charging defendants in the alleged abuse scandal.

IMPORTANT

The court said in its strongly worded opinion that it is essential for prosecutors to be able to proceed in their jobs without fear of lawsuits from the people they charge.

The U.S. Supreme Court in 1987 let stand the appeals court ruling that Kathleen Morris and others cannot be sued.

The falsely accused and arrested residents of Scott County, several who lost their jobs and homes and had to file for   bankruptcy, would received no compensation for their losses. The consequences of being falsely accused of child sexual abuse were devastating. Some never recovered. None ever forgave the officials responsible. **There was NO justice.**

After the judge's ruling, this letter to the editor expresses a reader's sentiment about the case. It was excerpted from the *Minneapolis Star Tribune* October 16, 1987 (three years after this whole mess started):

> "It was a sad day for society October 5 when the U.S. Supreme Court let stand an appeals court ruling that former Scott County Attorney Kathleen Morris cannot be sued for her (mis)conduct in the Jordan child sexual abuse scandal.
>
> A county attorney needs to be held accountable for his or her actions and should not be regarded as a 'sacred cow.' Taking the litigation process away from society gives American citizens no recourse when an innocent citizen is harmed by an unprofessional county attorney."
>
> –Joseph Brenny
> Staples, Minnesota

49

The Scars of Scott County

"A newspaper should be proud
of the enemies it makes."
– Joseph Pulitzer

This article published seven years after the charges were dropped so clearly shows the "scars" of the children and the adults, the financial and emotional upheavals... and the fact that the nightmare lingers in all their memories.

Written by Britt Robson for *Mpls.St.Paul* magazine:

Marlin Bentz was cleaning the house when the police came to take him away that winter day seven years ago. Walking past a window, he spotted a squad car parked at the bottom of the drive-way. Twelve-year-old Marlin was alone. His father was on his way home from his job at the Ford plant in St. Paul; his mother was working the second shift a at printing company in Chanhassen; his two brothers, Billy, 9, and Tony, 6, were playing at a neigh-bor's home.

The officers informed Marlin that they were there to take him and his brothers into protective custody. Arrest warrants had been issued for his parents, Robert and

Lois Bentz, each charged with 12 counts of criminal sexual conduct involving children.

This was not a total surprise. Nine days earlier, on Jan. 11, 1984, the Bentzes' good friends and next-door neighbors, Tom and Helen Brown, had been arrested on similar charges and separated from their two children. The Bentzes were the 10th and 11th people in and around Jordan–a town of about 2, 000 people 30 miles southwest of Minneapolis –to be charged with child sexual abuse within the past two months. Two years earlier Scott County attorney Kathleen Morris had made headlines and established her reputation by successfully prosecuting six members of the local Cermak family on sex-abuse charges. With Morris driving this new investigation, Scott County was enmeshed in its second major child-abuse scandal in three years.

The Bentz children were taken to the police station in Shakopee, the Scott County seat, where Marlin met Morris for the first time. The meeting established a pattern that would mark their relationship for months.

"Kathleen Morris told us why my parents were getting picked up, and I got pretty lippy with her,

saying my parents were innocent and asking where was her evidence," says Marlin, 19 now and living on his own in south Minneapolis. "And right away she let me know that if I didn't want to cooperate she was going to put me in a shelter. She said, 'Do you want to go to a shelter or to a foster home with your brother?' So I said, 'All right,' and kept quiet."

In a picture that accompanied the article…the caption read:

In the seven years since he was detained to be a Scott County sex-abuse witness, Marlin Bentz, 19 now, has struggled with drugs and antagonism toward women. Although questioned dozens of times, Marlin never accused his parents of abusing him or his brothers.

From that January day through the summer of 1984, Marlin endured isolation, coercion and deceit on the part of Morris and other officials in their concerted attempt to turn him into a witness against his parents. Yet he continued to insist that his parents were innocent. Meanwhile, Morris—who justified the arrests of dozens of people, the breakup of families and the enormous time and money spent investigating the cases on the basis of her often-repeated contention that "children do not lie"–refused to believe Marlin Bentz was telling the truth.

The events that collectively came to be known as "the Scott County case" make up one of the most bizarre, disturbing and emotional chapters in Minnesota history. Children as young as 18 months old were taken from their parents on the basis of fabricated stories coaxed from adolescents who themselves had been isolated for months and repeatedly questioned by zealous investigators. More than seven years later, the legacy of Scott County has been one of children crying for their parents in the middle of the night; of divorce and dysfunction among nearly all of the families involved; of perhaps permanent emotional damage to the accused and the accusers alike.

The Scott County case began with an ironclad indictment against an admitted pedophile, James Rud, who eventually was sentenced to 40 years in prison after pleading guilty to numerous counts of children sexual abuse. It ended two years later with a ruling by the governor-appointed Olson Commission that Kathleen Morris was twice guilty of malfeasance during her prosecu-

tion of Robert and Lois Bentz. The commission defined malfeasance as a willfully illegal, unlawful or wrongful act outside the scope of Morris' authority that interfered with the judicial process.

In all, Morris charged 24 adults in Scott County with sexually abusing children. Of those, only Rud was ever found guilty and only the Bentzes ever faced a trial, which ended in their acquittal on all counts. Shortly thereafter, Morris dropped all charges against the remaining 21 defendants, claiming that the child accusers who were the key witnesses could not be protected adequately and that continuation of the sex-abuse cases would interfere with "an active criminal investigation of great magnitude," which turned out to be unfounded allegations of murder made by many of the same children.

After Morris dropped the cases, Attorney General Skip Humphrey ordered an investigation by the FBI and the state Bureau of Criminal Apprehension. Their report, released in February 1985, concluded that the murder allegations were totally without substance. The report also said that the sex abuse cases should not be recharged because the key child witness had been subjected to repeated questioning and often had been informed about what other child witnesses were saying to Morris and her investigators, irreparable damaging their credibility.

When questioned by the Humphrey group, many of the children recanted their allegations. According to Humphrey's report, the credibility of the child witnesses was further eroded by a lack of corroborating evidence.

From almost every point of view, justice was not served in the Scott County case. "We have found that Kathleen Morris did not see that the guilty were prosecuted when she dismissed the 21 pending sex-abuse cases," the Olson Commission concluded. "Those defendants who were guilty went free, and those who were innocent were left without the opportunity to clear their names. The children who were victims became victims again."

The outrage over both the sexual abuse reported in the Scott County case and the way it was prosecuted eventually faded from public consciousness. Some took comfort from family-court ruling that denied parental custody to many of the first group of people arrested–those the investigators considered more likely to be guilty of abuse than the second wave of defendants. Others were reassured by the overwhelming defeat Morris suffered in her 1986 bid for reelection against a candidate fresh out of law school.

While it is appropriate to put the tragedy of Scott County behind us, it is also important to remember what was allowed to happen, so that it will not be repeated. While some legal changes now ensure greater sensitivity and effectiveness in the prosecution of child sexual abuse, government attorneys and investigators and therapists actually enjoy more immunity from the liability of their actions today than they did when the Scott County case was unfolding. In that respect, the scars borne by the families involved are even more painful.

[Photo caption] — Scott County Attorney Kathleen Morris (1984 photo) now practices law at a small Shakopee firm. She says she doesn't want to talk about what went wrong in her sex-abuse prosecutions: "The worst possible thing that could happen did happen: The children weren't protected. I have to live with that every day."

Two of those families are the Bentzes and Greg and Jane Myers and their three children. While the Bentzes suffered the indignity of a public trial, the Myerses are the lone family that continues to fight in the courts to clear their name. What follows is a partial account of what they endured and how they have struggled to cope with the memories of Scott County.

[Photo caption] — For Lois and Robert Bentz (top) and Jane and Greg Myers (above), the Scott County ordeal continues in huge legal bills, splintered families and social shame. (Photos are from 1985).

For Lois Bentz, the ordeal began about 5:30 p.m. on the day her sons were taken into custody, when the Shakopee police called to ask her and her husband to answer a warrant for their arrest. From that point, her emotions were consumed with the fear, embarrassment and helpless anger of her predicament, even as she focused on proving that she and her husband did not commit what is generally regarded as the most perverted crime in human society.

"When you go through something like this, you feel like a newborn–you feel absolutely that helpless," Lois says. She is sitting at her kitchen table, chain-smoking cigarettes, inhaling coffee and staring at the backs of her hands as she dredges up the past. "You have no control over and you feel like you have no future. I mean nothing; your whole world just stops. You go from day to day and sometimes hour to hour just eating, sleeping and breathing what is happening to you."

Making matters worse was the financial burden; shortly after they were arrested, the Bentzes had to pay a bail bondsman $5,000 to secure their freedom. Then there were the attorney's fees, the private investigator and miscellaneous expenses such as $750 for psychological tests to prove their stability. They took a second mortgage on their home, wiped out their savings, sold many of their possessions and still wound up owing thousands of dollars to their parents.

But it was the absence of the children that hurt the most. "There's a part of you that stays numb but that keeps saying [the authorities] are going to realize they made a mistake; they'll just call up and tell us to come and get our kids, no problem," Lois says. "And that didn't happen. It just kept getting worse."

From the police station, the Bentz boys were taken to a temporary foster home in Shakopee. Initially, they would go to the Scott County courthouse for weekly questioning, with Tony and Billy always interviewed together and Marlin interrogated alone. Three-and-a-half weeks later, on Valentine's Day, the younger boys were transferred to another foster home while Marlin stayed behind.

"They said it was because my brothers were scared of me, but the real reason was because they thought they could get Billy and Tony to talk if they weren't (living) with me," Marlin says. He has long, straight hair, a thin, wiry frame and an amiable sense of cocky insecurity.

From the onset, Marlin adamantly defended his parents' innocence, a position he says eventually exasperated Kathleen Morris. "She would throw her hands down on the table and say, 'When are you going to start talking?' in a high-pitched voice," he recalls. "She had her detectives around her and they were getting their two cents' worth in. It used to scare me. She was real forceful and demanding."

At the same time, the isolation was beginning to bother him. "After my brothers left, I didn't see anybody I really knew for about three months," he says. "I was really messed up, being away from my parents. At age 12, home is your whole world. I didn't want to be around all these strangers. My therapist was the one who was supposed to help me with this, and she wouldn't give me any help unless I started talking about my being abused."

Marlin began seeing Leslie Faricy, a therapist for Michael Shea and Associates family clinic, on Feb. 29, 1984. In early March, Marlin wrote a note to his father that he knew he couldn't send, first indicating that he had been told they would be apart for at least six months, then saying, "Dad, I want to come home so bad. Do everything you can and quick because I don't want to wait for six months." In a March 14 letter that Marlin dictated to Faricy and that was mailed to his parents, he asks, "Are you getting things done like talking to the judge? If you are found guilty and have to go to treatment, after that are we ever going to move?"

As the months dragged on, Marlin became more frustrated and lonely. On the morning of

May 8, he and his 11-year-old foster brother got hold of the family guns when no one else was home and shot out the windows of a "junker" car nearby. Later that day, in a letter to his parents, he wrote, "Happy Mother's day, Mom. I wish I could get you something. I'm sorry. I feel bad I never get you anything. Dad, it's your birthday this month. This is your first birthday we kids can't be there. I feel bad."

"The only reason I said anything is that they would say, 'If you want to get home, you've got to tell us that your mom and dad molested you, or else you'll never see your parents again.'"

– Billy Bentz.

On July 6, Faricy wrote her first comprehensive evaluation of Marlin in a letter to Assistant Scott County Attorney Miriam Wolf: "Test results indicate that Marlin is a rather frightened boy who often feels powerless and who perceives himself as encountering a dangerous world where there is a good deal of anger and violent behavior between people. He often feels that he must protect himself but that he doesn't know how to do that effectively…. He frequently experiences himself in a rather tenuous position with lit-

tle sense of security or safety… Marlin is a 13-year-old boy who is experiencing far more conflict and confusion than one would expect from a boy his age."

What is remarkable is that Faricy puts her conclusions solely in the context of a boy suspected of coming from an abusive family, without acknowledging that he had been separated from his parents for five weeks and his brothers for two weeks at the time he was tested, and had seen his parents for just one supervised visit over a 5-month period at the time she was writing to Wolf. She closes her report by saying, "Marlin very much needs to individuate from his father so that he is able to have his own feelings and not take on those of his dad."

Meanwhile, Marlin's parents had for months been trying to establish contact with their sons that went beyond the exchange of letters that were edited by therapists and investigators. Despite numerous annoyance calls and a death threat, they didn't change their phone number, hoping Marlin or Billy might call. As for a face-to-face meeting, "We couldn't get in, so we tried to get the grandparents in, an aunt–we even tried to get Father Tom

Carolan in just to reassure them
that we loved them," says Lois
Bentz. "And they wouldn't let
Father Tom in. I mean, they even
let POWs see priests."

One reason for the prosecution's
stonewalling became apparent
when a visit was granted between
Marlin and his parents on June 29,
with Robert Bentz's lawyer, Earl
Gray, also present.

"(The investigators) had been
telling me that my parents were
going to plea-bargain," Marlin
says. "But I talked to my dad's
attorney the day of the meeting,
and he said, 'No way. We're going
to trial.'" Faricy's notes mention
that Gray "was found cornering
Marlin in the waiting room" and
"had to be asked rather forcefully
to leave."

On July 27, 12 counts of interfa-
milial sexual abuse were added to
the charges against both Robert
and Lois Bentz: After more than
eight months away from his parents, 10-year-old Billy Bentz had
cracked.

Unlike his older brother,
Billy–now 16 and living with his
mother in Jordan–is not willing to
discuss in detail the time he spent
in foster homes. But the few
words he does are damning to the
way the process was conducted.

"The only reason I said anything
is that they would say, 'If you
want to get home, you've got to
tell us that your mom and dad
molested you, or else you'll never
see your parents again.' My foster
mom was the one; said, 'We're
going to have to have a little talk
after supper.' And we went in
another room, and she started
grabbing me and shaking me and
saying, 'Why don't you tell them
your mom and dad molested you,
and you can go home?'"

When Faricy showed Marlin a
newspaper detailing the new
charges against his parents, his
reaction led her to believe she had
made a breakthrough. "Marlin
was very angry with (his mother)
for lying to him," she wrote on
Aug. 10. Five days later, her notes
read, "Session was held…about
Marlin confronting his parents
with the sexual abuse. He was
uncomfortable in saying the
words but very clear that he wanted to have that session with his
parents to tell them that he did not
like what they had done to him."

But according to Marlin, he led
Faricy to draw those conclusions–without actually saying his
parents had done anything–to
ensure that his parental visit the
next day would not be canceled.

"The only way to make sure it was held was to say I would talk," he says.

Marlin got his meeting, but he dismayed his therapists by announcing that his parents were innocent. Consequently, he became the lead defense witness at the Bentz trial, although he was restricted simply to saying that he had never seen his parents abuse anyone. Billy also testified that he first incriminated his parents in response to questions from his foster parents. Foster parents legally are restricted from being interrogators for admissible evidence.

That left 6-year-old Tony Bentz and four other children witnesses, one of whom recanted part of his testimony under strong cross-examination from Robert Bentz's lawyer. Admitted child abuser James Rud also was a prosecution witness, but Rud couldn't even identify Robert Bentz in court when instructed to do so. In addition, both Robert and Lois took the stand on their own behalf and were not cross-examined by Morris. On Sept. 19, 1984, the jury voted to acquit on all charges.

During the Bentz trial, Morris successfully prevented defense lawyers from obtaining investiga-tors' notes that detailed lurid allegations by some of the child witnesses, including tales of murder and sexual mutilation. But following the Bentz trial, Morris faced a court order to release the notes to attorneys defending others indicted in the Scott County case.

Another court order would have enabled defense attorneys to questions the prosecution's child witnesses for up to four hours and have them evaluated by a psychologist of their choosing. Instead, Morris elected to drop all charges against the remaining 21 adult defendants. Although investigation of the murder allegations (which included everything from the shooting of a rock star to multiple slayings of children after a sexual orgy) had first been cursory and then dormant for many months, Morris referred to it as an "active criminal investigation…of great magnitude" and cited its prioritized importance as a reason for dismissing the sexual abuse charges. This was probably done to protect the credibility of the child witnesses and her own investigative team.

"I have no question in my mind that at the time she made her judgment to drop the cases, she knew that the criminal cases were gone," says Assistant Attorney General Norm Coleman, a coordinator of the Humphrey investigative team. "In fact, she originally only wanted to turn over the files for the family court cases; she said, 'These other (sex abuse) cases are dead.' And as a prosecutor, I can tell you that the murder cases just weren't there. There was no evidence."

One of the children who said he had seen murder and mutilation was Andy Myers, the 12-year-old stepson of Greg Myers, a Jordan police officer at the time, who had been arrested on Feb. 6, 1984 for child sexual abuse after being accused by a girl who would make similar charges against 19 others. Although Myers's wife, Jane, had not been implicated, Andy, his sister, Amy, 4, and brother, Brian, 18 months, were removed from their home that evening. The family attempted to keep mother and children together by proposing that Greg Myers live outside the home, but that was rejected by the county, as were proposed arrangements involving Andy's grandparents and even a foster home more than 80 miles from Jordan. Clearly Morris and investigators were as interested in having the children near at hand for questioning as they were in finding them a supportive living situation.

Andy was separated from his siblings that first night. The therapist to whom he was assigned, Thomas Price was not a licensed psychologist; his background included a master's degree in social work and years of experience in child protection. For nearly three months, Andy maintained that he never had been sexually abused. But the questioning continued.

Accordingly to a long article in the Star Tribune, Andy came to his allegations slowly, speaking in early April of "visions" and, more than two weeks later, on April 19, agreeing with Price's suggestion that those visions were memories of sexual abuse.

Greg Myers and the Myerses' attorney, Marc Kurzman, believe that Price pressured Andy into claiming he was abused, even after Price received a report from a licensed psychologist stating that Andy was on the verge of a nervous breakdown. They say that on the day Andy first said he was abused, Price had been in family court testifying against Jane Myers visitation. "After Price testified in family court, he brought

Andy to the courthouse that same day," Kurzman says. "He also went in and spoke to (another child who eventually became a key accuser in the case) even though he was not his therapist." Price categorically denies any coercion. He acknowledges reading a psychologist's report indicating Andy was under "severe stress," but he does not recollect whether it was before or after the April 19 court hearing. Price says the report was widely distributed to those involved in the Myers case, involving the judge who ruled against visitation for Jane Myers. "I was appointed by the court, and my actions were reviewed by the court many times, with questions with documents and blackboard drawings and charts and everything," Price says.

The bottom line was that Andy Myers's claim of sexual abuse reinforced the denial of visitation rights for Jane Myers.

Minnesota Bureau of Criminal Investigation documents show that Price continued to question Andy. According to the Star Tribune, Andy was questioned 45 times by Price and at least 29 times by detectives and other social workers before the end of the investigation. On May 3 Andy

named seven adults who had abused him, including his mother and father. Over the next two months, his allegations led to the arrest of his mother and six other adults not previously charged.

Yet according to both BCA agents and Kurzman, in early June Morris approached Greg Myers with an incredible offer: If Myers would plead guilty to a reduced misdemeanor charge and incriminate any of the other adults charged with abuse, his children would be returned to him immediately and Scott County would pay his moving expenses to another location and would assist him in establishing new identity.

Myers rejected the offer. "I tried to pound into him that he couldn't expect any more out of the system than this," Kurzman said. "But he said, 'I'm a police officer and I believe in the system.' And I said to myself, 'Oh boy, I've got an innocent client on my hands.' I tried to figure out something that would satisfy his sense of morality and the letter of the law–asking if he even saw someone casually rub their arm against a 12-year-old kid's buttocks. But he said no, he wouldn't lie."

As the summer progressed, Andy began to describe increasingly violent and macabre acts. "From July through September. he said he attended parties at which as many as 18 adults would torture, abuse and kill other children. He said he saw three children murdered at sex parties. He said he was forced to cut off a child's penis and to have sex with his family's dog and cat," wrote the Star Tribune, drawing on BCA documentation.

Despite such fantastic stories, Andy was scheduled to be a key prosecution witness in 11 child-abuse trials. When the Humphrey investigative team entered the case, they interviewed Andy on Nov. 2 and followed up on his murder allegations, finding them groundless. When confronted with their findings on Nov. 6, Andy recanted, saying he lied so he would not have to go home. Even though he clung to his allegation that he had been sexually abused by his father, the Humphrey Commission, believing Andy's creditability was damaged, declined to reintroduce charges.

Disappointed that there would be no public trial, Greg and Jane Myers turned their attention toward the family-court case that would determine the custody of their children. "It was our trial," Greg Myers says with quite pride. "It went for 5 weeks (beginning) in October. We had the attorney general right there in family court, where it takes less evidence to convict than it does in criminal court. We had the BCA there, and they testified that they believed 100 percent that we did not commit any sexual molestation of our children or anybody else's children.

"We also had psychologists testify on our behalf. They said Andy had post-traumatic stress syndrome, which is what people who have been in Vietnam get, or someone who has gone through a major crisis. They figured the turning point was when he was pulled away from his parents."

Dr. Harry Hoberman, an assistant professor of psychiatry and pediatrics at the University of Minnesota, was one of the two therapists who took over Andy's care from Price shortly before the Humphrey investigation. Hoberman agreed to speak generally about the two families he worked with from Scott County: "It has taken a terrible toll in the sense that basic principles of family life were compromised; notions of truth and honesty and integrity were shattered by the way the cases were handled from the children's perspective."

In February 1985–a year and seven days after they were removed from the Myers home– Amy and Brian were reunited with their parents. After recuperating in the child-psychiatry inpatient unit at University Hospital, Andy came home to his family that August.

Yet the joy of reunion for the families of Scott County soon evolved into a new set of problems. "You've wanted your kids for so long and all of a sudden they're home and you don't know what to do with them," says Lois Bentz, who greeted Marlin back on Jan. 4, 1985, with Billy and Tony arriving four days later. "God, they were different! When they left, they didn't dare swear at me. And they came back talking like truck drivers. And you're sitting there with this discipline routine you have used for years but you don't want to use it the second they get home and you don't know if you can use it anymore because these are different kids than the kids that left. They're hurt and hostile and rebellious and you know why; you've been hurt too."

The pure logistics of the separation also created problems, partic- ularly in education. "Tony, our youngest, flunked. He had a bit of dyslexia and was getting special help for it at the school here. But as I understand it, he ended up in about five different foster homes, and they flunked him in school. The other kids didn't do so well either," Lois says.

"But you know, my biggest con- cern is the trauma we don't see that might come later. You remember growing up and feeling like your parents could protect you from anything? Well, my kids had that illusion taken away."

A few days before Morris' 1986 reelection bid, the Bentzes sold their house, and Lois and the chil- dren moved to St. Francis, outside of Scott County. "I wasn't going to give her another four years at me and the kids," she says. Ten months later, at the urging of her children, Lois moved back to Jordan.

But it was a single woman. In January 1987, Lois was officially divorced from Robert Bentz. Although Marlin claims the mar- riage had not been strong even before the Scott County cases, Lois cites the stress of that time as the primary catalyst for the breakup.

"When you are under that kind

of pressure, you either grow together or grow apart," she says. "I mean, we spent our 15th anniversary in court. You can't take it out on the judicial system, so you take it out on each other. If you've seen those lists of the top 10 things that put stress in your life, we had most of these." Robert Bentz declined to comment for this story.

Lois and Marlin also found their relationship in tatters. "When I came back (home), I was pretty messed up," Marlin says. "My biggest fear was getting teased and seeing how people would look at us. And it was nice to come back and have the whole town greet you. But still felt disturbed about it. That stuff went worldwide; my parents talked to people from Spain and newspapers in other countries. I felt like the kid of the biggest molesters of the year. So I turned to drugs. Just pot and alcohol, but they can mess you up."

About two years ago, Lois kicked Marlin out of the house. "My mom and I don't get along too well," he says. It's O.K. now, but we don't talk much." A breakup with his girlfriend over his drug use has prompted a recent stab at sobriety, which had

lasted three months as of the first of the year. He currently lives in an apartment in Minneapolis and frequently spends time at his father's place in the city after working at construction during the day. His brother Billy stops by regularly.

Asked how he thinks his time in state custody has affected him, Marlin answers, "The big thing is women in authority. In general, I just don't like women. I can get along with them if they're nice, but women in authority is a problem. It's a prejudice I don't want or need."

Various backlashes against the Scott County case have occurred on a community and society-wide basis. "Immediately after those cases, you almost couldn't get a (child-abuse allegation) case charged; prosecutors were very leery to take them," says Michael Campion, who coordinated the BCA agents for the Humphrey investigative team and is currently an assistant superintendent for the agency.

"I think what happened (in Scott County) is that therapy got a bad name," Hoberman says. "Kids who are likely to need psychotherapy in the future have gotten a very negative sense of what it is, particularly in terms of its being so intrusive and non-trustworthy."

"The other Scott County tragedy," Kurzman says, "is that arguments are still made in child-abuse cases where the attorney will say that the allegations are fake and the evidence has been implanted in the kids just like in Scott County. And the jury remembers or has heard about Scott County and they buy the argument on the other side of the pendulum, from 'kids don't lie' to 'kids do lie.' We need to find the reasonable middle ground, where kids are [considered] human like the rest of us; they sometimes say things that are not true and sometimes say things because they think that's what they are suppose to be saying."

But the "reasonable middle ground" is nearly impossible to define when someone is alleging child abuse, for it remains an emotionally inflammatory and vastly underreported crime. The best example of its lightning-rod effect on people is, of course, Kathleen Morris. Seven years after Scott County, a few people still believe Morris was railroaded out of her own investigation or boxed into a corner by judges reflecting the social bias that children are second-class citizens with very limited rights, who are not to be trusted with such heavy-weight concerns as their own abuse.

Currently practicing law at a small firm in Shakopee, Morris gave only a tense, clipped response to a request for an interview: "I am not interested in rehashing it with the press in any way. The worst possible thing that could happen, happened: The children weren't protected. I have to live with that every day. And I am not interested in talking about it."

As the legal and moral center of the Scott County investigation, Morris also has to live with her own crucial role in the lack of protection for the children. "The real tragedy is that the children who were acknowledged victims of incest received very little help or were not provided with therapy," says Dr. Sharon Satterfield, a child psychiatrist at the University of Minnesota, who was director of the university's Program in Human Sexuality at the time of the Scott County case.

Morris also ducks the bigger questions that inevitably emerge in the aftermath of Scott County; Why did it happen that way and, more important, can it happen that way again?

Coleman, who coordinated the Humphrey investigation after Morris dropped the case, describes the metamorphosis he felt and saw in others. "When I got the files and read them over, I had to take long showers because of the ugly things that folks had done. And there were 10 veteran investigators from the FBI and 10 more from BCA who felt the same way. They were charged up to get these bad guys and put them away, because it was so horrible. But as we went along and saw how the cases were developed and how the statements were made and how on murder cases there weren't even reports made until five or six months later, then the investigators began to turn. And I think ultimately they felt that (Morris) was the bad guy. Because those kids were so screwed up, so hurt, so destroyed. And she was a big part of that.

"Somebody should have said, 'No! these kids are not going to be interviewed 50 times,'" he continues." "Someone should have said, 'Enough. No more.'"

Yet Coleman also said, "From the changes I've seen in the system, I don't believe the type of systematic response and disinte-

gration that you saw in Scott County can ever happen again."

In 1985, the Minnesota legislature responded to the Scott County case with a variety of bills. To minimize the chance for long separation of children from their parents, it established child-abuse cases as a priority in juvenile (or family) courts and required the court to set visitation rules when a child is outside the home. To avoid abuses in investigations, it set criteria for oral and taped interviews with child-abuse victims and prohibited mental-health treatment for alleged victims until probable cause for abuse had been established. It required all of Minnesota counties to establish specific jobs for child protection.

The silver lining of the Scott County case is probably the overall improved quality of Minnesota's child-abuse service network, provided it's not victimized by the state's current budget crunch.

Greg Myers turned down a plea bargain out of his sense of fairness and faith in justice only to watch his stepson unravel and accuse him of murder and sexual abuse. His wife's family goes back seven generations in Jordan, and most of the townspeople were very supportive of them through the investigation. But there were members of the Jordan police force who Greg suspects helped set him up for arrest, and when he returned to his old job he claims he was harassed in ways big and small. Finally, plagued by constant chest pains from stress, he quit the force and took a job as an environmental consultant in a Twin Cities suburb. He and his family live in another suburb, primarily because Andy did not want to return to Jordan.

His youngest son, Brian cried for his mother in the middle of the night during the first two winters after returning home, remembering his February separation. "He was a year and a half when he was taken and he was gone for a year. That's prime time in any kid's development," Greg says. "My daughter seems to be coping better, but I think there will be things that come up out of this as she grows into adolescence and realizes what sex really means, as opposed to what they told her."

As for Andy, now age 18, Greg says, "The process has been gradual. He remains a very emotional child who has a lot of bitter feelings with him still. We are the last ones to be in court, trying to make some of the individuals pay for what they did. We just got the (denial of the state court to hear the case) back, and my son sat down and wrote a seven-page letter on what happened that first evening. He told my wife he could probably quote every question asked of him in the course of that time. So it has been a very traumatic thing for him. I think he would love to tell the whole world what actually happened to him, and it would probably do him good at some time. But I don't know if he is ready yet."

The Myers' legal bills are "over half a million dollars, not to mention the money that I borrowed. I could easily be paying for the rest of my life," Greg says. To chip away at his debt and provide for his family, he works 12 to 14 hours per day. "It has taken my family life away from me," he says without a trace of irony.

Explaining why he did not want to talk as his brother and mother had, Billy Bentz says simply, "It doesn't do me or the family any good. I think we proved we were innocent to everybody, but there are those that don't think so. They can think what they want to think; we won't change their minds."

Feelings, judgments and ugly

memories persist, and pervade the lives of those who endured events in Jordan back in 1984. The company Greg Myers now works for does business with a lot of schools in the area. Because he doesn't want school personnel to be somehow caught by surprise that the guy working around their building is connected to the Scott County case, Myers frequently suffers the embarrassment of volunteering information about his past–innocent though it may be–to many people he barely knows. Meanwhile, somewhere in Minneapolis, Marlin Bentz is struggling to stay off drugs and tone down his resentment of women.

Regardless of their guilt or innocence, the people of the Scott County case are still serving time.

Reprinted with permission from *Mpls.St.Paul*.
Copyright by MSP Communications.

Now, the other side of the coin...

50

▼

Humphrey's Role

"A rich person does wrong, and even adds insults;
a poor person suffers wrong, and must add apologies."
— Sirach 13:3

Not everyone was satisfied with the Humphrey Report. Kathleen Morris said Humphrey lied to her and about her. Stanley Ezrol, who has been campaigning for Lyndon H. LaRouche in what seems like forever, has given permission to print part of a study titled: "Skip Humphrey and the Criminal Abuse of Power: Case Studies of Corruption, Cover-up, and Official Oppression in Minnesota," published January 1994.

Philip Valenti and a New Federalist investigative team did the study and produced the report. The New Federalist calls itself the "National Newspaper of the American System." One can subscribe to this newspaper by writing to The New Federalist, P.O. Box 889, Leesburg, VA 22075. The report calls upon the Minnesota State Legislature to launch an investigation of Attorney General Hubert Humphrey III as a preliminary to opening formal impeachment proceedings against him. Quote from the Preface: "As long as criminals are prosecutors, there can be no justice for anyone."

Skip Humphrey and the Criminal Abuse of Power: Case Studies of Corruption, Cover-up, and Official Oppression in Minnesota

By Philip Valenti and a New Federalist Investigative Team
Updated with new information, including Appendix on the
Humphrey Institute & OBE January 1994

(Used with permission)

Skip Humphrey, Protector of Sex Criminals: The Jordan Child Abuse Cover-up

Even the greatest financial frauds and swindles of the Humphrey/Pohlad-led new combination are over-shadowed by the cynical hypocrisy and personal moral corruption flaunted by Skip Humphrey and his minions, in the areas of child abuse and sex crimes generally.

On July 15, 1986, Cass County prosecutor and Humphrey protégé Michael Milligan resigned from office in disgrace, amid charges that he had raped a 22-year-old incest victim. Milligan reportedly had taken advantage of the young woman, after she had testified for him as a prosecution witness in a local murder trial.

Several outraged local and state law enforcement officers brought the case to the Office of the Attorney General, demanding prosecution, after Milligan's replace-ment washed his hands of it, citing a conflict of interest.

On behalf of Humphrey, Deputy Attorney General Thomas L. Fabel responded with a bald-faced political cover-up, issuing an official memorandum on August 13, 1986, declining to prosecute.

In the memorandum, Fabel pretended to be impressed by the victim's "sincerity and the obvious anguish which she has experienced, and claimed he was "accepting the complainant's version of these events and disregarding Milligan's statements and opinions which are inconsistent with that version."

He noted that "complainant describes the encounter as a struggle culminating in an involuntary act of intercourse imposed on her by Milligan," and recounted the circumstances in detail, including an act which most people would recognize as rape: "There he lay upon her in bed and partially penetrated her with his penis, while complainant resisted."

Fabel cynically claimed to feel "anger at Milligan," and "sympathy towards complainant," and denounced Milligan's behavior as "highly inappropriate, exploitive (sic), and if I may say so immoral," but still declined to prosecute, or even present the case before a grand jury, on the absurd and obscene premise that Milligan's attack did not result in "bodily harm"!

In Fabel's own words: "Following a most deliberate review of this case I must conclude that there is insufficient evidence to establish 'force' or 'coercion,' as those terms are defined by statute. The complainant states that she received no bodily harm on the night in November. She had no bruises, scratches, abrasions, or any other evidence of injury. She reports that even though she struggled with Milligan, she experienced no physical pain. The pain was more psychological: a sense of helplessness, a sense of again being victimized as she was earlier in life by her stepfather.

"Furthermore, complainant states that Milligan neither employed threats nor used any words suggesting that he would injure her or commit any other crime against her if she did not cooperate with him. To the contrary, he assured her repeatedly that he would not injure her and that the experience would not be painful...

"Having exhausted the possibilities provided by the statutory definitions of 'force' and 'coercion,' I must conclude that Milligan's conduct did not constitute a chargeable offense."

Scot-Free

Let off scot-free by his political godfather Skip Humphrey, Milligan went on to high-priced employment in a prominent DFL-connected law firm. Fabel later joined other DFL heavyweights in the Twin Cities firm of Lindquist and Vennum, where he continued a regular and generous political and financial supporter of Humphrey's ambitions.

Fabel, Milligan and Humphrey later teamed up in an all-out effort to destroy maverick Crow Wing County Attorney Jack Graham, after Graham spoke out in defense of Lyndon LaRouche, as we shall see below.

However, Humphrey's most abominable known cover-up of sex crimes by far, was his heavy-handed suppression of the massive Jordan, Minn, child sex-abuse case, combined with his relentless, years-long campaign to destroy the prosecutor who had initiated the investigation: then-Scott County Attorney Kathleen Morris.

Since that time, the existence of well-organized child kidnapping, prostitution, and ritual murder networks has been amply documented, particularly as a result of the so-called Franklin investigative committee of the Nebraska State Legislature. Former Nebraska State Senator John Decamp, a leading member of the Franklin Committee and attorney for two of the abuse victims, has related the facts of the case in his 1992 book, The Franklin Cover Up: Child Abuse, Satanism, and Murder in Nebraska

The Nebraska case

The Nebraska case broke in 1988 when federal agencies raided the Franklin Community Federal Credit Union in Omaha, and discovered a $40 million deficit. The Legislature's investigation of Franklin manager and Republican Party influential Lawrence E. King, Jr., led to evidence of organized child prostitution, drug-trafficking, and other atrocities, involving high-level law enforcement and political figures and members of the U.S. financial elite.

DeCamp's aggressive public exposure of the facts led to the conviction of Omaha World-Herald society columnist Peter Citron for sex crimes involving male minors, while other offenders received high-level protection, including from the Omaha-based regional FBI head Nick O'Hara (currently stationed in Minneapolis). At least 15 key figures in the case have died violent or mysterious deaths, including Franklin Committee investigator Gary Caradori and his young son, when Caradori's small plane crashed in July 1990.

DeCamp's two clients, former child-victims Alisha Owen and Paul Bonacci, have stuck to their testimony throughout, and have continued to provide extremely valuable information, including about Minnesota, as we shall see.

DeCamp himself is careful to distinguish between phony, concocted allegations of "child abuse," manipulated by zealous social workers to break up families, and organized child sex-abuse rings on the Franklin model.

"It has been my policy and belief, as it is now," Decamp wrote in The Franklin Cover-Up (p. xxiii), "that there is nothing worse than child abuse, with the possible exception of falsely accusing people of child abuse... I am the lawyer for the National Child Abuse Defense and Resource Center of Nebraska, which fights against false accusations of child abuse... By contrast with these cases of fantasy, I can say without reservation that in one Franklin related instance after another, there was sufficient evidence and corroboration available for anyone seeing it, to back up the victims' tales" (emphasis in original).

The Jordan Case

The case in Jordan, Minn. broke in October 1983, when 26-year-old trash collector James Rud and his 17-year-old brother were arrested on charges of sexual and physical abuse of several children, all of whom lived in the Valley Green Trailer Park in Jordan. Rud had been convicted on child sex-abuse charges at least twice before, in Newport News, Va. in 1978, and Dakota County,

Minn. in 1980.

By December, Rud had been charged on a total of 110 counts of criminal sexual conduct, as more children came forward with shocking testimony including vivid stories of posing for pornographic photographs and murders of children.

By the time Rud finally pleaded guilty to 10 counts of first degree criminal sexual conduct in August 1984, some 24 adults had been charged as alleged participants in two interconnected sex rings involving at least 40 child-victims. Those charged included a Scott County deputy sheriff and a Jordan police officer. Rud promised to testify against other defendants as part of his plea agreement.

Scott County prosecutor Kathleen Morris had been elected in 1978, and quickly established a reputation for rigorous exercise of her duties, and for political independence. She successfully prosecuted one of the first organized-child-sex-abuse cases in the country in 1981, and was mentioned in some circles as a possible future candidate for Attorney General.

Evidence of large-scale, ritualistic sexual abuse of children in Jordan was overwhelming.

Jordan elementary school teachers said they had noticed extreme behavior problems on the part of many of the children who later testified to sexual abuse, and medical reports showed that many of the children had also suffered massive physical damage. The Minneapolis Star-Tribune reported on Oct. 21, 1984 that "one of the victims in the current cases, for example, has had her genital and rectal organs so badly damaged that she can't control either her urination or defecation."

The Children's Testimony

Minneapolis psychologist Susan Phipps-Yonas who interviewed many of the child-witnesses, is reported in the Star-Tribune on Oct. 18, 1984 to have said, "I find the children's stories very persuasive. There is enough consistency in the details of the stories to make one believe the things they describe really did happen.... They're extraordinarily upset when they recount these things. They'd have to be world-class actors to be so convincing if it wasn't true."

Clinical psychologist Michael Shea, who had several of the children in therapy, also believed their testimony, telling people graphic detail about sexual acts, which are outside their experience. "And they certainly can't be coerced, or bribed or brainwashed into making statements about their parents."

Phipps-Yonas and other interviewers also believed the children's detailed accounts of being photographed for pornography, with large sums of money often paid to their parents, a sign of possible organized-crime involvement. At least three children separately told consistent stories of murders to different investigators.

One interviewer said a child-witness told of a boy being stabbed repeatedly, until he went into convulsions and died. "I personally believe that this kid actually saw someone die," the interviewer insisted. "If you haven't seen someone die you don't know what it looks like. It's not like 'Gunsmoke,' where they hold their chest and fall down" (Minneapolis Star-Tribune, Oct. 18, 1984).

Signs of an organized effort to destroy Morris' prosecution surfaced soon after the first case, that of Robert and Lois Bentz, went to trial. Morris' case was sabotaged at the outset by Rud, who deliberately made false and contradictory statements to the media, and pretended not to recognize Robert

Bentz from the witness stand. The District court later sentenced Rud to 40 years in prison, after ruling that Rud "knowingly violated the plea agreement by making false statements to authorities and destroying his usefulness as a witness in subsequent sexual abuse prosecutions."

With Rud self-discredited, Morris had to rely on the testimony of the children themselves. Twin Cities attorney Earl Gray, representing the Bentzes, drove the children to tears with a vicious cross-examination, characterized by one reporter as "browbeating," which horrified even other defense attorneys present for the spectacle. (Minneapolis Star-Tribune, Oct. 16, 1984).

Morris said later that she was admonished in advance by trial Judge Martin Mansur not to raise repeated objections against these tactics in court.

People magazine reported (Oct. 22, 1984), "During the grueling cross-examination, defense attorneys succeeded in shaking some of the young witnesses' stories by hammering away at dates, places, and word meanings. However, a 12-year-old girl steadfastly refused to waver in her testimony. When a defense attorney accused her of lying, she snapped: 'You're just helping Bob and Lois (Bentz) to get out of this stuff this child-abusing stuff, I'm not lying, you guys are. Its the truth, they hurt us.' Later she rushed tearfully into the arms of a social worker."

The Defense Tactics

Gray later showed up as a defense attorney for DFL/Humphrey insider and Midwest Federal Savings and Loan Vice President Robert Mampel, convicted on fraud charges in 1991 along with Humphrey loyalist Hal Greenwood. According to the Minneapolis Star-Tribune (Oct. 16, 1984), Gray arrogantly defended his obscene trial tactics "by saying that he knows of no law that says that child witnesses need be questioned any differently than adults." In closing arguments, Gray charged that Morris had "brainwashed" the children and "concocted" the charges for political gain.

Significantly, among the defense witnesses called by Gray was Minnesota psychologist Ralph Underwager, a member of the False Memory Syndrome Foundation advisory board and a staff member of the Institute for Psychological Therapies in

Northfield, Minn. (Minneapolis Star-Tribune, Sept. 8, 1984).

Underwager was later exposed as a defender of sex with children, also called pedophilia, in a 1993 interview published in Paidika, The Journal of Paedophilia, a Dutch magazine connected to the North American Man/Boy Love Association (NAMBLA). In the interview, Underwager declared, "What I think is that pedophiles can make the assertion that the pursuit of intimacy and love is what they choose. With boldness, they can say, 'I believe this is in fact part of God's wills" (Minneapolis Star-Tribune, Oct. 12, 1993).

The Bentzes were ultimately acquitted on half of the original charges; Judge Mansur had dismissed the rest before the case went to the jury. According to the Minneapolis Star-Tribune of Oct. 16,1984, "Jurors in the case said afterward that they believed children were abused, but were not convinced that the Bentzes had done it."

Morris' Decision

With the prospect of traumatized children being publicly ridiculed and browbeaten by defense attorneys over months and years of further trials, Morris reached a dramatic decision announced on Oct. 15, 1984, to drop all charges against the two remaining defendants, and to seek protection of the children through proceedings in family court, leaving open the option of possibly reinstating criminal charges later on. Morris' decision was also forced by a judge's ruling, requiring her to turn over to defense attorneys 126 pages of investigators' notes, which would have destroyed the ongoing probe of the child-murder allegations.

With newspapers the next day blaring front-page headlines, "Jordan sex charges dropped," and with at least one former defendant appearing on television to appeal to the Attorney General to intervene, Skip Humphrey seized the opportunity to go after Morris with a high-profile press conference, pronouncing that "the recent events in Scott County have cast a dark shadow on our criminal justice.'"

"I would like to make it clear that I am not investigating Kathleen Morris," Humphrey lied. In 1985 testimony, Humphrey admitted that "his office began researching how to remove Scott County Attorney Kathleen Morris from office the day after she dismissed 21 sexual abuse cases last year" (Minneapolis Star-Tribune, Aug. 17, 1985).

That same day, Gray and other attorneys made headlines by filing multimillion-dollar lawsuits against Scott County and Morris personally, for supposedly violating their clients' constitutional rights. Three years later, after Morris had been safely railroaded out of office, every single one of these suits was dismissed as groundless by federal judges.

Humphrey's grandstanding tactics were denounced at the time by Star-Tribune columnist Jim Klobuchar, who attacked Humphrey for publicity-seeking and for politicizing the legal process: "It's hard to see how you advance the cause of dispassionate slice very far by making the Scott County attorney publicly countable to Skip Humphrey in the midst of the shock waves" (Minneapolis Star-Tribune, Oct. 18, 1984).

Morris Defeated, NAMBLA Crows

Under incredible pressure personally, with public denunciations of her mounting hour-by-hour, Morris was persuaded to turn all the cases over to the Office of the Attorney General, believing this would remove her "personality"

as an issue and benefit the children. The announcement was made at an Oct. 16, 1984 joint press conference at the state capital, with the treacherous Humphrey praising Morris: "I applaud the actions of Ms. Morris and her staff today. I believe that the steps we have taken will do much to advance the cause of justice" (Minneapolis Star-Tribune, Oct. 19, 1984).

Morris believed that she had an agreement from Humphrey to pursue the cases. She explained, as the Oct. 19, 1984 Star-Tribune reported: "This is something I requested the Attorney General's office to do. I shouldn't be the focus. Children should be the focus because children are the ones that are getting hurt out there. Not me."

Ominously, Humphrey's takeover was celebrated in the pages of the January-February 1985 issue of the NAMBLA Bulletin: Voice of the North American Man/Boy Love Association, under the headline: "R. Kathleen Morris, Witch Finder General of Minnesota Calls It Quits!"

NAMBLA is a notorious organization of pedophiles, which traffics in children and lobbies to legalize sex with minors, under the obscene slogan, "sex before eight, or else it's too late." Both NAMBLA, and the national homosexual political lobby called the Human Rights Campaign Fund, have multiple connections to Minnesota and Humphrey's circles.

NAMBLA co-founder David Thorstad, a native of Thief River Fails, Minn., was a Socialist Workers Party candidate for Congress in 1968 and for mayor of Minneapolis in 1969. At the height of the Jordan controversy, Thorstad appeared in Minneapolis to defend "man-boy sex" at a June 21, 1984 public meeting at the Hennepin County Government Center (Minneapolis Star-Tribune, June 22, 1984). The meeting was sponsored by the Minnesota Gay Defense Fund, run by Phil Wilkie, a grandson of Wendell Wilkie who is listed in 1987 as a member of the NAMBLA steering committee (NAMBLA Bulletin, January-February 1987).

Some Background

The Human Rights Campaign Fund was founded in Washington, D.C. in 1980 by Minnesotan Stephen Endean, and included NAMBLA members. Endean's Fund was publicly embraced by Walter Mondale in 1984, and

endorsed his presidential campaign–so that the Jordan investigation, if pursued, might have had the potential to blow up Mondale's candidacy.

When Endears died of AIDS in 1993, a Sept. 26 memorial service in his honor was attended by declared homosexual politicians, including U.S. Rep. Barney Frank and Minnesota DFL legislators Rep. Karen Clark and Sen. Allan Spear, the latter being the first openly homosexual president of a State Senate in the country. Also prominently listed as attending Endean's memorial was Skip Humphrey (Minneapolis Star-Tribune, Sept. 20, 1993).

No sooner had Humphrey taken control of the Jordan cases, than the FBI announced it was entering the investigations along with state authorities. Alarm bells went off in knowledgeable quarters when the involvement of FBI psychologists became known, "including one from the FBI behavioral sciences unit at Quantico, Virginia. This individual was also familiar with similar investigations around the country," according to the Attorney General's Report on Scott County Investigations, Feb. 12, 1985.

Sources have identified the

unnamed FBI agent as Kenneth Lanning, who later became infamous for dismissing evidence of Satanic ritual abuse in America with the statement that "far more crime and child abuse has been committed in the name of God, Jesus, and Mohammed than has ever been committed in the name of Satan." Lanning insists that charges of organized sex abuse rings are a diversion from the "real crisis," namely abuse within the family, requiring totalitarian-style monitoring of the home and seizure of children by the state on the slimmest pretext.

Lanning's FBI agenda was later fully endorsed by Humphrey and his allies in the Anti-Defamation League.

On Feb. 12, 1985, Humphrey released his long-awaited "Report On Scott County Investigations" at a high-profile capital press conference. Based on the "findings" of FBI and state investigators, and backed by Deputy Attorney General Tom Fabel, Norm Coleman, and other officials, Humphrey's report concluded on pages 16-17 "that there was no credible evidence of murders in Scott County connected to the activities of any child sex-abuse ring. In addition, no reliable evi-

dence of the existence of pornographic materials was discovered. Finally...there is presently a lack of credible evidence which would provide a basis for pursuing any criminal charges in these cases" (emphasis added).

Whitewash

Humphrey stated emphatically, as reported in the Star-Tribune, Feb. 13, 1985: "I will not file any new criminal charges in these cases," nor would he bring the evidence before a grand jury."

On top of this total whitewash of major crimes, Humphrey called for the "healing process" to begin, announcing that all of the children would be returned home, despite the admission by Bureau of Criminal Apprehension Superintendent Jack Erskine that "only 16 to 19 children had been abused" (emphasis added) (Minneapolis Star-Tribune, Feb. 13, 1985).

Media commentators attacked Kathleen Morris for "over-zealous" prosecutions, with some implying that she got "carried away" because she was a woman. At the same time, Humphrey protégé and then-Crow Wing County Attorney Steve Rathke was quoted in the Feb. 13, 1985 Star-Tribune, calling for Morris to resign, saying, "It seems crummy to knock a person when they're down, but there's no other alternative. I hope she resigns."

Morris countered with a point-by-point refutation of Humphrey's Report, declaring, "I believe that children can be believed and that I do not intend to abandon them. Also, I resent Mr. Humphrey's politically motivated attack on the efforts of honest and hard-working Scott County employees and authorities, independent therapists, physicians, and foster parents in trying to prevent further harm to innocent children" (Minneapolis Star-Tribune, Feb. 14, 1985).

Morris also revealed that the cowardly, treacherous Humphrey had phoned her one-half hour before his press conference, asking if he could announce her resignation! She refused: "1 said (to Humphrey) that I was disappointed that I learned from the media about the press conference. And then I get a call from him at 12:30 so he could cover his rear," she told the Star-Tribune on Feb. 13, 1985.

With Morris refusing to break, DFL Governor Rudy Perpich announced that there would be no investigation of Morris unless citizens petitioned for it according to a Minnesota statute then governing removal of elected officials (Minneapolis Star-Tribune, Feb. 14, 1985).

'Malfeasance'?

Within a few weeks, Perpich received petitions supposedly collected by former Scott County defendants, charging Morris with malfeasance for initiating criminal prosecutions without probable cause. Perpich appointed a three-member commission to investigate the, charges, and Humphrey named Mankato attorney Kelton Gage as special counsel to the commission.

Humphrey had good reason to be confident of Gage's loyalties: His firm represents the Archer Daniels Midland food cartel, owned by Humphrey family intimate and ADL moneybags Dwayne Andrews.

On June 12, 1985, one day before the hearings against Morris were scheduled to begin in St. Paul, Gage announced that he had revised the original petition. Now, instead of accusing Morris of wrongdoing for overzealously pursuing groundless prosecutions, Gage attacked Morris for not prosecuting the cases aggressively enough! Gage's new petition now asserted, "The evidence in many of the criminal cases was sufficient to obtain convictions" (emphasis added) (Minneapolis Star-Tribune, June 13,1985).

Morris' attorney Stephen Doyle denounced the bizarre turn of events, declaring, "We've been on one of the most incredible fishing expeditions that I've ever experienced....The entire focus was how (Morris) screwed the case up. Now they want her thrown out of office for not prosecuting the charges. It's a 180-degree turnabout" (Minneapolis Star-Tribune, June 13, 1 985).

After eight weeks of highly publicized hearings and months of negative propaganda in the press. Perpich's commission found Morris guilty of acts of malfeasance, charging that she could have successfully prosecuted some of the child abuse cases!

When asked if these conclusions conflicted with Humphrey's decision not to seek any criminal charges, commission chairman Lynn Olson explained that several child-witnesses had recanted their testimony after Humphrey took over the cases (Minneapolis Star-Tribune, Oct. 11, 1985).

Somehow, the children's stories fell apart only after they were interviewed by the FBI and Humphrey investigators.

Perpich and his commission declined to remove Morris from office outright, but said the issue should be settled by the political process. Morris was defeated for re-election in 1986 by the 28-year-old Humphrey-backed James Terwedo, who had graduated from law school just two years before.

Humphrey's "Blue Ribbon"

Humphrey followed up the railroading of Morris by appointing a "blue ribbon" committee to formulate policy on sexual abuse of children. The committee was co-chaired by ADL honorary vice chairman and Humphrey Institute senior fellow Geri Joseph; and Marvin Borman, counsel to Joseph's husband Burton, who was a former ADL national chairman and Humphrey insider.

Humphrey's committee called the Attorney General's Task Force on Child Abuse Within the Family, buried evidence of organized child sex-abuse rings, and adopted the totalitarian anti-family agenda of the FBI's Kenneth Lanning.

Norm Coleman, an Assistant Attorney General who had coordinated the Jordan cover-up for Humphrey, was later rewarded with Humphrey's endorsement for mayor of St. Paul in 1993. With the backing of Humphrey's personal network of cronies, Coleman defeated the DFL-endorsed candidate in the November election, leading to demands within the DFL Party itself for the downfall of the treasonous Humphrey in 1994.

The enormity of Humphrey's crime in suppressing the Jordan cases, was unexpectedly confirmed in Nebraska in 1991. In his book The Franklin Cover-Up, John De ramp recounts several discussions between his client, child-abuse victim Paul Bonacci, and Missing Children's Foundation investigator Roy Stephens. Decamp writes:

"Paul Bonacci identified by name, from pictures, some of the same individuals Morris had been investigating. Some of Bonacci's conversations with Stephens about these events have been transcribed:

"RS: You know anybody else who hurts children or takes kids and sells them or takes pornography of them?"

"PB: I don't know what their names are and they're all mainly not even from...."

"RS: From this area? Where are

they from?"

"'PB: Minnesota and California."

"P.5: Do you know where or who?"

"PB: In Minnesota there was one guy named James Rud. He lived with his mom and dad, cause I remember we went out to his place one time in a trailer."

"RS: And that's in Minnesota?"

"PB: Yeah, that was in Jordan, Minnesota."

A second exchange between Bonacci and Stephens, recorded on September 28, 1991, shed more light on the events in Jordan.

"RS: What do you remember about this little boy named Joey?"

"PB: Joey? Oh, that's what I wanted to tell you about ... Jordan, Minnesota."

"RS: Jordan? That's where he came from?"

"PB: Well, he wasn't kidnapped, his parents let him go, 'cause his parents were friends with Emilio and they had some strange...."

"RS: It's okay."

"PB: That there's a bunch of parents, that are not just parents but other people in that town that were abusing kids.... Bob Bentz, that's the one I told you about that had the two [inaudible]."

"RS: And this guy's name was Bob?

"PB: Uh-huh. Bentz."

"RS: How do you spell it? Bentz."

"PB: B-e-n-t-z."

"RS: And he's in Jordan? When was this?"

"PB: Mmmmm, that was in '82."

Stephens had asked Bonacci to draw up a list of both abusers and victims. Later in the same conversation, Stephens went through the written list out loud.

"RS: Okay. What do you have written here? What does this say? Who is this Bob? Is that his wife's name? Lois? Bob and Lois Bentz? They had three sons? Okay. This is the Bob you told me about."

"PB: Uh-huh [yes]."

"RS: And Joey is theirs? Okay, and Jim Rud is the guy who lives with his mom and dad at the Valley Green Trailer Park?"

"PB: Yeah. 'Cause I remember one of the games we played was called hide and seek basketball."

"RS: Hide and seek basketball? How do you play that? You're not talking about regular basketball, are you?"

"PB: No, it's sex…A lot of people lived in Jordan that were doing that (child abuse). 'Cause when we were up there [inaudible] they tortured a couple (of children) that came in (The Franklin Cover-Up, pp. 236-237).

Morris Judges Humphrey

Kathleen Morris herself pronounced judgment on the treacherous Humphrey in a Sept. 6, 1987 interview with the Star-Tribune:

"I don't apologize for what I did in the Scott County cases. I don't regret any of my decisions. The only decision I regret is trusting Hubert Humphrey….

"In retrospect that's my only mistake… And I'll go to my grave regretting that… "He lied to me. And he lied to the people on my staff. And he lied to the public. And now we've got kids home. And you talk about being hurt. My God. You think you can believe the Attorney General. What a joke."

Referring to Humphrey's obsession with winning his father's former seat in the U.S. Senate, Morris said, "It never dawned on me that to be Senator is more important than to just make sure kids aren't hurt anymore. And it was."

The question of what high-level sex criminals, including among his circles of power and wealth, Humphrey was trying to protect in suppressing the Jordan investigations, remains to be answered.

51

▼

Recent Movies About Child Sexual Abuse

"If you know somebody is going to be awfully annoyed by something you write, that's obviously very satisfying. And if they howl with rage or cry, that's honey."
– A.N. Wilson

- Capturing the Friedmans
- Stevie
- Mystic River

In the *Minneapolis Star Tribune* October 16, 1994, Lois Bentz said she was interviewed by a writer for a screenplay based on her story. Her experience of false accusation, arrest, jail, bail, lawyers' fees, children placed in foster care, trial and acquittal of all charges–and the hassle of getting their children returned from foster care, would make a dramatic stage play or movie.

She said the writer couldn't get a producer to buy her story as every producer wanted a story with a happy ending. Lois

Bentz said, "There are no happy endings in this."

Recently some movies dealing with child abuse have been made. They do not have happy endings, but have received some critical acclaim and monetary success.

Capturing the Friedmans

Capturing the Friedmans is a recent documentary film reflective of some aspects of the Jordan child sexual abuse scandal of 1984. This film won the Grand Jury prize at the 2003 Sundance Film Festival. Similar to the Jordan cases, this non-fiction feature film explores one of the most publicized criminal cases in American history.

Frank Rich of the *New York Times* said, "One of the most compelling American films I've seen in ages."

Peter Travers of *Rolling Stone* said, "This movie will pin you to your seat."

Roger Ebert of *Ebert & Roper* said, "Two thumbs up! This is an amazing film."

Mary F. Pols of *Contra Costa Times* added, "If you are at a cocktail party and you're chatting with two people who've seen *Capturing the Friedmans* and you haven't, consider yourself conversationally dead in the water."

Much of the movie is from home movies taken by family members in the throes of allegations and sexual misconduct charges against father figure, Arnold Friedman and his youngest son, Jesse Friedman. Like Jordan, the community of Great Neck, Long Island was caught up in this sex scandal of epic proportions. Like Jordan, the case was national news.

The film is about child abuse. Mild-mannered pedophile, Arnold Friedman, is a respected member of his community with a thriving computer class for young boys in his home.

In 1984, the same year as the Jordan scandal, Arnold

ordered a child pornography magazine from the Netherlands that the federal authorities intercepted at New York City's JFK Airport. A fed then pretended to be a fellow pedophile. He wrote many letters to Arnold, one persuaded him to put the contraband in the mail to him.

The day before Thanksgiving in 1987, the police shattered the front door of the Friedman home with a battering ram. They arrested almost everyone in the house and searched the home and boxed up the family's possessions.

The Friedman family included Elaine and Arnold and their three boys, David, Seth and Jesse, in that birth order. None of them would ever have a normal life again as they became encumbered with suspicions of a child pornography ring, child sexual abuse, and the legal and judicial demands of the allegations.

Suspicions of a child pornography ring and child pornographic photos and literature are also a part of the Jordan story. And some of the characters in this film are reminiscent of the people involved in the Jordan cases.

Elaine Friedman, Arnold's wife, divorced him when he was convicted and sentenced to prison. She said she didn't see any abuse at the Friedman house, but the doubt and turmoil took its toll on the family unit. Like the Friedmans, several divorces resulted from the Jordan allegations and investigations and arrest, even though charges were dismissed.

Arnold's brother, Howard Friedman, could not believe his brother was capable of the child sexual abuse. Initially, he insisted the police made a mistake. After completing the film, he resumed contact with Elaine Friedman and talked about the fate of his nephew, Jesse.

Similar to the Friedmans, several family members of the accused in Jordan have worked for years to reestablish and regain trust and respect within their families.

Debbie Nathan, a famous investigative journalist, said that originally the entire family expressed a feeling of innocence. Nathan was one of the first journalists to question the sex-abuse hysteria that splintered more that one community in the mid-80s.

Nathan, who co-authored the book, *Satan's Silence: Ritual Abuse and the Making of a Modern American Witch Hunt*, remains a friend and is involved in the Friedman's lives. A few investigative reporters have maintained a dialogue with some of the formerly accused in Scott County.

Judd Maltin was Jesse's best friend and said he was at the Friedman house three or four days a week and none of the allegations against Jesse ever happened. Many children in Jordan, who were friends of the children of the accused, said they visited the homes often and saw no signs of child sexual abuse.

Judge Abby Boklan said of the Friedmans: "There was never any doubt in my mind as to their guilt."

The courts say that a judge is supposed to be impartial to the case as it is being heard. If a judge begins the case with guilt in his mind, then it becomes a self-fulfilling prophecy that the accused will suffer. I wonder if the judges in Scott County who issued the arrest warrants for the Jordan citizens had any doubts about the guilt or innocence of those charged with child sexual abuse.

New York Detective Lloyd Doppman said, "Children want to please you. Very often they want to give answers you want or they think you want."

Defense attorneys and some psychologists claim kids said things in the Jordan cases to please the police investigators and Morris. Later these children recanted their allegations or told different stories to different investigators.

In the Friedman movie, the detectives incriminate themselves by describing wildly biased interviewing techniques. One parent describes the police interview as browbeating– "We know what happened! Tell us!" Some children who   testified in the Friedman case now say they lied. The children of the accused in Jordan have told me they were coerced and manipulated by the investigators to say things that weren't true.

Postal Inspector John McDermott, involved with the Friedman case, said, "I remember walking in there and saying 'God damn–we could have a problem here.'"

Jordan police and other Scott County investigators did not seize pornographic material and use as evidence to make a case of child sexual abuse. Why?

Peter Panaro, Jesse Friedman's lawyer, said, "You have to understand, this is a 19-year-old kid who's now facing the most heinous crime known to man. And everyone in the world slowly, but surely, was tuning against him."

Jordan defendants claim that little by little the community turned against them. Biased media coverage caused former friends and acquaintances to side with the police and the news reports.

Scott Banks, Judge Boklan's former legal secretary, wondered how could this go on in this house for so long and not come out?

In Jordan, the question of how could something like child sexual abuse go on for so long in this community took on a special meaning–a school teacher confessed to molesting   students for twenty years at the high school before being found out.

In January 2003, Judge Thomas Howe sentenced Jordan High School teacher James Mark Simon to 86 months in prison for Criminal Sexual Conduct. Simon was ordered to pay restitution for the victim's counseling expenses. Upon his release from prison, he must register as a sex offender and provide his DNA sample.

Retired New York Detective Sergeant Frances Galasso was the chief detective who led the police effort. She was the driving force behind the investigation that is the centerpiece of the Friedman story. She said, "You always want to be very careful about how you proceed, because one thing you worry about–I know I worried about it all the time is–just charging somebody with this kind of crime is enough to ruin their lives."

Unlike Fran Galasso's concern about making a false accusation, the people involved in the Jordan cases–the police, the judges issuing warrants, County Attorney Morris, and other professionals–accused and arrested Scott County residents with little or no evidence. They had no concern for the rights of the accused, and they didn't care how many lives they ruined.

New York Assistant District Attorney Joseph Onorat said, "Because Arnold Friedman, the father, did it, a reasonable human expectation was that the son Jesse did it also. Guilt by association was difficult for Jesse to overcome."

Many in Jordan felt the guilt by association. Negative comments and innuendos about Jordan still pops up today, more than 20 years after all the charges were dismissed. Yes, many lives were affected. Some ruined.

Arnold Friedman, sentenced to ten to thirty years, committed suicide in prison.

Son Jesse, on the advice of his lawyer, who felt that a fair trial was impossible with all the publicity given to the case, also pled guilty in hopes of receiving a light sentence. He also claimed his father, Arnold, molested him (a claim he now says is simply not true) in the hopes of receiving mercy from the court. He was sentenced to six to 18 years in prison and released on parole in 2001, after being incarcerated for 13 years.

He went to prison at age 19 and got out at age 32. He

moved to Manhattan and is classified as a sex offender. He wears an electronic ankle bracelet so the police can track his movements.

Harvey Silvergate, criminal-defense lawyer and civil liberties lawyer, watched the Friedman documentary and said, "It didn't take me long to recognize not only the telltale signs of a concocted prosecution—including young witnesses who had been induced and even coerced into giving false testimony–but also signs of what criminal lawyers refer to as a 'bullshit pact,' in which a defendant pleads guilty to a crime that he did not commit to gain a lighter sentence or to get prosecutors to drop criminal charges against a loved one."

Jesse Friedman has set up Web site and is working to free himself from the false accusation and conviction of child sexual abuse. Those falsely accused of child sexual abuse in Jordan are still trying to free themselves from the false accusations brought against them by Scott County Attorney Kathleen Morris.

What follows here is a personal letter from Jesse Friedman, who was found guilty along with his father, of child sexual abuse–guilt by association or relationship, he claims.

One of these Days I'm Gonna Sit Down and Write Myself a Letter

by Jesse Friedman

When I was eighteen, in 1987, my father was arrested and charged with molesting children who were students enrolled in an after-school computer instruction program in our home. I was also arrested, charged as his co-defendant, with 243 counts of sodomy and sexual abuse, which never occurred.

Before a year had passed there was a third co-defendant arrested, and two others who were accused of being part of a sex ring, but who were never arrested. Seventeen children testified before a Grand Jury, but the police eventually claimed that as many 500 children, over as many as five years, were victimized by my father and me. After thirteen years in prison the documentary, "Capturing the Friedmans," would be made about my family and the case.

I often wonder about the other people across the country who were also victims of mass-hysteria multiple-victim multiple-offender sex abuse cases. I know most of their names, and I trust they know mine. The names of the cities are etched in my mind: Wenatchee, Jordan, Edenton, Bakersfield, and now Great Neck is on that list too.

I ride the bus, gazing out the window, thinking about this "exclusive" club of which I am a member. I wonder how many of us there are. I wonder if they suffer the same traumas I now suffer. There are many people in my life who support me, and carry me through the internal traumas that I suffer, but they cannot completely know the horrors in my mind. I wonder about the others. I wonder about Kelly Michaels, and Ray Buckey; I wonder about Gerald Amirault and John Stoll. I wonder about the McCuans and the Kniffens.

We should all get together and have a convention once a year to create some support group for healing. I wonder if upon meeting there would be some unspoken bond between us, and if others would intrinsically understand the private nightmare in my head.

Maybe we would look in each other's eyes with knowing and understanding of where we each have been. We could compare nightmares. Certainly there are things I've learned about my own healing which could be helpful to someone else, just as others certainly must have some insights about their own healing which has escaped me.

I am barred from contacting anyone else because I am on parole. Besides, the pull of wanting to leave that part of our lives behind us, and in the past, is strong. It is sad because I think we could help each other.

People often ask me, amazed, about my lack of anger toward the police. I attempt to explain how it is that I don't demonstrate any resentment toward the accusers who ruined my life.

I realized that hate only hurts me. The people who harmed me did not care about any hate I might have for them. If I continued to be angry about what happened and angry at the people who harmed me, it would only turn me into an angry person. I did not want that to happen. The best revenge was to overcome. My primary concern has always been not to allow prison to beat me down, to destroy my soul, to suck the life out of me. If it did, then they would win. Surviving prison, and surviving prison by overcoming the difficulties, and not someone destroyed by the experience, would mean they did not win. I vowed never to allow them to win.

There is no one for me to point a finger at and blame for what happened to my life. The children did not set out to tell lies about me. The police did not set out to send an innocent man to prison. They were doing their job, going after someone who they thought was a child molester. They believed the children were molested and conducted their interviews with the children in the manner they believed was the best way to talk to children, to help the children "remember" the abuse that the children initially denied had ever taken place.

The parents were lied to by the police. The parents were told by the police that their children were molested. Even if some parents questioned whether their own child had been harmed, everyone believed that something terrible had happened to other children (because clearly the police would not arrest someone for child molestation if it were not true).

There was a sense of collective hysteria akin to "The Emperor's New Clothes." Everyone was thankful that nothing terrible had happened to their son, in the classes their son attended, but believed and were outraged that other children in other classes were molested. Sadly, everyone believed that something terrible happed to other children. Therefore nobody was willing to come forward and put their children on the witnesses stand as a defense witness.

The criminal justice system is not perfect, but it is the best system we have. Since it happens to be a human system, based on people, there is no way it can ever be perfect. Sadly, because of the number of people involved (police, D.A., judges, attorneys, etcetera), there are more risks of human error at each stage. With two million people behind bars, even if the system were 99.9% accurate, how many innocent people might there be in prison? And nothing is 99.9% accurate. Still, it is the best system we have and the best system we know how to make.

People are very uncomfortable with the notion that nothing happened. People are much more apt to rationalize that, "Something must have happened, but that the case got all blown out of proportions."

It is more comfortable to go to sleep at night believing that "something must have happened" because this all could not simply have come from nothing. I don't mean to sound cynical, but this is all just a question of gravity. Yes, gravity.

Do you realize that the Earth is hurtling around and around at about 1,000 miles an hour? We all go to bed and night and wake up in the morning trusting that gravity is going to hold us in place and we are not going to be hurled off into the darkness of space. If there were any doubt of this fact at all, then all of society would cease to function. There would be no way to go about our daily lives if everyone were walking around clutching hand-railings worrying that at any moment gravity is going to stop working.

We have to believe that police do not go around just randomly arresting people for no good reason, for crimes that never occurred. If our trust in the system broke down, our society would cease to function.

Life has not been easy since my release from prison. The adjustment has been horrific and more difficult than my wildest expectations. Getting out of prison was a hundred times more difficult than going to prison. It took me eight months before I was able to do the things I do daily without having to think through every last step. It took about eight months before things like buying some groceries or doing my laundry did not take a half a day. Daily life is better now, but I still have the onus of Parole with a noose around my neck, and will have for some years still to come.

Restaurant menus were and still are quite difficult for me. The obvious reason would be that after 13 years of not having any choices about what to eat that I was daunted by choices. Nope, that's not it. The problem is not the choice, but the   question. My brother David would sympathize and encourage me to, "Order what you like?" The problem has been that I don't know what I like. I have not had a lifetime of experiences, and trying different things, to find out what I like and what I don't like. I don't really know who I am anymore.

The media storm surrounding the film was fun in some ways, and not so much in others. It has been a distraction from the business of trying to move on with my life. I struggle almost daily with figuring out who I am, and what my life is to become.

This Neil Young song snippet has been playing in my head all day. "One of these days I'm going to sit down and write a long letter." I began to wonder, what would I write to my younger self if I were able?

What would I most want to tell myself? What I do I think my younger self most needs to learn? Are those two things necessarily the same?

> Dear Jesse,
>
> Don't let them take your soul. They can take your freedom. They can take your family, and friends, tarnish your name, and brand you with labels. But those names are not you. Those labels mean little. Friends come and friends go. Freedom lies within; always within. They can't steal your heart.
>
> You will lose every friend you've ever known. They will all fade from your life. There is no need to cling to those friendships. You have no need in your life for fair-weather friends. Don't identify yourself by who your friends are. Concentrate on making you a strong person and you'll never be lacking for friendships.
>
> Most people are ignorant of anything that happens farther than three feet away from their faces. People are not bad just because they are neglectful. Most people simply don't know how to do good things because they are so busy doing other things. People are distracted. That does not make them bad people.
>
> A terrible thing is about to happen to you, but nothing bad is

going to harm you. There will be no pain that you will be unable to endure, and no scar that will not heal. The Bible says that God promises not to test us beyond that which we can stand. It is a charming thought to think of God inflicting (or allowing) suffering and pain, but promising that nothing will befall the faithful beyond that which they will be able to endure.

Every storm has a beginning and an end. Some even have a calming eye to them. You appreciate the predictability and elegance of a hurricane. Life storms can share that same beauty. Ships batten down and ride out storms. So can you, and so you shall. So I have, and so I will again.

Thirteen years in prison is a long time, but you get into a routine, and time passes. You do a lot of growing up. There are good days and bad days just as if you were not in prison. Being a convicted child molester is not easy, especially not one so publicly well known, but you can't allow that to stop making the most of your life as possible. You have work with what you have and build a life for yourself.

Every day of your life is a day of your life. Make of it what you wish, but don't waste it. You will try to learn something new everyday. You will try to do something productive every day. You will never allow your life to stagnate as so many others in prison do with their lives.

The best that a child molester can hope for in prison is to be left alone and treated like a leper. Mostly the only people who will talk to a child molester are other child molesters. Earning respect will take diligence, commitment, and fortitude of character, but you will earn respect from other inmates and staff. You keep to yourself, hope that nobody knows who you are, try to make a few friends. Then someone finds out about you, there is some trouble, you get shipped to another prison where hopefully nobody knows who you are, you keep to yourself and make a few friends. Then someone learns who you are, decides to make some trouble, and you get sent to a different prison to start over again.

When you are asked, and you will be asked –repeatedly– "How do you think you've changed because of being arrested and going to prison?" You will answer by paraphrasing Richard

Bach. (Don't worry about not knowing who he is. He will write your favorite book shortly.) "I gave my life to become the   person I am today. Was it worth the price I paid?"

I am the product of my experiences. I am who I am because of the journey I have taken. If I like who I am, and if the person I become at the end of my journey is who I want to be, then what does it matter the road I've taken? If the end of the journey is successful then the trip was worth it.

And you really believe that.

But you really didn't have a choice.

We always have a choice. We always have a choice about how to view life; how to respond to life; and how we feel about our life. We may not have a choice about things that happen to us, but   everything we do or feel is a choice.

I am hopeful about the future, but then I've always been hopeful about the future. My life is by far "fixed" or made whole. My friends like to point out that perspective is everything, and that is true. From where I was three years ago in prison things are   pretty good, even though they are still quite difficult. It was not an easy journey but it was a rewarding one. There are still a great many weights I am forced to carry.

From where I am sitting the view from my window is much nicer today than it was three years ago, so I try not to complain that much. I am trying to learn how to be happy for the first time in my life. I try staying focused on that, and not let life become too oppressive.

With love and respect,
-- Jesse
11/28/04

Stevie

In 2003, Steve James, best known for his Oscar-nominated basketball film, "Hoop Dreams," produced a documentary called "Stevie." Roger Ebert, *Chicago Sun-Times* film critic said of this film, "Impossible to forget."

In 1982, when Steve James was 27, he became a mentor and advocate for a 11-year-old Stevie Fielding through the Big Brothers organization. James regularly spent time with Stevie when the boy was between the ages of 11 and 13. For three years James volunteered one afternoon a week hoping to provide a positive role model for the needy, vulnerable boy. It was not the rewarding, hopeful and uplifting experience the Big Brothers idea would lead you to believe. After three years, James moved to Chicago and his only contact with the boy was an annual Christmas card.

Stevie had been an abused child. He was placed in various foster homes and soon engaged in a life of petty and serious crime.

A decade after he stopped mentoring Stevie Fielding, Steve James returned with a camera crew to rural Pomona, Illinois to record his reunion with his "little brother." For five years he recorded a portrait of a life gone haywire and the moral confusion affecting the community.

Stevie had become an adult. His choices became more alarming and destructive. He abused drugs and couldn't hold a job. Two years into James' documentary film, Stevie was accused of sexually assaulting his 8-year-old cousin.

James' film does not encourage hope. What Lois Bentz would say, "There is no happy ending."

Stevie ends up fighting lawyers who are trying to help him. He refuses counseling for his sex crime and turns down a plea bargain that would spare him a lengthy prison term.

In the film, Stevie's small-town postmaster asks, "It take a village to raise a child. What do you do when a village fails?"

Some have asked the same question of the village of Jordan.

Mystic River

"Mystic River," a movie made from the book by Dennis Lehane, directed by Clint Eastwood, deals with the consequences of child sexual molestation. The lives of three boys are deeply affected when one of them is abducted and molested. Although they have grown apart in adulthood, the movie focuses on what happened twenty-five years after the molestation, when their shared past resurfaces. The movie depicts fearful suspicions, unhealthy relationships, marital discord, violence and even murder resulting from child sexual abuse.

A young man from Jordan told me that although he was not sexually abused, he was taken from his parents and placed in a foster home. He has had dreams and nightmares of killing "the cops, the shrinks, his foster parents, and the monster Kathleen Morris and others who put him and his parents through hell." His telling and retelling of being repeatedly interrogated was Kafka-esque (nightmare-like, bizarre). He has a sense of impending disaster. If it happened once, could the police come again and arrest his parents on trumped-up charges?

Consequences of the Jordan sex scandal: drug abuse, treatment center successes and failures, depression, attempted suicides, divorce, mental illness, misdemeanor and felonious crime, and unemployment.

What lies ahead for the people who were sexually abused then, as children? What lies ahead for those who were not sexually abused but were directly or indirectly involved in the scandal? Some psychologists believe that children who were coerced into making false statements may suffer more long-term damage than those who were physically molested.

A tagline in "Mystic River" is, "We bury our sins, we wash

them clean." This didn't happen in "Mystic River." New sins were added to the old ones. Same in Jordan.

John Anderson of *Newsday* called "Mystic River" "a masterpiece." Kenneth Turan of the Los Angeles Times said, "Eastwood's best since 'Unforgiven.'" Jeanne Wolf of Jeanne Wolf's Hollywood said, "A movie so powerful you won't be able to forget it."

"Mystic River's" star, Sean Penn, won an Oscar for best actor for his role in which he plays the tormented father of a murdered girl in Boston. Co-star Tim Robbins won the Oscar for best supporting actor for his gut-wrenching performance as the suspected killer of his friend's daughter. Robbin's complex character evolves from his boyhood sexual abuse.

Robbins delivered this message when he received his Oscar. "In this movie, I play a victim of abuse and violence, and if you are out there and have had that tragedy befall you, there is no shame or weakness in seeking help and counseling. It sometimes is the strongest thing you can do to stop the violence."

Many of the children involved in Jordan's scandal and many of the falsely accused have sought help and counseling. It is unclear whether therapy and counseling have been helpful or harmful. The majority of the people I have interviewed said the counseling, therapy, anger management classes, forgiveness classes, discussions and seminars have not helped. They felt the professionals were not genuinely interested in how they were coping. They described psychologists as being more interested n getting paid and what the limits were on their insurance coverage.

These wounded people have not yet found their "healer." Maybe some wounds never heal. Some scars were concealed and covered up while others are loud and visible. Some anger and resentment subtly sneaks into many conversations about the injustice.

"Mystic River" is a violent movie–with no happy ending. I believe the final act of the Jordan scandal is yet to be acted out and recorded.

52

▼

More About Jordan
and the Author

*"I am responsible for speaking what I perceive to be the
truth, not what I think others may want to hear."*
– Tom Dubbe

Twenty-eight years before the Jordan Child sexual abuse scandal of 1984, I graduated from Jordan High School. I was expelled about as much as I was enrolled, but that has not diminished in any way my appreciation for good old JHS. I was born and raised in Jordan. Jordan is my hometown. I'm proud of my Jordan heritage.

Thomas Wolf in *Look Homeward Angel* said, "You can't go home again." Most of us make geographical changes, but we never totally leave our hometown. We carry memories, values, beliefs, scars and blessings wherever we go and for as long as we live. After graduating from high school, I moved from Jordan to college, military service, married life, and a business career. I was fortunate to earn some degrees and titles so that I can now put some letters before or after my name.

During my research for this book, I discovered many Jordan residents who were maligned by the so-called professionals during the 1984 investigations of child sexual abuse, are very suspicious of people with degrees and titles. To them, it seems a degree or a title signals "less trustworthy."

The Jordan I experienced and appreciate is reflective of the old African Proverb: "It takes a village to raise a child." Hillary Clinton popularized this proverb in her speeches and her book. The kind, decent and caring people of Jordan detoured me from my penchant for delinquency that may well have led me to lengthy incarceration in unfriendly places. I know I grew up in a life-giving, life-saving small town. I am grateful.

My hometown, the Jordan I grew up in was a nirvana. The accusations of child sexual abuse, the "scandal" of 1984 turned Jordan into a dystopia.

Author Tom Dubbe was born and raised in Jordan.

53

▼

Resurrection and Restoration of Jordan

*"Those who cannot remember the past
are condemned to repeat it."*
– George Santayana

Some local residents in 1984 were not quite ready to let their town continue to be scandalized and demoralized. A community festival began in 1984 and has been held every year since. The festival was the brainchild of Paul Sunder, editor of the *Jordan Independent* and Bob Wittman, Director of Community Education and Recreation. The two men felt there was a need to resurrect the community spirit of residents following the plethora or negative publicity heaped upon the city by the sex abuse cases.

The festival received its permanent name from a local resident Cele Pekarka. It is now called Heimatfest. (high-mutt-fest). Cele explained there are little festivals all over Germany and they are called Heimatfest Albend, which meant "home-town night festival." Since this event is held during the day in

Jordan, the Albend (evening) was dropped.

The Jordan I moved from in the middle 1950s had a population of about 1400. At the time of the child abuse scandal in 1984, the population had grown to more than 2660. Today more than 4,000 people call Jordan their home.

54
▼

From the Past...

"Why shouldn't truth be stranger than fiction?
Fiction after all has to make sense."
– Mark Twain

Jordan had long been a tightly knit community built around a history of tough pioneers and hard-working farmers. Everyone knew everyone and it was a supportive community for raising your cattle, soybeans, or children. Community members had a mutual respect for each other and trust of the community in its entirety. People were good neighbors and helped each other out.

The investigation brought to the residents a level of distrust and uncertainty amid the mounting allegations of child abuse that one could not even have fathomed before all this happened. People began to wonder things about their neighbors. Whispers followed those accused–guilty or not. And the whispers became so loud that it burned the ears and reputations of not only all accused, but those that had the misfortune to part of the hysteria that overtook the town and surrounding farm community.

But it didn't stop with subtle whispers. Innocents were

jeered and ridiculed. Neighbors who lived, worked, and shopped next to each other for years, were now shunned and blackballed by some of the closest friends they'd had throughout their lives. The trauma left them scarred then–and scarred now.

And Jordan would never be the same community again.

55
▼

The Future "Must-Dos"

"Where is there dignity unless there is honesty."
– Marcus Tullius Cicero

We must never slide into indifference about the heinous crime of child sexual abuse. Kind hearts and gentle spirits must not become calloused and hardened. Children deserve our love and protection. Without headline sensationalism, or any political agenda, we must do the right thing and arrest and convict child abusers.

It is more than just our duty–it is our moral obligation. There is an intelligent and legal way of gathering evidence. With thorough investigation and gathering sufficient evidence, prosecutors can charge child abusers with criminal charges, bring them to trial and obtain convictions that will put the offenders in jail for a long time.

A botched prosecution by an overzealous, incompetent, or dishonest prosecutor indelibly stains the criminal justice system. Worse yet, abusers are not punished or jailed and children are returned to the abusers and may suffer more and even harsher abuse.

Epilogue

"Cowardice ask the question, 'Is it safe?
Expedience ask the question, 'Is it politic?
Vanity ask the question, 'Is it popular?
But conscience ask the question, 'Is it right?'"
– Martin Luther King

A matter of conscience: If I thought someone was falsely accused of a crime (criminal sexual abuse), would I step forward and proclaim my opinion? If I suspected someone of a crime (criminal sexual abuse), would I confront the criminal or report my suspicions to the police?

Some children in Scott County were sexually abused. Some innocent people were falsely accused. Sloppy police work, and an overzealous prosecutor who was found guilty of malfeasance and lying to a judge, are primarily responsible for the Scott County child sexual abuse scandal.

County commissioners, judges, lawyers, psychologists, teachers, social workers, medical doctors, State and Federal political office holders, clergy, reporters, and a host of others, played a role in the debacle by what they did or what they failed to do.

It is never too late to admit wrongdoing, and make amends to those who have been harmed. Selective loss of memory and remaining silent and secretive is unhealthy. The nightmare will end when the truth is fully known and openly discussed.

The real trial of the Jordan child sexual abuse cases was a trial of our justice system.

Margaret A. Hagen, Ph.D. author of *Whores of the Court* says, "A society that does not believe in its justice system is a doomed society."

We must do all we can to prevent child abuse. We must insist upon competent and thorough investigations. We must demand fair and just prosecution. Since 1984, some child protection laws have been introduced and strengthened. Better training for police investigators has been developed. Technical advances such as video taping, data processing, DNA testing help identify, arrest and convict sexual abusers.

With all the improved and additional tools now available to prosecutors, the fundamental concept of "innocent until proven guilty" must be the guiding principle.

Dean Tong, author of *Elusive Innocence* said: "We will not win the war against child abuse until we first win the battle against false accusation."

People magazine published a special year-end double issue December 1984 with an article on "The 25 Most Intriguing People of 1984 & Faces to Watch in 1985." The cover is graced with photos of Mary Lou Retton, Farrah Fawcett, Geraldine Ferraro, and Tina Turner. Included in the article with Bruce Springsteen, Michael Jackson, Richard Gere, Clint Eastwood and Betty Ford is Kathleen Morris.

The article highlights the level of fame and public attention showered on the Jordan sexual abuse case.

Many on the list of intriguing people continued to be intriguing or notorious, and grow more famous. Kathleen Morris did not.

The victims, the accused and arrested parents, and the children who were made to tell horrific lies about their parents–all have nightmares. And still, the sleepy little town has its secrets!

I should have started with this statement from one of the child victims I interviewed. But... it is a most appropriate ending to *Nightmares and Secrets*.

"Look, Mister,
just because I am from Jordan
don't mean I'm a piece of shit."

Bibliography

Recommended Reading: Books

No Crueler Tyrannies, Accusation, False Witness, and Other Terrors of Our Times
Dorothy Rabinowitz, 2003 Free Press
ISBN 0743228340
Pulitzer Prize Wall Street Journal editorialist Rabinowitz writes about false accusations of sex crimes and failed justice. Tells how counselors used leading questions and anatomically correct dolls to encourage children to falsely accuse teachers.

Elusive Innocence, Survival Guide for the Falsely Accused
Dean Tong, 2001 Huntington House Publishers
ISBN 1563841908
Having been falsely accused himself, the author gives the pitfalls and shows how to combat and defeat false accusations. The book is a powerful and compelling expose? that is the training manual for the defense of those falsely accused. Shows the destruction that is incurred by families due to false accusation of child abuse.

Kinsey: Crimes and Consequences
Judith A. Reisman 1998 Institute for Media Education
ASIN 0966663407
Dr. Reisman calls Dr. Kinsey a misogynist and pederast and said he

should have spent his years in jail instead of being lauded as "the father of sexology."

From Scandal to Hope
Benedict J. Groeschel 2002 Our Sunday Visitor
ISBN 1931709696
This prolific writer, theologian, and psychologist has the courage to say that ordinary people and professionals have failed to protect children from sexual abuse.

The Myth of Repressed Memory: False Memories and Allegations of Sexual Abuse
Dr. Elizabeth Loftus, 1994, St. Martins Press 1st edition.
ASIN 0312114540.
The author does not completely dismiss the theory of repressed memory. However, she contends that often counselors are inadvertently instilling "memories" of sexual abuse in their patients.

The Unknown Darkness: Profiling Predators Among Us
Greg O. McCray 2003 William Morrow
ISBN 0060509570
Tells how the FBI's behavioral science unit works. Explores the strengths and pitfalls of modern criminal investigation.

Satan's Silence, Ritual Abuse and the Making of a Modern American Witch Hunt
Debbie Nathan and Michael Snedeker 2001 Authors Choice Press
ISBN 0595189555
This is a cautionary study about the detrimental effects of modern-day hysteria. Cites alleged child abuse cases in which unethical practices had been use to gather evidence against innocent people.

The Franklin Cover-up: Child Abuse, Satanism, and Murder in Nebraska
John W. Decamp 1996 AWT 2nd edition ISBN 0963215809
Shocking allegations of child abuse, money   laundering, drug running and government's cover-ups both big and small. Makes connection between child sexual abuse and murder in Nebraska and Jordan, Minnesota.

Child Sexual Abuse and False Memory Syndrome
Edited by Robert A. Baker 1998 Prometheus Books
ISBN 1573921823
This compendium of 32 lucid articles aims to help those involved identify instances of child sexual abuse while protecting innocent adults who may be wrongfully accused. This book is for professionals, legal experts, victims and their families.

Predators: Pedophiles, Rapist, and Other Sex Offender: Who They Are, How They Operate, and How We Can Protect Ourselves and Our Children
Anna C. Salter 2004 Basic Books
ISBN 0465071732
Dr. Salter contends most sex crimes are premeditated and carefully planned, and fewer than 5% of sexual predators are caught. Author offers some specific strategies to avoid high-risk situations.

Whores of the Court: The Fraud of Psychiatric Testimony and the Rape of American Justice.
Margaret A. Hagen 1997 Regan Books 1st edition
ISBN 0060391979
Unmasking some legal psycho-expertise as a total fraud, Dr. Hagen instructs reader to protect themselves and their families from being victimized by psychological testimony in the courtroom. Incalculable harm has been done to millions of Americans by the purveyors of psychological pseudoscience who have invaded our courtrooms.

Smoke and Mirrors: The Devastating Effect of False Sexual Claims
Terence W. Campbell, 1998 Insight Books Inc.
ASIN 0306459841
An uncompromising examination of how false allegations originate, gather momentum and too often culminate by ripping apart lives of innocent people. Psychologist Dr. Campbell castigates his own profession for its role in false sexual abuse claims that have put innocent people behind bars, ruined families and damaged patients in therapy.

The Trial
Franz Kafka 1995 Schocken Definitive edition
ISBN 0805210407
With great skill, Kafka captures the essence of a man unjustly arrested.

This novel is a must read for every American interested in preserving our democracy and freedoms.

The Crucible
Arthur Miller 2003 Penguin Books
ISBN 0142437336
This play about the Salem witchcraft trials is chilling in the fact that these sorts of witch hunts occur today in all different areas of society. Miller's play shows how easily   people can be swayed, with the barest of evidence something that is false. "The Crucible" is extremely well-written and informative, and almost too frighteningly real.

Who's Looking Out For You
Bill O'Reilly 2003 Broadway
ISBN 0767913795
The underlying theme of the book is trust. O'Reilly points out that our government and legal system are not always trustworthy. He mentions that psychologist do not deserve our trust.

Accusations of Child Sexual Abuse
Hollida Wakefield and Ralph C. Underwager 1988 C.C. Thomas
ISBN 0398054231
Wakefield and Underwager were among the first to warn of the danger of uncautious over reaction to allegations of child sexual abuse. This classic work should be read by anyone interested in the issues around child abuse allegations. If you are falsely accused, this book can help save you from much suffering, loss of children, loss of health, loss of job, loss of social standing, etc.

Chasing the Devil
Dave Reichert 2004 Little Brown Company Time Warner Books
ISBN 0-36-15632-9.
Story of Sheriff Dave Reichert's relentless pursuit–a 21-year odyssey, an epic hunt for American's most heinous serial killer, the Green River Killer, Gary Ridgeway. Inaccurate media coverage, political conniving or interagency police department policies and blunders could not deter the sheriff's quest for justice.

GREED, RAGE and Love Gone Wrong
Bruce Rubenstein 2004 University of Minnesota Press
ISBN 08166443377.

This excellent reporter puts the reader at the scene of Minnesota's most notorious murders. Eight of the ten stories in this book were previously published in newspapers and periodicals. Mr. Rubenstein cites some police incompetence and perhaps more sinister cover ups. Bruce Rubenstein is an excellent reporter and writer and wrote many articles about the Scott County child sexual abuse cases in 1984.

Walking With the Devil
Michael W. Quinn 2004 Quinn and Associates
ISBN 097591250X.
Mike Quinn has been a cop for 25 years and writes passionately and candidly. The subtitle of his book, "What Bad Cops Don't Want You to Know and Good Cops Won't Tell You" explains why cops should not be trusted. This is a must read for every cop, lawyer, judge and anyone who has been mistreated and abused by the police.

The Reign of Error: Psychiatry, Authority and Law
Lee Coleman, M.D. 1985 Beacon Press
ISBN: 0807004790.
Coleman, a practicing psychiatrist says that if society is to ever deal effectively with crime and violence, it must strip psychiatry of its legal "authority." Psychiatrists have no valid expertise to justify their legal power, especially in the area of child protective services.

Living Justice: Love Freedom, and the Making of the Exonerated
Jessie Blank Eric Jensen 2005 ATRIA Books
ISBN: 074348356
A powerful reminder of how tragically unjust our justice system can be. Innocent people have been arrested, tried and convicted. Some sentenced to death. Recently a few have been exonerated.

Newspaper Bibliography

Bruce Rubenstein, <u>Parents Tell Story of How Their Children Were Abused</u>, *Shakopee Valley News* 4-4-1984

Paul McEnroe & Joe Rigert, <u>Decade Ago, Morris Also Rowed Against Tide</u>, *Minneapolis Star Tribune* copyright 1984

E.R. Shipp, <u>Town in Dread of Murder Rumor As Sex Cases End</u>, *New York Times* (Special to the *New York Times*) 10-25-1984

Scott Vance Sex Ring Attention Angers Town, Denver Post 10-18-1984

Eileen Ogintz, Sex Scandal Robs Town's Innocence, *Chicago Tribune* 9-2-1984

Joe Rigert, Paul McEnroe, Josephine Marcotty, Sex Abuse Probe Called Faulty; Let Healing Start Humphrey Urges, *Minneapolis Star Tribune* 2-13-1985

Eric Black, Lawyers Accuse Morris of Destroying Evidence, *Minneapolis Star Tribune* 2-13-1985

Josephine Marcotty & Dennis J. McGrath, Morris Says She Doesn't Intend To Step Down, *Minneapolis Star Tribune* 2-13-1985

Lori Sturdevant, Weeks Ago, It Was Clear The Evidence Wasn't There, *Minneapolis Star Tribune* 2-13-1985

David Peterson, Judges, Lawyers Voice Concern About Child Witnesses, *Minneapolis Star Tribune* 2-13-1985

David Peterson & Joe Rigert, True Believers Ignored Need For Supporting Evidence, *Minneapolis Star Tribune* 2-13-1985

Mike Kasuba & Kevin Diaz, There's Relief in Jordan—But Mostly Just Weariness, *Minneapolis Star Tribune* 2-13-1985

Dan Oberdorfer, 7 Civil Suits By Accused Proceed. *Minneapolis Star Tribune* 2-13-1985

Marci Brown, Bentzes Found Not Guilty, Vow To Get Children Home, *Jordan Independent* 9-26-1984

Bruce Rubenstein, Sex Abuse Case Analysis: Was Bentz Trial a Witch Hunt? *Jordan Independent* 9-26-1984

Marci Brown, Once friends of their prosecutor, accused Jordan couple claims innocence, wants children back, *Shakopee Valley News* 8-15-1984

Marci Brown, Morris takes files from courthouse, *Jordan Independent* 11-12-1986

Unidentified, Insurance firm cancels $5 million Scott County Liability policy last week, *Jordan Independent* 10-24-1984

Joe Rigert & Paul McEnroe Scott County Document shows wild, inconsistent tales, Minneapolis Star Tribune 11-30-1984

Joe Rigert, Credibility of children becomes major concern in Scott County cases, *Minneapolis Star Tribune* 11-15-1984

Paul McEnroe, Divers search river near Jordan for bodies of 2 boys, *Minneapolis Star Tribune* 11-3-1984

Joe Rigert, Documents describe stress among children linked to Jordan cases, *Minneapolis Star Tribune* 10-24-1984

Unidentified, Deputy testifies in Buchan sex case, *Minneapolis Star Tribune* 10-4-1984

Unidentified, Jury selection completed in child sex case, *Minneapolis Star Tribune* 10-18-1984

Cheryl Johnson, Commissioners call for review of Morris' budget increase, *Minneapolis Star Tribune* 10-18-1984

Unidentified, Scott County deputy to return to work, *Minneapolis Star Tribune* 10-18-1984

Unidentified, Shakopee man, 52, is eighth adult charged in Scott County sex case, *Minneapolis Star Tribune* 11-23-1984

Unidentified, 2 more children cited as abuse victims, *Minneapolis Star Tribune* 11-22-1983

Dennis J. McGrath & Mike Kasuba, Scott County murder stories called untrue, *Minneapolis Star Tribune* 11-15-1984

Joe Rigert, Two children recant sex stories; officials worry about others, *Minneapolis Star Tribune* 12-15-1984

Unidentified, Meeting crowd claims pair not guilty, blames county attorney for press coverage, *Jordan Independent* 1-19-1984

Marci Brown, Myers attorney trying to get charges dropped in child sex abuse case, *Jordan Independent* 9-5-1984

Marci Brown, Trial date set Oct 1 for Myers, *Jordan Independent* 9-12-1984

Unidentified, <u>Jordan couple arrested in sexual abuse case; brings number to thirteen</u>, *Jordan Independent* 1-26-1984

Bruce Rubenstein, <u>Jury in deliberation over verdict in Bentz child sex abuse case</u>, *Jordan Independent* 1-26-1984

Mary Jo Mosher, <u>Jordan Policeman Greg Myers charged with sex crimes</u>, *Jordan Independent* 2-16-1984

Mary Jo Mosher & Patrick Boulay, <u>Eight-year Jordan policeman charged with sex crimes</u>, *Jordan Independent* 2-9-1984

Patrick Boulay, <u>Arrest in sex abuse ring reaches 14</u>, *Jordan Independent* 2-2-1984

Patrick Boulay, <u>Scott County woman arrested for alleged sex crimes</u>, *Jordan Independent* 11-24-1983

Mary Jo Mosher, <u>Build trust relationships with children so they'll talk about crime</u>, *Jordan Independent* 10-20-1983

Unidentified, <u>New charges filed against James Rud</u>, *Jordan Independent* 10-12-1983

Unidentified, <u>Recent arrest of couple for criminal sexual conduct stirs controversy. Jordan couple arrested on criminal sexual conduct charges involving seven children</u>, *Jordan Independent* 1-19-1984

Marci Brown, <u>Myers attorney attacks Rud statement at pre-trial hearing</u>, *Jordan Independent* 8-22-1984

Bruce Rubenstein, <u>First child sex abuse trail began Monday in Carver County</u>, *Jordan Independent* 8-22-1984

Unidentified, <u>James Rud pleads guilty to 10 criminal sexual abuse charges</u>, *Jordan Independent* 8-22-1984

Patrick Boulay, <u>Trial date set for August 20 for Robert and Lois Bentz in County-wide sex abuse case</u>, *Jordan Independent* 8-8-1984

Patrick Boulay, <u>Three adults arrested as part of ongoing county child sex abuse investigation</u>, *Jordan Independent* 6-6-1984

Bruce Rubenstein, <u>Several defendants in child sex abuse cases speak their minds</u>, *Jordan Independent* 4-11-1984

Unidentified, Shakopee woman is 17th sex ring suspect, *Jordan Independent* 4-4-1984

Bruce Rubenstein, Elaborate social denial system occurs with child sexual abuse, *Jordan Independent* 4-4-1984

Unidentified, Sixteenth suspect arrested in child sexual abuse case, *Jordan Independent* 3-1-1984

Josephine Marcotty, Stripped of family, identity and dignity, *Minneapolis Star Tribune* 9-16-1984

David Peterson, Child abuse cases remain tricky legal terrain, *Minneapolis Star Tribune* 9-16-1984

Josephine Marcotty, Pain, rage over false accusations linger, *Minneapolis Star Tribune* 9-16-1984

David Peterson, Morris out of limelight but still practicing law, *Minneapolis Star Tribune* 9-16-1984

David J. McGrath, Jordan residents working to regain their civic pride, *Minneapolis Star Tribune* 2-16-1984

Dan Oberdorfer, Court hears arguments on sites in sex cases, *Minneapolis Star Tribune* 5-14-1986

Dan Oberdorfer,, Court upholds dismissal of lawyers indictment, *Minneapolis Star Tribune* 5-13-1986

Mike Kasuba, Humphrey offers new plan for recall of county officials, *Minneapolis Star Tribune* 2-11-1086

Dan Oberdorfer, Morris assailed over grand jury probe, *Minneapolis Star Tribune,* 10-18-1986

Dan Oberdorfer, Judge halts probe of Morris' opponent, *Minneapolis Star Tribune* 10-17-1986

Dan Cassano, Child in Scott County case may go home, *Minneapolis Star Tribune* 4-7-1987

Unidentified, Children say pornography made, children slain, in Scott County, Resource Center News November 1984

Marci Brown, <u>Myers' attorney wants judge taken off child sex case</u>, *Shakopee Valley News* 9-19-1984

Joe Rigert & Paul McEnroe, <u>Children questioned over alleged deaths in Scott County case</u>, *Minneapolis Star Tribune*11-9-1984

Gary Dawson, <u>Child Abuse Cases Pose Legal Dilemma--Are accused parents caught in undue rush to judgement?</u> *St. Paul Pioneer Press* Focus 6-10-1984

Gregor W. Pinney & Dan Oberdorfer, <u>Morris removes herself from next sex-abuse trial</u>, *Minneapolis Star Tribune* 9-27-1984

Josephine Marcotty, <u>Both Bentzes deny abusing children</u>, *Minneapolis Star Tribune* 9-11-1984

Joe Rigert, <u>Jordan Cases Unusual</u>, *Minneapolis Star Tribune* 11-4-1984

Jim Dawson, <u>3 couples sue Scott County for millions</u>, *Minneapolis Star Tribune* 11-20-1984

Marci Brown, <u>Admission of lies may be reason investigation dropped</u>, *Jordan Independent* 11-24-1984

Marci Brown, <u>Buchan and Brown children reunited with their parents</u>, *Jordan Independent* 11-7-1984

Marci Brown, <u>Search for bodies to be conducted in Minnesota River north of Jordan</u>, *Jordan Independent* 11-7-1984

Bruce Rubenstein, <u>Investigators have physical evidence in some sex cases</u>, *Jordan Independent* 10-17-1984

Marci Brown, <u>Myers' files $34 million lawsuit against county; Kathleen Morris</u>, *Jordan Independent* 10-17-1984

Bruce Rubenstein, <u>Observations given on Scott County sex abuse cases</u>, *Jordan Independent,* 10-17-1984

Unidentified, <u>Bentzes back in court trying to regain custody</u>, *Jordan Independent* 10-10-1984

Bruce Rubenstein, <u>Bentz sex abuse trial continues this week with state rebuttal of defense arguments</u>, *Jordan Independent* 9-12-1984

Unidentified, <u>Another suspect is charged in Jordan sex case</u>, *Minneapolis Star Tribune* 12-1-1983

Paul McEnroe, <u>Sex-abuse charges against Rud total 108</u>, *Minneapolis Star Tribune* 11-19-1983

Paul McEnroe, <u>Sex case linked to as many as 30 children</u>, *Minneapolis Star Tribune* 10-17-1983

Unidentified, <u>Jordan/Rud charged in 110 counts</u>, *Minneapolis Star Tribune* 12-2-1983

Recommended Reading:
Magazines/Periodicals

People Magazine, December 24-31, 1984 "The 25 Most Intriguing People of 1984." Article by Civia Tamarkin with photographs by Taro Yamasaki under the heading, "KATHLEEN MORRIS, the controversial prosecutor vows to continue the legal fight against sexual abuse of children."

US Magazine, June 18, 1984, Article by Karolyn Ide with photographs by Marty Katz under the heading of "JUSTICE IN JORDAN Amid a nationwide outcry, an outraged prosecutor makes child abusers unwelcome in Jordan."

Twin City Reader, Volume 9, Issue 6 February 8-14, 1984, Cover photo of Kathleen Morris by Greg Helgeson with color-enhanced attention-grabbing heading: "KATHLEEN MORRIS, AT THE EYE OF THE STORM, Scott County Residents Wonder Who's Next." Lengthy article by Teri Mach titled, "Scott County Attorney Kathleen Morris On the Defensive." Dramatic photographs by Greg Helgeson.

Sunday Magazine, Star Tribune, September 6, 1986, Article by Kay Miller with photographs by Stormi Greener. Tells about Kathleen Morris' new career as a private lawyer in practice with Miriam Wolf, her former assistant. Article headline quotes Kathleen Morris, "I Still Believe The Children" with this subtitle, "Kathleen Morris was under fire from many directions for her handling of the Scott County child-abuse cases, and she was voted out of office. But she is unrepentant. Everything she did, she says, was for the children.

Mpls.St.Paul, March 199,1 Cover Content Highlight: "HOW THE INNOCENT WERE HURT AND THE GUILTY WENT FREE IN SCOTT COUNTY'S INFAMOUS SEX-ABUSE CASES." In-depth article by Britt Robson about the consequences suffered by some of the accused parents and their children during and after the 1984 debacle. Concludes: "Regardless of their guilt or innocence, the people of Scott County are still serving time."

To order copies of *NIGHTMARES AND SECRETS, The Real Story of the 1984 Child Sexual Abuse Scandal in Jordan, Minnesota*, mail this order form along with a check or money order made out to:

Memorial Press
P.O. Box 131
333 - 10th Avenue East
Shakopee, MN   55379

ORDER FORM

Name _____

Address _____

_____

City/State _____ Zip _____

Phone # _____

❏ Please send me _____ copies at $24.95 each
of *NIGHTMARES AND SECRETS, The Real Story
of the 1984 Child Sexual Abuse Scandal in Jordan,
Minnesota* for a total of $ _____

❏ Add $3.00 shipping and handling for the first book $ _____

❏ Plus $1.00 for each additional book $ _____

Total $ _____

For large quantities, contact the publisher for discount.

~

Visit **www.tomdubbe.com** for
special offers and promotions.

~

To order copies of *NIGHTMARES AND SECRETS, The Real Story of the 1984 Child Sexual Abuse Scandal in Jordan, Minnesota,* mail this order form along with a check or money order made out to:

Memorial Press
P.O. Box 131
333 - 10th Avenue East
Shakopee, MN   55379

ORDER FORM

Name _____

Address _____

_____

City/State _____ Zip _____

Phone # _____

❏ Please send me _____ copies at $24.95 each
  of *NIGHTMARES AND SECRETS, The Real Story
  of the 1984 Child Sexual Abuse Scandal in Jordan,
  Minnesota* for a total of $ _____

❏ Add $3.00 shipping and handling for the first book $ _____

❏ Plus $1.00 for each additional book $ _____

                                            Total $ _____

For large quantities, contact the publisher for discount.

∼

Visit **www.tomdubbe.com** for
special offers and promotions.

∼